# NUT**CASES**

# European Union Law

## SIXTH EDITION

by
**PENNY KENT**
LLB, LLM, Solicitor
Principal Lecturer
Middlesex University

D0416568

**SWEET & MAXWELL**          THOMSON REUTERS

First edition – 1997
Reprinted – 1999
Second edition – 2000
Reprinted – 2002
Third edition – 2003
Fourth edition – 2006
Fifth edition – 2009

Published in 2012 by Sweet & Maxwell part of Thomson Reuters (Professional) UK Limited
(Registered in England and Wales, Company No. 1679046. Registered Office and address
for service: Aldgate House, 33 Aldgate High Street, London EC3N 1DL)

For further information on our products and services, visit
*www.sweetandmaxwell.co.uk*

Typeset by YHT Ltd
Printed in Great Britain by
Ashford Colour Press, Gosport, Hants

*No natural forests were destroyed to make this product;*
*only farmed timber was used and re-planted*

A CIP catalogue record for this book is available from the British Library.

ISBN: 9780414023260

# Contents

# Using this Book

Welcome to our new look **NUTCASE** revision series. We have revamped and improved the existing design and layout and added new features, according to student feedback.

**NEW DETAILED TABLE OF CONTENTS** for easy navigation.

**REDESIGNED TABLE OF CASES** for easy reference.

**NEW CHAPTER INTRODUCTIONS** to outline
the key concepts covered and condense
complex and important information.

...egal Order of the EC and EU     **1**

**INTRODUCTION**

The present European Community (EC) and European Union (EU) originated in
the European Economic Community (EEC), created in 1957 by the Treaty of
Rome (EEC Treaty). The Treaty provided for a customs union and a common
market (the free movement of goods, persons, services and capital) for the six
signatory states (Germany, France, Italy, Belgium, the Netherlands and
Luxembourg). These states also created the European Coal and Steel Community
(ºSC, wound up in 2002) and the European Atomic Energy Authority (Euratom).
'United Kingdom, Denmark and Ireland joined in 1973. The United Kingdom
d the European Communities Act (ECA 1972) in 1972 to give effect to its
ºs under EC law. Further accessions took place in 1981 (Greece); *
ºrtugal); 1995 (Austria, Sweden and Finland); 2004 (Cyp*
ºstonia, Hungary, Poland, Latvia, Lithuania, M*
º* (Bulgaria and Romania).
º which are

...en deciding whether the .
y and precision of the rule infringed, w
...ther or not the error of law was excusable, the ,
...stitution, and non-compliance by the court in its c
to the ECJ under art.234(3).

**THINK POINTS**

Why is direct effect a concept of central importance
think the time is right to extend horizontal effect to c

How and in which decisions did the ECJ use art. 1(
develop the concepts of indirect effect and state '

**NEW BOXED "THINK POINTS"** at
the end of each chapter with
further case analysis and
questions to encourage critical
thinking.

...456/98) it held that the n...
...s of domestic law, predating or post...
...pret those provisions, as far as possible, in ...
...rpose of the directive, so that those provisions .
...consistent with the result pursued by the directive. In
SA v Quintero and Salvat Editores SA v Prades (Joined
C-244/98), it repeated this formula, adding (in the context c
Terms Directive 93/113) that the requirement to interpre
the directive requires the national court, in particular, to fa
tion which would allow it to decline of its own motion the ju
on it by an unfair term.

[4]   The ECJ confirmed in Maria Pupino (Case C-105
nterpret national law in line with EC law applies in the a
operation. The EC had adopted a Framework D
* to guarantee victims the opportunity to be h
·ly vulnerable victims must benefit f
···text of criminal proce·

**NEW COLOUR CODING** throughout
to help distinguish cases and
legislation from the narrative.
At the first mention, cases are
highlighted in colour and italicised
and legislation is highlighted in
colour and emboldened.

# Table of Cases

# Table of European Legislation

# Table of Abbreviations

| | | | |
|---|---|---|---|
| CAP | Common Agricultural Policy | EFTA | European Free Trade Association |
| CCT | Common Customs Tariff | EMU | European Monetary Union |
| CET | Common External Tariff | | |
| CFI | Court of First Instance | EP | European Parliament |
| CMLR | Common Market Law Reports | EPU | European Political Union |
| EC | European Community/ Communities | EU | European Union |
| | | EURAToM | European Atomic Energy Authority |
| ECA | European Communities Act | IGC | Intergovernmental Conference |
| ECB | European Central Bank | | |
| ECHR | European Convention for the Protection of Human Rights and Fundamental Freedoms | O.J. | Official Journal |
| | | SEA | Single European Act |
| | | TEC | Treaty establishing the European Community |
| ECJ | European Court of Justice | TEU | Treaty on European Union |
| ECR | European Court Reports | | |
| ECSC | European Coal and Steel Community | TFEU | Treaty on the Functioning of the European Union |
| EEA | European Economic Area | TN | Treaty of Nice |
| | | ToA | Treaty of Amsterdam |
| EEC | European Economic Community | ToL | Treaty of Lisbon |

# Legal Order of the EU

## INTRODUCTION

The European Union (EU) is governed by two treaties, both with legal force: the Treaty on European Union (TEU) and the Treaty on the Functioning of the European Union (TFEU). These treaties have been in force since December 1, 2009, when the Treaty of Lisbon came into effect.

The EU developed from the European Economic Community (EEC), which was created in 1957 by the Treaty of Rome (EEC Treaty). The **EEC Treaty** provided for a customs union and a common market (the free movement of goods, persons, services and capital) for the six signatory states (Germany, France, Italy, Belgium, the Netherlands and Luxembourg). These states also created the European Coal and Steel Community (ECSC, wound up in 2002) and the European Atomic Energy Authority (Euratom). The United Kingdom, Denmark and Ireland joined in 1973. The United Kingdom enacted the European Communities Act (ECA 1972) to give effect to its obligations under the **Treaty of Rome**. Further accessions took place in 1981 (Greece); 1986 (Spain and Portugal); 1995 (Austria, Sweden and Finland); 2004 (Cyprus, the Czech Republic, Estonia, Hungary, Poland, Latvia, Lithuania, Malta, Slovenia and Slovakia), and 2007 (Bulgaria and Romania).

Seven main institutions are entrusted with carrying out the tasks of the EU: the European Council (heads of state or government, of the Member States, its President and the High Representative of the Union for Foreign Affairs and Security Policy); the Council of the EU (an ad hoc body of ministers from the Member States responsible for the adoption of legislation); the Commission (a permanent body which proposes legislation and monitors the implementation of EU law); the European Parliament (EP) (directly elected since 1979 but with a limited role in the legislative process); the Court of Justice (the final authority on matters of EU law, assisted by the General Court); the European Central Bank; and the Court of Auditors.

The **Treaty of Rome** was amended on a number of occasions, notably in 1986 by the Single European Act (SEA), providing for the completion of the single or internal market within which goods, persons, services and capital may circulate freely. In 1993 the Maastricht Treaty introduced the commitment to political union (EPU) and monetary union (EMU).

Before amendment by the **Treaty of Lisbon**, the **Treaty on European**

Union (TEU) provided for the EU to operate through a three-pillar system. The first pillar, the EC, was governed by law under the Treaty establishing the European Community (TEC), whereas Pillar Two, the Common Foreign and Security Policy (CFSP), and Pillar Three, Police and Judicial Co-operation (CJP) were covered by the TEU, with decisions taken by intergovernmental co-operation. The Maastricht Treaty enabled states to "opt out" of various areas, such as EMU, as the UK chose to do. The Treaty was amended on three further occasions: in 1997 by the Treaty of Amsterdam (ToA) when the Treaty provisions were renumbered, in 2001 by the Treaty of Nice (TN) and most recently in 2009 by the Treaty of Lisbon (TL or 'Reform Treaty'), adopted after the failure to ratify the Constitutional Treaty (CT) following negative results in referenda in France and the Netherlands in 2005. The TEU was retained and amended by the Treaty of Lisbon, while the TEC was renamed the Treaty on the Functioning of the European Union (TFEU). The three pillar system was amalgamated into a single pillar, the Union (EU), by the Treaty of Lisbon, which renumbered the Treaty provisions once more. The new, post-Lisbon, numbering is used throughout this book, followed by the previous number in brackets, where appropriate: see, for example, art.34 TFEU (ex 28). References to '[EU]' indicate that the decision predated the creation of the EU (i.e. during the existence of the EEC or EC).

## THE NEW LEGAL ORDER

**Key Principle**
The Union is a new legal order in both international law and the national legal systems of the Member States.

VAN GEND EN LOOS V NEDERLANDSE ADMINISTRATIE DER BELASTINGE (CASE 26/62) 1963
Van Gend en Loos, a firm of importers, was required to pay customs duty on urea-formaldehyde (glue) imported from Germany into the Netherlands under a law adopted after the creation of the EEC (now EU). The importers challenged the payment in the Dutch courts on the basis that the extra duty infringed art.30 TFEU (ex 25) prohibiting the introduction of new customs duties). The Dutch court referred questions to the ECJ for interpretation under art.267 TFEU (ex 234) procedure.

**Held**
❖ (ECJ) (1) The "Community" (now the EU) is a new legal order in international law, on behalf of which states have limited their sovereign rights in

certain fields and whose subjects comprise not only states but also individuals.

(2) Article 30 TFEU produces direct effects in the relationship between the Member States and their subjects, creating individual rights which national courts must protect. [1963] E.C.R. 1.

## Commentary

The "new legal order" is recognised in international law as a treaty between sovereign states but also takes effect within the domestic legal systems of the Member States. The order is characterised by the concepts of direct effect and the supremacy of EU law over national law. Where a provision of EU law is directly effective it creates rights and duties which are directly enforceable by individuals before the national courts. The ECJ stated in *Van Gend en Loos* that to create direct effects a provision must be clear, unconditional and require no further action by Member States.

## SUPREMACY AND DIRECT EFFECT

### Key Principle

The Treaties (**TEU** and **TFEU**) are an integral part of the legal system of the Member States and must be applied in their courts.

> COSTA V ENEL (CASE 6/64) 1964
> Ente Nazional Energia Elettrica (ENEL) was created by the Italian government under a law passed in 1962 to nationalise the electricity industry. Costa refused to pay his electricity bill, on the basis that the nationalisation infringed the Italian constitution and various provisions of the **Treaty of Rome.**

### Held

❖ (ECJ) The transfer by Member States from their domestic legal systems to the [EU] system of rights and duties carries with it a permanent limitation of their sovereign rights, against which a later, unilateral act incompatible with [EU] law cannot prevail. [1964] E.C.R. 585.

> ITALIAN MINISTER OF FINANCE V SIMMENTHAL (CASE 106/77) 1978
> An Italian law introduced after joining the EC (now EU) required veterinary inspections of beef and veal. The law was challenged before the Italian courts as contrary to art.34 TFEU (ex 28) (prohibiting quantitative restrictions on imports and measures having equivalent effect).

**Held**

❖ (ECJ) A national court in such circumstances should not apply conflicting national legislation, even in situations where it was adopted after joining the Community (now EU); it should not wait for the decision of a higher national court before acting. [1978] E.C.R. 629.

**Commentary**

[1] The ECJ reconsidered *Simmenthal* in *Ministero delle Finanze v In.Co.Ge.90* (Joined Cases C-10–22/97) 1998, holding that it does not follow from *Simmenthal* that the conflicting national law should be regarded as non-existent. The Court held that where a national law is adopted after an EU law with which it is incompatible, it is for the national authorities to decide on its reclassification.

[2] The art.267 preliminary reference procedure enables the ECJ to interpret or consider the validity of EU law (see Ch.7). The ECJ has used this procedure to develop the concept of the "new legal order" and to provide authoritative rulings, which apply uniformly throughout all the Member States. The United Kingdom recognised the direct effect of EU law in s.2(1) of the **European Communities Act 1972**.

[3] The supremacy of EU law over national law has been apparent from the early decisions of the ECJ. The attempt to provide explicitly for the precedence of EU law was perceived as having contributed to the rejection of the **Constitutional Treaty (CT)** by the people of France and the Netherlands in 2005. After the failure of the **CT**, the **Treaty of Lisbon** provided more diplomatically for primacy by adopting a declaration which recalls that the Treaties and law adopted under them have primacy over the laws of the Member States "in accordance with the well-settled case law of the Court of Justice".

## INTERIM RELIEF

**Key Principle**

The full effectiveness of EU law would be impaired if a rule of national law could prevent a court considering a matter governed by EU law from granting interim relief.

R. v SECRETARY OF STATE FOR TRANSPORT EX P. FACTORTAME
(CASE C-213/89) 1990
Following concern about the tenuous nature of the link between the owners of a number of fishing vessels and the United Kingdom, the

Merchant Shipping Act 1988 was adopted, setting out stringent rules for the registration of fishing vessels as British. Many vessels owned by Spanish nationals previously registered as British no longer qualified and thus could not share in the UK fishing quota under the common fisheries policy. The unsuccessful applicants sought judicial review in the United Kingdom and suspension of the relevant parts of the 1988 Act, arguing that the Act contravened various provisions of the Treaty. An injunction against the Secretary of State was refused. The House of Lords referred questions for interpretation to the ECJ under art.267.

**Held**

❖ (ECJ) A national law should be set aside where it prevents the granting of interim relief in a dispute governed by EU law. [1990] E.C.R. I-2433.

**Commentary**

[1] The ruling of the ECJ followed the interim decision of the same court in an enforcement action brought by the Commission against the United Kingdom under art.258 TFEU (ex 226): *Commission v UK* (Case C-246/89R), ordering the United Kingdom to suspend the operation of the offending sections of the 1988 Act. The House of Lords applied the decision and set aside the rule that an interim injunction cannot be granted against the Crown in *R. v Secretary of State for Transport Ex p. Factortame* (1991). The ECJ later ruled on the interpretation of the substantive provisions of the Treaty (in Case C-221/89R), holding that arts 49 TFEU (ex 43) etc. were infringed in circumstances where registration was made more difficult for nationals from other Member States than for nationals from the host state.

[2] The ECJ ruled on the status of a requirement for interlocutory (interim) proceedings in *Melki and Abdeli* (Joined Cases C-188 &189/10. It held that a national requirement for an interlocutory procedure to review the constitutionality of a national law before making a reference to the ECJ did not infringe EU law provided national courts were free to apply any necessary measures to protect rights under EU law and disapply conflicting national measures at the end of the interlocutory proceedings.

# THE DIRECT EFFECT OF REGULATIONS, DIRECTIVES AND DECISIONS

**Key Principle**

Regulations, directives and decisions are capable of creating direct effects.

### GRAD V FINANZAMT TRAUNSTEIN (CASE 9/70) 1970

A haulage contractor challenged a German transport tax on the basis that it infringed a decision addressed to the Member States on VAT and a harmonisation directive imposing a deadline for implementation of the decision.

### Held

❖ (ECJ) (1) The wording of art.288 TFEU (ex 249) does not prevent individuals from relying in the national courts on decisions addressed to Member States. (2) The decision was directly effective; the directive merely fixed the date on which the VAT regime in the decision took effect. [1970] E.C.R. 825.

### Commentary

The ECJ adopted the same reasoning in *Van Duyn v Home Office* (Case 41/74), holding that directives can be directly effective. Regulations are stated in art.189 to be "of general application". If they are also clear and unconditional, they may be directly effective: *Leonesio v Italian Ministry of Agriculture* (Case 93/71).

### Key Principle

A directive containing a deadline for implementation is only capable of creating direct effects from the date of the deadline.

### PUBBLICO MINISTERO V RATTI (CASE 148/78) 1979

Ratti, a manufacturer of solvents in Italy, was charged with failure to comply with Italian labelling legislation. He claimed that his products were labelled according to EC (now EU) standards contained in two directives.

### Held

❖ (ECJ) As the deadline for implementation had been reached in relation to one but not both of the directives, only the directive for which the deadline had expired could be relied upon to create direct effects (and thus to provide a defence to one of the criminal charges). [1972] E.C.R. 119.

### Commentary

If no deadline is specified in a directive it takes effect on publication in the Official Journal.

# VERTICAL AND HORIZONTAL DIRECT EFFECTS

## Key Principle
Treaty provisions are capable of creating direct effects both vertically between the state and individuals and horizontally between individuals.

> DEFRENNE V SABENA (CASE 43/75) 1976
> Ms D, an airline stewardess employed by the Belgian airline Sabena, was paid less and had to retire earlier than male stewards. She claimed that this amounted to a breach of art.157 TFEU (ex141) (providing for equal pay for equal work).

## Held
❖ Article 157 creates direct effects both vertically and horizontally. [1976] E.C.R. 455.

## Commentary
The ruling in *Defrenne* was limited to Treaty provisions. **It meant that Treaty provisions may be relied upon in the national courts against both the state and private individuals where the requirements for direct effect are satisfied.** However, art.157 was treated as directly effective only from the date of the judgment. This ruling on temporal effect was unusual but not unique and was based on the need for legal certainty. See also *Barber v Guardian Royal Exchange* (Case C-262/88) (see p.196).

## Key Principle
Directives are capable of creating direct effects vertically but not horizontally.

> MARSHALL V SOUTH WEST HAMPSHIRE AREA HEALTH AUTHORITY (NO.1) (CASE 152/84) 1986
> Ms M sought to rely on art.5 of the Equal Treatment Directive 76/207 when she was required to retire at 60 when men did not have to retire until the age of 65. The House of Lords referred questions to the ECJ.

## Held
❖ (ECJ) (1) Distinguishing between retirement ages for men and women contravenes art.5 of the directive.
(2) The obligation in a directive is addressed to Member States and cannot be enforced against individuals.

(3) As an area health authority is a public body, the obligation not to discriminate may be enforced directly against that body. [1986] E.C.R. 723.

## Commentary .................................................................................................

[1] *Marshall* established for the first time that **directives are not enforceable directly against individuals,** unless the individual is a public body (or "emanation of the state").

[2] In *Foster v British Gas* (Case C-188/89) the ECJ held that a directive may be enforced against a body responsible for providing a public service under state control, possessing special powers greater than those normally applicable between individuals (e.g. privatised utilities such as gas, water and electricity). In *NUT v St Mary's Church of England Junior School* the Court of Appeal in the UK held that the governors of a church school were a public body as they were charged by the state with running the school.

[3] The limitation on the direct effect of directives was upheld in *Faccini Dori v Recreb* (Case C-91/92). (Ms FD could not rely on the cooling-off period in a consumer protection directive against an Italian company when she sought to cancel a contract for a language course entered into on Milan Station.)

[4] The lack of horizontal direct effect in directives was again confirmed in *El Corte Ingles SA v Rivero* (Case C-192/94). In this case it was held that art.169 TFEU (ex 153) (providing that the EU shall contribute to the attainment of a high level of consumer protection) cannot justify the direct effect of a directive on consumer protection which has not been transposed into national law.

[5] In *Wells v Secretary of State for Transport, Local Government and the Regions* (Case C-201/02) the ECJ held that vertical effect may be invoked against the state even where it gives rise to adverse consequences for individuals. In this case a landowner sought to rely on a directive to prevent the owner of a nearby quarry from extracting minerals from it. The ECJ recognised that the directive could be invoked, even though such reliance would have adverse consequences for third parties.

[6] The ECJ held in *Carp* (Case C-80/06) that a *decision* does not create horizontal direct effects (in the context of an art.267 ruling on **Decision 1999/ 93** on the procedure for attesting conformity of construction products under a directive). In this case, a decision had been addressed to the Member States but could not be relied upon by individuals in the context of legal proceedings against another individual for breach of contract.

# THE DIRECT EFFECT OF GENERAL PRINCIPLES OF LAW

## Key Principle
The general principles of law are capable of creating direct effects.

GRAD WERNER MANGOLD V RÜDIGER HELM (CASE C-144/04) 2005
A German law adopted in 2000 authorised the conclusion of fixed-term contracts of employment once the worker has reached the age of 52, except in specific cases of continuous employment. Mr Mangold, a 56-year-old lawyer, entered into a contract in Germany by which he was employed by Mr Helm for a fixed period from July 2003 until February 2004. He brought proceedings arising from the contract before the German courts which referred several questions to the ECJ for clarification on the interpretation of Directive 2000/78.

## Held
❖ (ECJ) The principle of non-discrimination on grounds of age is a general principle of EU law. The purpose of **Directive 2000/78** is to lay down a general framework for certain forms of discrimination, including in particular discrimination on grounds of age, as regards employment and occupation. A difference of treatment on grounds directly of age constitutes direct discrimination prohibited by Community law, unless it is objectively and reasonably justified by a legitimate aim, particularly by legitimate employment policy and labour market objectives. The means to achieve such objectives must be appropriate and necessary.

## Commentary
[1] The ECJ recognised in *Mangold* that the purpose of the German legislation was to promote the integration into working life of unemployed older workers, in so far as they met difficulties in finding work. While such an objective could be objectively and reasonably justified, the German provision exceeded what was appropriate and necessary to achieve this objective.

[2] While *Mangold* was not cited in several later decisions on age discrimination, it was upheld in *Kücükdeveci* (Case C-555/07), where the ECJ held that non-discrimination on grounds of age is a general principle of EU law (see Ch.14).

# INDIRECT EFFECT

### Key Principle

Where a directive is indirectly effective (i.e. not directly effective) national legislation must be interpreted in the light of the wording and purpose of the directive.

> ### VON COLSON AND KAMANN V LAND NORDRHEIN-WESTFALEN (CASE 14/83) 1984
>
> Ms Von Colson and Ms Kamann had applied for posts as social workers in a German prison. Although they had been placed at the top of the list of applicants by the social work committee, the officials responsible for recruitment refused to appoint the two women, because of the problems and risks associated with working in a male prison. They claimed that they should be granted a contract of employment or damages under art.6 of **Directive 76/207**. The German courts made an art.267 reference.

### Held

❖ (ECJ) (1) Article 6 of **Directive 76/207** does not satisfy the requirements for creating direct effects.

(2) The duty of Member States to achieve the results envisaged by the directive and their duty under art.10 EC (now 4 TEU) to ensure fulfilment of that obligation binds all authorities within the Member States including the courts. National courts must interpret and apply legislation adopted to implement a directive in the light of the wording and purpose of the directive in order to achieve the objective of the directive. [1986] E.C.R. 1891.

### Commentary

[1] Rather than treating the question as one concerned with the supremacy of EU law over national law, the ECJ developed a rule of construction in *Von Colson* derived from art.288 (directive binding on Member State to whom addressed, with choice of form and method left to the national authorities) and art.10 EC (now 4 TEU).

[2] In *Kolpinghuis Nijmegen* (Case 80/86) the ECJ repeated the formula in *Von Colson* but added that a directive cannot independently create criminal liability where its provisions are infringed. See also *Arcaro* (Case C-168/95) in which the ECJ held that, where a Member State has failed to transpose a directive, the obligation to interpret national law in line with EC law reaches a limit. An unimplemented directive may not, of itself, serve to determine or aggravate criminal liability of persons acting in contravention of the directive.

For an application of the principle in the context of the First Companies Directive 68/151, see Berlusconi (Joined Cases C-387, 391 and 403/02).

[3] UK law provides for the implementation of indirectly effective EU law in s.2(2) of the **ECA 1972**.

[4] **Directive 76/207** was repealed and replaced in August 2009 by Directive 2006/54 (see Ch.14).

## Key Principle
The obligation to interpret national law to comply with a directive applies regardless of whether the national law was adopted before or after the directive.

> MARLEASING SA v LA COMMERCIAL INTERNACIONAL DE ALIMTACION SA (CASE C-106/89) 1990
> Marleasing SA had sued La Commercial and several other companies in the Spanish courts. M claimed that the defendant companies had been established by Barviesa, who owed M large sums of money, in order to put his assets beyond the reach of his creditors. M sought a declaration that the contract establishing the companies was void for lack of cause under the Spanish Civil Code. La Commercial claimed that the action should be dismissed because lack of cause was not listed in art.11 of Directive 68/151, which listed nullity grounds exhaustively. An art.267 reference was made.

## Held
❖ (ECJ) In applying national law, whether the provisions in question were adopted before or after the directive, the national court must interpret it, as far as possible, in the light of the wording and purpose of the directive in order to achieve the result pursued by the directive and to comply with art.288(3)TFEU (ex 249(3)). [1990] E.C.R. I-4135.

## Commentary
[1] It follows from the ruling in *Marleasing* that the Spanish Civil Code had to be interpreted in line with the directive, thus excluding lack of cause as a ground for annulment of the contract.

[2] The obligation to interpret national law to conform with an EU obligation is stated to apply "as far as possible".

[3] In *Wagner Miret v Fondo de Garantia Salarial* (Case C-334/92) the ECJ accepted that it was impossible to interpret pre-existing legislation so as to comply with Directive 80/987 on the protection of employees in the event of their employer's insolvency. In such circumstances the state may be obliged to compensate the applicant for his loss under the Francovich principle (see p.15).

**Key Principle**

It is for the national courts to decide in each case whether it is possible to interpret national law to accord with a directive or whether it would distort the meaning of the national law.

> WEBB V EMO AIR CARGO (UK) LTD 1992
> Ms Webb was engaged by EMO for an indefinite term while another employee was on maternity leave. She was dismissed when she found that she, too, was pregnant. The House of Lords had to consider whether EMO was entitled to dismiss Ms Webb. This required the court to decide whether it could construe the Sex Discrimination Act 1975 in accord with the **Equal Treatment Directive 76/207**. The House of Lords referred questions to the ECJ.

**Held**

❖ (HL) It is for the UK court to construe domestic legislation in any field covered by an EC (now EU) directive so as to accord with the interpretation of the directive as laid down by the ECJ, if that can be done without distorting the meaning of the domestic legislation. [1993] 1 C.M.L.R. 259.

**Commentary**

[1] The ECJ ruled that it was a breach of **Directive 76/207** to dismiss a female employee who was pregnant and who had been recruited for an unlimited term, even if she had been engaged as a maternity leave replacement (see p.297). The House of Lords applied the ruling in *Webb v EMO Air Cargo (No.2)* in 1995 and interpreted the UK law in accordance with the directive.

[2] *Webb v EMO* represents a clear statement by the House of Lords of the duty of the UK courts to give effect to EU law when interpreting national law. *Webb* was decided after *Marleasing* and should be contrasted with its earlier decision in *Duke v Reliance Systems* (HL, 1988) in which it had held that it would distort the meaning of the **Sex Discrimination Act 1975** to interpret it so as to give effect to **Directive 76/207**.

[3] The ECJ upheld the liberal approach to statutory interpretation exemplified by cases such as *Marleasing* in two decisions. In *Centrosteel Srl v Adipol GmbH* (Case C-456/98) it held that the national court is bound, when applying provisions of domestic law, predating or postdating the relevant directive, to interpret those provisions, as far as possible, in the light of the wording and purpose of the directive, so that those provisions are applied in a manner consistent with the result pursued by the directive. In *Oceano Grupo Editorial SA v Quintero* and *Salvat Editores SA v Prades* (Joined Cases C-240/98 and C-244/98), it repeated this formula, adding (in the context of the Unfair Contract Terms Directive 93/13) that the requirement to interpret in conformity with the directive requires the national court, in particular, to favour the interpretation which would allow it to decline of its own motion the jurisdiction conferred on it by an unfair term.

[4] The ECJ confirmed in *Maria Pupino* (Case C-105/03) that the duty to interpret national law in line with EU law applies in the area of Police and Judicial Co-operation. The EU had adopted a Framework Decision (similar to a directive, but adopted under the old third pillar) requiring Member States to guarantee victims the opportunity to be heard in criminal proceedings. Particularly vulnerable victims must benefit from specific treatment. This case arose in the context of criminal proceedings against a former nursery school teacher accused of various abusive practices against the children in her care, all of whom were under five years old at the time. The defendant opposed the Public Prosecutor's request for special arrangements to take the testimony of eight children who were witnesses and victims, arguing that it contravened Italian law. The national court made a reference to the ECJ under art.267. (The ECJ had jurisdiction to give preliminary rulings on Framework Decisions prior to the **Treaty of Lisbon** where a Member State declared that it accepted this jurisdiction. Italy had made such a declaration.) The ECJ held that the national court must interpret national law as far as possible in conformity with the wording and purpose of the Framework Decision, in order to attain the result which it envisaged. The national court must be able to authorise young children claiming mistreatment to give their testimony in accordance with arrangements providing for a suitable level of protection.

**Key Principle**
National provisions must not make it practically impossible or excessively difficult to exercise rights conferred by EU law.

METALLGESELLSCHAFT LTD, HOECHST AG AND HOECHST UK v
COMMISSIONERS OF INLAND REVENUE AND HM ATTORNEY GENERAL
(JOINED CASES C-397/98 AND C-410/98) 2001
The applicants were subsidiaries whose parent companies were not
resident within the same Member States (the UK and Germany). The
subsidiaries challenged the resulting imposition of discriminatory
corporation tax (ACT), seeking restitution or compensation in the form
of interest which would otherwise have been due.

### Held

❖ (ECJ) art.49 TFEU (ex 43) requires that resident subsidiaries and their non-
resident parent should have an effective legal remedy in order to obtain
reimbursement or reparation of the financial loss suffered and from which the
Member State concerned has benefited as a result of the advance payment of
corporation tax by the subsidiaries.

### Commentary

[1] The ECJ did not accept the UK's argument that the applicant should have
refused to comply with national tax law, seeking a remedy through directly
effective EU law.

[2] An individual may not be prohibited from relying on art.101 TFEU (ex 81)
(see Ch.12) merely because he was a party to an anti-competitive agreement,
unless he was significantly responsible for the breach.

### Key Principle

The duty to interpret national law in accordance with EU law applies not only
to implementing legislation but to the whole system of national law.

PFEIFFER V ROTES CROSS (CASES C-397/01) 2004
Emergency workers employed by the Red Cross, a private body, in
Germany brought an action claiming that they were required to work for
more than 48 hours a week, contrary to the Working Time Directive 93/
104.

### Held

❖ (ECJ) (art.267) The directive had vertical effect only and so could not be
relied upon by individuals in such circumstances. The national courts are
required to interpret national law as far as possible in accordance with the
Directive, taking national law as a whole into consideration, not merely the
implementing provision.

**Commentary**

[1] The ruling was based on the obligation of the Member States to give full effectiveness to EU law, setting aside any conflicting provisions of national law.

[2] As a result of the ruling, national courts must make use of all available approaches to statutory interpretation. In practice, this is likely to mean making full use of a purposive rather than literal approach to interpretation.

## STATE LIABILITY FOR BREACH OF EU LAW

**Key Principle**

A Member State will be liable for non-implementation of a directive in certain circumstances.

> FRANCOVICH, BONIFACI AND OTHERS V ITALY (CASES C-6 AND 9/90) 1991
> Italy had failed to implement **Directive 80/987** on the protection of workers in the event of insolvency. (The directive required the guarantee of payments of outstanding claims for remuneration and the creation of guarantee institutions to meet those claims.) Italy's breach was established by the ECJ in *Commission v Italy* (Case 22/87). Francovich and Bonifaci had outstanding claims against a company declared bankrupt in 1985. Unable to recover against the company they brought actions in the Italian courts against Italy, requesting that Italy should pay them compensation in the light of the obligation in the directive. Both national courts referred questions to the ECJ to determine the extent of a Member State's liability.

**Held**

❖ (ECJ) Member States are obliged to compensate individuals for breaches of EU law for which they are responsible if three conditions are satisfied:
   (1) the objective of the directive must include the conferring of rights for the benefit of individuals;
   (2) the content of the rights must be identifiable from the directive;
   (3) there must be a causal link between the breach and the damage. [1991] E.C.R. I-5357.

**Commentary**

[1] The ECJ in *Francovich* stated that the full effectiveness of EU law would be impaired if individuals were unable to obtain compensation when their rights were infringed by a breach attributable to a Member State. The principle of

state liability is inherent in the scheme of the Treaty. The duty on Member States to compensate derives from art.4 TEU (ex 10 TEC) which obliges them to ensure fulfilment of their obligations under [EU] law.

[2] State liability under *Francovich* applies to obligations which may not be directly effective and provides a remedy in the event of non-implementation (or inadequate implementation) of EU law. Thus it prevents a state from relying on its own default in implementing EU law.

[3] The ruling has been of immense importance and has been extended and clarified in a number of later rulings.

[4] The High Court in *Three Rivers District Council v Governor and Company of the Bank of England* (1997) held that no action for state liability arose out of the First Banking Directive (the directive at issue in *Francovich*) as the directive did not intend to confer rights on individuals. This decision is hard to reconcile with that of the Italian court in *Francovich*, where the court found that the directive did confer rights on the individual members of a group, but that the applicant himself was outside the group.

**Key Principle**

States are liable for breaches of EU law where the breach is sufficiently serious.

BRASSERIE DU PÊCHEUR SA V GERMANY (CASE C-46/93) AND R. V SECRETARY OF STATE FOR TRANSPORT EX P. FACTORTAME LTD (No.3) (JOINED CASES C-46/93 AND C-48/93) 1996

These cases both concerned the question of the extent of state liability where legislation had been adopted in contravention of directly effective rights. *Brasserie du Pêcheur* arose out of a claim by a French brewery against Germany for losses incurred as a result of the German beer purity laws which had been found by the ECJ to infringe art.34 TFEU (ex 28) (Case 178/84). *Factortame* (see p.xx) had led to a finding that the Merchant Shipping Act 1988 infringed EU law. The Spanish trawler owners claimed compensation from the UK courts. An art.267 reference was made to the ECJ.

**Held**

❖ (ECJ) Where a Member State acts in a field where it has a wide discretion, it will be liable to an individual for breach of EU law provided:

(1) the rule of law infringed is intended to confer rights on individuals;

(2) the breach is sufficiently serious;

(3) there is a direct causal link between the breach and the damage. [1996] ECR I-1029; [1996] 1 C.M.L.R. 889.

## Commentary

[1] The first and third conditions correspond to *Francovich*. However, the position of the Member States was compared with that of the EU institutions under art.349 TFEU (ex 288). The EU institutions are liable in relation to legislative measures involving choices of economic policy where the breach is "sufficiently serious", i.e. when it is "manifest and grave" under the "Schöppenstedt Formula": see p.73.

[2] It was held that reparation may not be made conditional on fault or on a prior finding by the ECJ and that the amount must be commensurate with the damage sustained. No temporal restriction was placed on the effect of the judgment.

[3] The German Federal Court applied the ruling of the ECJ in *Brasserie du Pêcheur v Germany* in 1996. It held that there was no direct causal link between the breach of art.34 TFEU (ex 28) and the applicant's loss. It also found that the infringement in relation to additives was not sufficiently serious. The brewer's claim against the German government thus failed.

[4] The United Kingdom Divisional Court in *Factortame (No.5)* held in 1997 that the trawler owners were entitled to damages, but not to punitive damages. The House of Lords upheld the earlier findings of fault by the British government, namely that there had been a sufficiently serious breach, leaving unchanged the earlier ruling on damages: *R. v Secretary of State for Transport Ex p. Factortame* (Decision of October 28, 1999) HL.

[5] A national requirement to exhaust domestic remedies before bringing an action against the state for breach of EU law contravenes the principle of equivalence: *Transportse Urbanos y Servicios Generales v. Administración del Estado* (Case C-118/08). Member States must not make it any more difficult to bring an action for state liability under EU law than for a comparable action under national law.

**Key Principle** ........................................................................................

Incorrect implementation of an imprecisely worded directive does not necessarily give rise to state liability.

R. v HM TREASURY EX P. BRITISH TELECOMMUNICATIONS PLC
(CASE C-392/93) 1996

BT claimed that the United Kingdom had incorrectly implemented Directive 90/531 covering the procurement (purchasing) procedures of bodies contracting in the telecommunications sector (e.g. BT and Mercury). In particular, BT alleged that the procedures adopted by the United Kingdom for exemption had put BT at a competitive disadvantage. The United Kingdom court referred questions to the ECJ.

**Held** ........................................................................................

❖ (ECJ) The three conditions in *Brasserie du Pêcheur/Factortame* must be satisfied. However, when transposing the directive into national law, the United Kingdom government had not gravely and manifestly disregarded the limits on the exercise of their power. The breach was not sufficiently serious to impose liability. [1996] All E.R. (EC) 411.

**Commentary** ........................................................................................

[1] The ECJ appears in *Ex p. British Telecommunications* to have accepted that the breach was not sufficiently serious because the obligation in the directive was imprecisely worded and could reasonably have borne the interpretation placed on it by the United Kingdom government. No guidance had been provided to the United Kingdom by the ECJ and the Commission had not objected to the United Kingdom's implementing regulations.

[2] See also *Denkavit International v Bundesamt für Ernahring* (Cases C-283, 291 and 292/94) which also involved incorrect transposition of a directive. The ECJ finding that the breach was not sufficiently serious to lead to liability on the part of Germany was influenced by the fact that most other Member States had adopted a similar approach to Germany's.

**Key Principle** ........................................................................................

The mere fact of infringement of EU law may be enough to establish the existence of a sufficiently serious breach were the Member State has little or no discretion.

## R. v Minister of Agriculture, Fisheries and Food Ex p. Hedley Lomas (Ireland) Ltd (Case C-5/94) 1996

MAFF refused to grant licences to enable Hedley Lomas to export live sheep to Spain because it considered that Spain had not implemented properly an EU directive dealing with the pre-slaughter condition of certain animals. The Commission investigated but found no breach by Spain. It informed the United Kingdom that its export ban infringed art.35 TFEU and was not justified under art.36. When proceedings were brought in the United Kingdom courts, an art.267 reference was made.

**Held**

❖ (ECJ) (1) Recourse to art.36 TFEU is impossible where harmonisation has occurred.

(2) A Member State may not act unilaterally to avoid a breach of EU law by another Member State.

(3) Where a Member State does not have to make legislative choices or has only reduced discretion, the mere fact of infringement of EU law may be enough to establish a sufficiently serious breach.

(4) It is for the national court to determine whether there is a causal link between duty and the damage.

(5) If state liability is established, the state must make good any loss in accordance with its domestic law on liability. [1996] All E.R. (EC) 493.

**Commentary**

[1] See also *Dillenkofer v Federal Republic of Germany* (Joined Cases C-178, etc./94): intentional fault is not an essential precondition to state liability. Here, the German government had failed to implement the Package Holidays Directive by the deadline. The ECJ held that failure to implement a directive on time was a sufficiently serious breach.

[2] In *Rechberger v Austria* (Case C-140/97), in another case involving the **Package Holidays Directive**, the ECJ found that incorrect transposition of the directive, preventing reimbursement of money in the event of the insolvency of the travel organiser, was a sufficiently serious breach. Austria had no margin of discretion over the implementation of the directive.

[3] In *Konle v Austria* (Case C-302/97) the ECJ sought to clarify the position on state liability for breach of EU law by states with a federal structure (like Austria). The ECJ held that it is for each Member State to ensure that individuals obtain compensation for damage caused to them by breach of EU law, whichever public authority is responsible for the breach and for payment of compensation. There is no need under EU law to change the law relating to

the distribution of power and responsibility within public bodies, provided it is no more difficult for an individual to bring an action for state liability for breach of EU law than to bring an action in relation to rights deriving under national law.

[4] The ECJ provided further guidance as to discretion in relation to what is a sufficiently serious breach in *Haim v Kassenzahnärztliche Vereinigung Nordrhein* (Case 424/97). It held that the existence and scope of discretion must be determined by EC and not national law. It follows that discretion conferred on an individual by national law is irrelevant. EU law does not preclude a public law body, in addition to the Member State, from being liable to make reparation for loss and damage caused to individuals as a result of measures which it took in breach of EU law.

## Key Principle

Losses arising from judicial decisions may, in principle, give rise to state liability.

### KÖBLER V AUSTRIA (CASE C-224/01) 2003

The case arose out of a claim by an Austrian professor for recognition of time spent working in universities in other EU Member States for the purpose of a long service increment. (Austrian law required 10 years as a professor at an Austrian university to qualify.) The national court withdrew a request for a preliminary ruling from the ECJ. As a result, the applicant lost the increment. The applicant sued the Austrian government for infringement of state liability. This time a preliminary reference was made to the ECJ.

## Held

❖ (ECJ) State liability can arise from an infringement of EU law by a decision of a national court of last resort only exceptionally where the court has manifestly infringed the law. Various factors should be considered when deciding whether the breach was manifest, namely the degree of clarity and precision of the rule infringed, whether the breach was intentional, whether or not the error of law was excusable, the position taken by an EU institution, and non-compliance by the court in its obligation to make a referral to the ECJ under art.267(3).

**Commentary** ...............................................................................................

In principle, *Köbler* opens up the possibility of an applicant claiming damages against a national court which wrongly refuses to make a preliminary
reference to the ECJ.

---

**THINK POINT**

Why is direct effect a concept of central importance in EU law? Do you
think the time is right to extend horizontal effect to directives?

How and in which decisions did the ECJ use art.4 TEU (ex 10 TEC) to
develop the concepts of indirect effect and state liability?

# The Institutions of the EU

## INTRODUCTION

The tasks of the EU are entrusted by art.13 TEU to seven institutions, namely the European Parliament (EP), the European Council, the Council, the Commission, the Court of Justice, the European Central Bank (ECB) and the Court of Auditors. Of these, the Council wields the most political power, although the influence of the EP continues to increase.

Article 15 TEU provides for regular summit meetings of the European Council, made up of the Heads of State of the Member States, the President of the Commission and the High Representative of the Union (see below). The role of the European Council is strategic rather than legislative.

The EP is a directly elected body, meeting in Strasbourg, with some committee session in Brussels. MEPs sit in political groupings, reflecting traditional ideological divisions. Seats are not evenly distributed according to population, resulting in a better representation of small states relative to large states.

Most secondary legislation is adopted jointly by the Council and the EP under the ordinary legislative procedure set out in art.294 TFEU (ex 251), although some measures are adopted by the Council alone under a special procedure where the Treaties provide, after consultation between the EP, Council and Commission.

Membership of the Council fluctuates, depending on the subject matter under discussion (e.g. foreign ministers meeting as the General Affairs and External Relations Council). Most voting is by qualified majority (QMV), involving the weighting of votes by approximate reference to population. A few areas still require a unanimous vote, or (rarely) a simple majority.

The Commission is based in Brussels where it meets weekly in private, taking decisions by simple majority. It is led by the President of the Commission. The **Treaty of Lisbon** introduced a new role of High Representative who presides over foreign policy and is the Vice President of the Commission. Members of the Commission (one per Member State, including the President and the High Commissioner) are appointed for a five-year term. The Commission's functions are wider than those of a national civil service, as it is responsible for promoting the integration of the EU. The Commission has three main functions: as initiator of Community legislation (it drafts legislative proposals for submission to the Council and the EP), as guardian of the Treaties to ensure that EU law is observed (it may bring enforcement proceedings against defaulting Member States under art.258 TFEU (ex 226) and as the executive of the EU (it implements policies decided by the Council). In addition it negotiates international treaties and drafts the Budget. In both cases, the Council concludes the matter after consultation with the EP. The Commission also has limited powers to adopt legislation through a process known as "Comitology" under delegation from the Council and the EP.

The European Court consists of two courts, the Court of Justice (ECJ) and the General Court (known as the CFI before the **Treaty of Lisbon**). Both sit in Luxembourg. The ECJ at present consists of one judge per Member State (art.19 TEU). As it is no longer practical for the ECJ to hear many cases as a full court of 27 judges, many cases are now heard in chambers of three or five judges, or in a Grand Chamber of 13 judges. The Court issues a single judgment, binding on all the Member States, with no provision for dissent. It may be assisted in its task by the Opinion of the Advocate General, a neutral official of the Court, who makes non-binding submissions about the issues in question. Simpler cases may not require such submissions. The main areas of the Court's jurisdiction are preliminary rulings under art.267 TFEU (ex 234), a particularly significant mechanism which has enabled the Court to develop the law (see Ch.7), enforcement under arts 258–260 TFEU (ex 226–228) (see Ch.4), judicial review of the acts of the EU institutions under arts 263 TFEU (ex 230), 265 TFEU (ex 232) and 277 TFEU (ex 241) (see Ch.5), and actions relating to the non-contractual liability of the EU institutions under art.340 TFEU (ex 288) (see Ch.6).

The General Court acts as a court of first instance, with appeal against its decision to the ECJ. It hears actions under arts 263, 265, etc., brought by individuals, unless the matter is in an area assigned to a judicial panel (e.g. staff cases), from which there is an appeal to the General Court. It comprises at least one judge per Member State (art.19 TEU). Although the General Court is empowered to hear preliminary references under art.267 in specific areas provided by the Court's statute, such rulings are likely to be the exception rather than the norm.

The Court of Auditors was set up in 1975 to control and supervise the implementation of the Budget and to audit the accounts of the EU institutions. The European Central Bank operates as a central bank for Member States participating in EMU and issues euros.

This chapter focuses on choice of legal base and transparency to illustrate the inter-relationship of the EU institutions.

# THE EUROPEAN PARLIAMENT

### Key Principle
Failure to consult the EP, where required by the Treaty, is a breach of an essential procedural requirement.

> ROQUETTE FRÈRES SA v COUNCIL (CASE 138/79) 1980
> The Council adopted a regulation before it had received the opinion of the EP under art.40 TFEU (ex 34(3)). It was challenged by a producer affected by the measure.

### Held
❖ (ECJ) Consultation under art.40 (3) is the means whereby the EP participates in the legislative process of the [EU]. Failure to consult was a breach of an essential procedural requirement, as a result of which the measure concerned was void. [1980] E.C.R. 3393.

### Commentary
The ECJ stated in *Roquette Frères* that consultation "reflects at Community [EU] level the fundamental democratic principle that the peoples should take part in the exercise of power through the intermediary of an intermediate assembly".

### Key Principle
If the Council or Commission fails to act, in infringement of the Treaties, the EP may bring an action in the ECJ: art.265.

> EP v COUNCIL (CASE 13/83) 1985
> The EP sought a declaration that the Council had infringed the **[EEC] Treaty** by failing to adopt a Common Transport Policy. The Council objected, claiming that the EP lacked competence to bring an action under art.265.

### Held
❖ (ECJ) The EP had capacity to bring an action under art.265 and had observed the conditions of that provision in bringing the action. The action was upheld in part, but rejected where the obligation was too vague to be enforceable. (See p.xx.)

# THE COUNCIL

## Key Principle

If action by the EU is necessary, in the course of the operation of the policies defined in the Treaties, to attain one of the objectives set out in the Treaties, and the Treaties have not provided the necessary powers, the Council, acting unanimously, shall adopt the appropriate measures acting on a proposal from the Commission and after consulting the EP: art.352 TFEU (ex 308).

> ### COMMISSION V COUNCIL (CASE 45/86) 1987
>
> The Commission brought annulment proceedings under art.263 (see Ch.5) against two regulations adopted by the Council relating to generalised tariff preferences for products from developing countries. The Commission claimed that there was no explicit legal basis stated in the measures. The Council argued that it had intended to base the measures on both arts 207 TFEU (ex 133) (the Common Commercial Policy) and 352 TFEU (ex 308).

## Held

❖ (ECJ) It follows from the wording of art.352 that its use as the legal basis for a measure is justified only where no other provision of the Treaty gives the [EU] institutions the necessary power to adopt the measure in question. As art.207 would have provided an appropriate legal basis, the Council was not justified in relying on art.352. [1987] E.C.R. 1493.

## Commentary

The choice of legal basis determines the procedure which is followed in the adoption of the measure. Article 352, unlike art.207, requires unanimity in the Council, thus making it possible for individual states to veto a proposed measure.

## Key Principle

The choice of legal base must be based on objective factors which are amenable to judicial review.

> ### COMMISSION V COUNCIL (CASE C-300/89) 1991
>
> The Commission brought annulment proceedings under art.263 against the Council in relation to a directive harmonising programmes to eliminate pollution caused by waste from the titanium dioxide industry. The directive in question had been based on art.192 (ex 175) which

enabled the Council to adopt measures relating to environment protection by unanimity, on a proposal from the Commission after consulting the EP and the Economic and Social Committee. The
Commission claimed that the measure should have been adopted
under art.114 TFEU (ex 95) as a single market measure (under the now-
defunct co-operation procedure, which required qualified majority
voting and two consultations with the EP).

## Held

❖ (ECJ) The measure should have been based on art.114, not art.192. [1991]
E.C.R. I-2867.

## Commentary

[1] While the directive displayed features relating both to the environment
and to the establishment and functioning of the internal market, recourse to
a dual basis was excluded by the ECJ. An EU measure cannot be treated as an
environmental measure merely because it pursues objectives of environmental protection. Action to harmonise national rules on industrial production with a view to eliminating distortion of competition is covered by art.114.

[2] This case was considered before amendment by the **Maastricht Treaty**,
which introduced the co-decision (now the ordinary) procedure. The new
procedure provided for legislation to be jointly adopted by the EP and
Council. As it governed both the adoption of internal market rules under
art.114, as well as environmental measures under art.192, the choice of legal
base became less significant.

[3] In *EP v Council* (Case C-42/97) the EP, by contrast, sought to argue that a
Council decision on the adoption of a programme to promote linguistic
diversity in the EC should have a dual legal base. The ECJ concluded that the
effects on culture were only indirectly incidental; the measure was essentially
economic. As a result, it was appropriate for the measure to have been based
on art.173 TFEU (ex 157) on industry rather than art.167 TFEU (ex 151) on
culture.

[4] The EP mounted another challenge to a measure adopted by the Council in
*EP v Council* (Joined Cases C-164 and 165/97). The regulations in question
had been adopted under art.43 TFEU (ex 37) (CAP), but the EP claimed they
should have been adopted under art.192 TFEU (ex 175) (environment), as they
were intended to protect forests in the EC from atmospheric pollution and
fire. This time the ECJ held that the measures were primarily environmental,

even though there would have been repercussions for agriculture, and allowed the EP's application.

[5] *Netherlands v EP and Council* (Case C-377/98) arose out of a challenge by the Netherlands (a long-standing opponent of genetic manipulation of animals and plants) to **Directive 98/44** on the legal protection of biotechnical inventions. The directive lists which inventions involving plants, animals or the human body may be patented. Member States are required to allow the patenting of inventions with an industrial application, making it possible to use biological material. The Dutch government sought to annul the directive, claiming that it should not be possible to patent plant, animal or human material. It was supported in the action by Italy and Norway. A number of grounds were used including the use of wrong legal base (now art.114 TFEU (ex 95)). The ECJ dismissed all the claims, holding that the measure was an internal market measure and so properly adopted under the correct legal base, compliance with subsidiary was implicit in the recitals to the directive: there was no uncertainty, no breach of international law, no infringement of rights of human dignity and no breach of procedural rules.

[6] In *R. v Secretary of State for Health Ex p. British American Tobacco (Investments) Ltd* (Case C-491/01) the legal base of a directive was again at issue, this time in relation to tobacco advertising. The case arose under an art.267 reference from proceedings before the High Court in which judicial review was sought in relation to the intention and/or obligation of the UK government to transpose the directive into UK law. **Directive 90/239** was adopted under (old) arts 95 and 133 (now arts 114 and 207 TFEU), recasting an earlier directive, providing a stronger health warning. The national court sought to clarify whether the directive was invalid, by lacking an appropriate legal base. The ECJ found that where an EC act has a twofold purpose and one of these is predominant, the act must be founded on that as the predominant one. Where, exceptionally, the act pursues several objectives which are indissolubly linked, it may have several legal bases. In the case in question, art.95 was found to be the correct legal base. The incorrect reference to art.133 did not, however, make the directive invalid. It was no more than a formal defect. Having found, in addition, that there were no breaches of the principles of subsidiarity and proportionality (amongst other matters), the ECJ ruled that the directive was valid.

**Key Principle** ........................................................................................

Where the Treaty confers a specific task on the Commission, it also confers on it the powers which are indispensable to carry out the task.

**Key Principle** ........................................................................................

The Commission shall have the task of promoting close co-operation between Member States in the social field. To this end the Commission shall act in close contact with Member States by making studies, delivering opinions and arranging consultations both on problems arising at national level and on those of concern to international organisations: art.153 TFEU (ex 137).

GERMANY, FRANCE, NETHERLANDS, DENMARK AND THE UNITED KINGDOM V COMMISSION (JOINED CASES 281, 283 AND 287/85) 1987
Germany and the other applicant states sought annulment of Decision 85/381 under art.263 in relation to the migration policy of non-member countries. The challenge was brought on the grounds that such a policy was outside the social field and that the arrangement of consultation under art.153 did not empower the Commission to adopt binding measures.

**Held** ........................................................................................

❖ (ECJ) (1) The promotion of the integration into the workforce of non-member countries must be held to be within the social field within the meaning of art.153, in so far as it is linked to employment.

(2) The promotion of cultural integration goes beyond the social field but may be justified under art.153(2) (power to arrange consultations). [1987] E.C.R. 3203.

**Commentary** ........................................................................................

The ECJ exercised care in this judgment to make it clear that the Commission's power to take binding decisions (not explicitly provided in art.153) is limited to procedural matters.

**Key Principle** ........................................................................................

Citizens of the EU and natural or legal persons residing or having a registered office in one of the Member States shall have a right of access to EP, Council or Commission documents: art.15(3) TFEU (ex 255).

**Key Principle**

The public shall have access to measures adopted by the Council unless the release of such documents would undermine the protection of the public interest, individual privacy, commercial and industrial secrecy, the EU's financial interests or confidentiality requested by natural or legal persons: art.1, Decision 93/731.

> CARVEL & GUARDIAN NEWSPAPERS V COUNCIL (CASE T-194/94) 1995
> Carvel, the European Affairs Editor of the *Guardian*, requested various documents relating to meetings of the Social Affairs and Justice Council in 1993 and the Agriculture Committee in 1994. The Council's Secretariat refused, stating that the documents related directly to the deliberations of the Council and could not be disclosed. The applicants challenged the decision under art.263.

**Held**

❖ (CFI) **Decision 93/731** requires the balancing of the applicants' interests in gaining access with the Council's interests in maintaining confidentiality. By automatically refusing access to the documents the Council had failed to exercise discretion in accordance with the decision. [1995] 3 C.M.L.R. 359.

**Commentary**

[1] After the ruling of the CFI, the Council agreed to facilitate the release of minutes of meetings, to broadcast debates on matters of public interest and to release details of votes on legislative acts. Carvel remains dissatisfied and is pursuing a further action against the Council.

[2] The principle in art.15 TFEU is subject to the Council's power in art.15(2) to determine the "general principles and limits on grounds of public and private interest governing the right of access to documents".

[3] *In Svenska Journalistforbundet v Council* (Case T(174/95) the CFI interpreted art.1 of the regulation as meaning that the Council must consider in relation to each document requested whether disclosure would undermine one of the matters referred to in para.1 of the Code of Conduct concerning Public Access to Council and Commission Documents (including public interest, protection of the individual and privacy, etc.). Similar considerations govern the release of Commission documents: *Interporc v Commission* (Case T-124/96).

[4] In *Council v Hautala* (Case C-353/99P) the Council appealed against a decision of the CFI which had annulled its decision to refuse Ms Hautala, an

MEP, access to a report on conventional arms policy. The refusal was based on **Decision 93/731** regarding public access to documents, under which the Council may refuse access to a document in order to protect public interest in the field of international relations. The Council stated that the report contained sensitive information which would harm the EU's relations with non-Member States. The ECJ emphasised that the public should have the widest possible access to Council and Commission documents. If a document contains confidential information, partial access must be considered. Refusal of partial access was a disproportionate measure. The Council may not systematically limit the public's right of access to documents.

[5] In *Skoma Lux* (Case C-161/06) the ECJ held that lack of publication of legislation in the *Official Journal of the European Union* in one of the official languages of the Member States renders the obligations in that legislation unenforceable against individuals in that State, even though the individual could have learned of the legislation by other means. (In this case, a regulation had not been translated into Czech.)

## THINK POINT

How does the case law of the ECJ demonstrate the importance of the legal base of a measure relative to the role of the EC institutions in the legislative process?

Do you think the ECJ has got the balance right between the interests of the individual and the public in relation to disclosure of documents?

# Fundamental Rights and General Principles

## INTRODUCTION

The **TEU** and the **TFEU** are framework treaties, providing basic rules which require supplementing by secondary legislation and judicial interpretation. The term "general principles" refers to the body of principles decided by the ECJ in interpreting the primary and secondary law of the EU. Authority may be found in the Treaty for the role of general principles in art.263 which enables the ECJ to annul measures on grounds including infringement of the Treaties or rule relating to their application, and in art.340 which provides that the non-contractual liability of the EU institutions is determined in accordance with the general principles common to the law of the Member States. The case law of the ECJ shows that general principles may also derive from international law, particularly the European Convention on Human Rights and Fundamental Freedoms (see below). General principles include fundamental rights, legal certainty, proportionality, equality, procedural rights and subsidiarity.

**Key Principle**

Fundamental rights and the general principles of EU law are protected by the ECJ.

> STAUDER V CITY OF ULM (CASE 29/69) 1969
> A Commission regulation provided for the recipients of welfare benefits to receive free butter. When the scheme was implemented, the German government required beneficiaries to produce a coupon bearing their name and address. Stauder claimed that the German decision implementing the scheme infringed the general principles of EC [now EU] law. An art.267 reference was made to the ECJ by the German administrative court.

**Held**

❖ (ECJ) The provision in issue contained nothing capable of prejudicing the fundamental human rights enshrined in the general principles of EU law and protected by the Court. [1969] E.C.R. 419.

**Commentary** .........................................................................................

[1] The tentative statement in *Stauder* is the first acknowledgment by the ECJ that fundamental rights are recognised by EU law. In its subsequent case law the ECJ has developed its approach to fundamental rights, providing a mechanism to review that validity of action by the EU institutions and by the Member States. Fundamental rights and general principles are most often invoked in annulment proceedings under art.263 (see Ch.5), to claim damages under art.340 (see Ch.6) and as a guide to the interpretation of EU law (see Ch.1).

[2] General principles derive from:

- (a) international law (e.g. the **European Convention on Human Rights (ECHR)**);
- (b) principles which are accepted by the domestic legal systems of the Member States; and
- (c) the decisions of the ECJ.

[3] The Charter of Fundamental Rights was proclaimed at the Nice European Summit in December 1999. It was based on existing law from various sources, particularly the **ECHR**. The Charter is divided into seven chapters headed Dignity (including freedom from torture and slavery), Freedoms (liberty, association, expression, property, private and family life), Equality (similar to art.19 TFEU (ex 13), with further references to rights of children, the elderly and persons with disabilities), Solidarity (labour rights based on the earlier European Social Charter), Citizens' Rights (EU citizenship, right to good administration, access to documents), Justice (e.g. right to a fair trial) and, finally, General Clauses on the scope of Charter. Article 6(1) TEU provides for the Charter to have "the same legal effect as the Treaties". The UK and Poland signed a Protocol declaring that the Charter does not extend the ability of the ECJ or the Member States to find that laws of administrative provisions conflict with fundamental rights under the Charter.

. . . . . . . . . . . . . . . . . . . . . . . . . . . . . . . . . . . . . . . . . . . . . . . . . . . . . . . . . . . . . . . . . . . . . . . . . .

## RELATIONSHIP BETWEEN THE CHARTER OF FUNDAMENTAL RIGHTS AND THE GENERAL PRINCIPLES OF EU LAW

**Key Principle** .........................................................................................

Rights under the Charter of Fundamental Rights have the same status in EU law as the Treaties.

Regulations under the Common Agricultural Policy required the publication of information on the recipients of aid to be made available to the public through websites operated by national governments. This requirement for transparency conflicted with the right to the protection of personal data under the Charter. The German court referred to the ECJ under art.267.

**Held**

❖ (ECJ) (1) Publication on a website of data naming the beneficiaries of funding interfered with the rights of those beneficiaries to a private life in general and to protection of their personal data in particular. Interference with such rights would only be justified where it is provided for by law, respects the essence of those rights and is proportionate.

(2) While taxpayers in a democratic society have a right to information about the use of public funds, the Council and Commission must maintain a proper balance between the various interests involved, and should find out, before publication of such data on a website, whether such action went further than was necessary.

**Commentary**

We can expect to see far more frequent references to the rights under the Charter following the **Treaty of Lisbon,** particularly in the context of access to effective judicial protection under art.47 of the Charter. See, for example, *DEB Deutscher Energiehandels-und-Beratungsgesellschaft* (Case C-279/09), in which the ECJ brought an action for state liability against Germany arising from that country's delay in transposing Directive 98/30 on common rules for the internal market in natural gas. The ECJ held that account must be taken of rights under the Charter, particularly art.47(3) which provides that legal aid shall be available to those lacking sufficient resources in so far as it is necessary to enable them to ensure effective access to justice. However, it is for the national courts to determine whether the conditions for the grant of legal aid limit access to the courts, undermining the right, whether the conditions pursue a legitimate aim, and whether the means are proportionate to the aims. The ECJ then lists the factors that the national court should take into account, including the importance of the issue at stake and the complexity of the applicable law. (See p.41 on previous case law on the right to effective judicial control.)

**Key Principle** ...........................................................................................

Respect for fundamental rights forms an integral part of the general principles of law protected by the ECJ.

---

INTERNATIONALE HANDELSGESELLSCHAFT MBH V EINFUHR- UND
VORRATSSTELLE FÜR GETREIDE UND FUTTERMITTEL (CASE 11/70) 1970
The applicants had obtained a licence to export maize from Germany, conditional under an EU regulation on lodging a deposit which acted as a guarantee that the exportation would be carried out while the licence was valid. As the exportation was not completed during the validity of the licence, the German administrative authorities ordered the forfeiture of a large part of the deposit. The applicants challenged the forfeiture on the basis that it contravened certain principles of German law in the Frankfurt administrative court, which made an art.267 reference to the ECJ.

**Held** .................................................................................................

❖ (ECJ) (1) The validity of a measure of [EU] law cannot be affected by allegations that it contravenes national fundamental rights or national constitutional principles.

(2) The protection of fundamental rights, while inspired by the constitutional traditions common to the Member States, must be ensured within the framework and structure of the objectives of the [EU]. [1970] E.C.R. 1125.

**Commentary** ...................................................................................

[1] See also *Nold v Commission* (Case 4/73) in which the ECJ declared that it would not uphold measures which are incompatible with fundamental rights recognised and protected by the constitutions of the Member States.

[2] In the early years the German Constitutional Court did not accept the supremacy of EU law on fundamental rights expressed in decisions such as *Handelsgesellschaft*. This view was modified in *Wünsche Handelsgesellschaft* (1987) where the German court accepted that the protection of fundamental rights under EC law had reached the level of German law. However, in *Brunner v EU Treaty* (1994) the Constitutional Court reasserted its right to review the legitimacy of EC law (see Ch.1).

[3] In *Connolly v Commission* (Case C-274/99P), Bernard Connolly, then a high-ranking official in the Commission, for personal reasons, published a book in 1995 entitled *The Rotten Heart of Europe*, which was highly critical of the Commission. After being removed from his post in 1996 he sought unsuccessfully to annul the decision ordering the removal before the CFI. He

then appealed to the ECJ which upheld the decision of the CFI. The ECJ reaffirmed its support for fundamental rights including freedom of expression under the **ECHR**, but held that the protection of the rights of the institutions responsible for carrying out tasks in the public interest justifies the restriction. The ECJ was required to strike a fair balance between the individual's fundamental right to freedom of expression and the legitimate concern of the institutions to ensure that their officials and employees fulfil their duties.

## LEGAL CERTAINTY

### Non-retroactivity

**Key Principle**
Penal provisions may not take effect retroactively.

> R. v KIRK (CASE 63/83) 1984
> Captain Kirk, a Danish fisherman, was charged with fishing in the United Kingdom's 12-mile coastal fishing zone, contrary to United Kingdom law. Although the United Kingdom was entitled under the Act of Accession to exclude non-United Kingdom fishing vessels from the 12-mile zone until December 31, 1982, Captain Kirk had been fishing on January 6, 1983. The [EU] subsequently adopted a regulation permitting the United Kingdom to maintain the exclusion for a further 10 years, backdated to January 1, 1983. The United Kingdom court made an art.267 reference.

**Held**
❖ (ECJ) Non-retroactivity of penal provisions is common to all the Member States and enshrined in art.7 of the **ECHR**. It is one of the general principles of EU law. [1984] E.C.R. 2689.

**Commentary**
[1] The duty to interpret national law in accordance with EU law reaches its limits in the context of the general principles of law, particularly the principle of non-retroactivity. In X (Case C-60/02), the Austrian court sought clarification of the legality of imposing penalties for breach of EU law. This action arose out of a request by Rolex for a judicial investigation into persons unknown, following the discovery of a consignment of counterfeit watches in transit between Italy and Poland. Austrian law only permitted a judicial review where the conduct involved a criminal offence. The importation and exportation of counterfeit goods was an offence. Mere transit was not an offence

under Austrian law, although it was an offence under an EU regulation. The ECJ held that, if the national court considered that mere transit was not an office, the principle of non-retroactivity of penalties would prohibit the imposition of criminal penalties for such conduct, even though the national law was contrary to EU law.

[2] The ECJ has upheld a number of individual provisions of the **ECHR** as general principles of EU law: see e.g. *National Panasonic (UK) Ltd v Commission* (Case 136/79): art.8 (right to privacy); *VBVB v Commission* (Cases 43 and 63/82): art.10 (right to expression).

[3] The EU recognises the importance in art.2 TEU of respect for human dignity, freedom, democracy, equality, the rule of law and respect for human rights including the rights of persons belonging to minorities. Article 6(1) **TEU** provides that the Union recognises the rights, freedoms and principles set out in the Charter of Fundamental Rights 2000.

[4] After amendment by the **Treaty of Lisbon**, art.6(2) **TEU** requires the EU to accede to the **ECHR**. A Protocol to the **ToL** provides that accession to the **ECHR** must be agreed unanimously.

[5] Article 7(1) **TEU** empowers the Council to determine that a Member State has committed a persistent and serious breach of human rights, in which case it may decide to suspend the voting rights of the offending state.

[6] The EU itself was found to be in breach of the **ECHR** in *Matthews*. The applicant, a resident of Gibraltar, brought a claim before the European Court of Human Rights (ECtHR) following her exclusion from voting in the EP. The ECtHR ruled in 1999 that the limited status for Gibraltar residents provided by the Direct Elections Act 1976 infringed art.3 of Protocol 1 of the **ECHR** (right to free elections). As the Act was in fact a Treaty, the ECJ did not have the capacity to review it, thus depriving the applicant of a remedy if she had not pursued her claim before the Court of Human Rights. For a further decision arising from these facts, see *Spain v UK* (Case C-145/04) (Ch.4).

## LEGITIMATE EXPECTATIONS

### Key Principle

EU measures must not infringe the legitimate expectations of those concerned in the absence of overriding public interest.

Mulder and other milk producers decided not to deliver milk for five years under an EC [now EU] scheme to reduce an excess supply of milk. After that time they were unable to resume deliveries because provision under an [EU] regulation was based on a reference year during the five years of non-delivery.

**Held**

❖ (ECJ) Where a producer has been encouraged by an [EU] provision to suspend marketing in the general interest and against the payment of a premium he may legitimately expect not to be subjected to restrictions because he has acted on the provision. [1988] E.C.R. 2321.

**Commentary**

An expectation is only legitimate where it is reasonable rather than speculative. Challenges to EU legislation based on a breach of legitimate expectations rarely succeed.

## PROPORTIONALITY

**Key Principle**

Measures should not exceed what is appropriate and necessary to achieve the objectives in question.

R. V INTERVENTION BOARD FOR AGRICULTURAL PRODUCE EX P. MAN (SUGAR) (CASE 181/84) 1986
As a result of applying for an export licence four hours late the Commission ruled that the entire deposit was forfeit under the terms of a regulation. The Divisional Court in the United Kingdom made an art.267 reference.

**Held**

❖ (ECJ) The forfeiture of the entire deposit was a disproportionate penalty for a minor breach. The regulation was annulled to the extent that it required the forfeiture. [1985] E.C.R. 2889.

**Commentary**

[1] Proportionality, like a number of other general principles, derives from German law, although there are some similarities with reasonableness in English law. Proportionality operates by weighing the objectives of legislation

against the means by which they are achieved. The principle operates to restrain public authorities from imposing unnecessarily restrictive measures.

[2] Proportionality is frequently invoked in the context of single market measures. Under the *Cassis de Dijon* principle (see p.xx) restrictions on imports may be permissible if necessary to justify a mandatory requirement provided they are not disproportionate. (In *Cassis* (Case-120/78) it was disproportionate to ban the sale of drinks below a certain alcohol level. Labelling would have provided the customer with sufficient information.) Proportionality is incorporated in the principle of subsidiarity under art.4 TEU (ex 5) (see p.42).

## EQUALITY

**Key Principle**
Persons in similar situations should be treated alike unless differential treatment is objectively justified.

> SABBATINI V EP (CASE 20/71) 1972
> Mrs Sabbatini sought the annulment of decisions whereby the expatriation allowance she had previously received from the EP was withdrawn following her marriage. The allowance was payable to the "head of the family", normally considered to be the husband except in cases of serious illness or invalidity.

**Held**
❖ (ECJ) Determination of the status of expatriate must be dependent on uniform criteria, irrespective of sex. The decisions taken with regard to the applicant were annulled. [1972] E.C.R. 345.

**Commentary**
[1] The **TFEU** recognises the principle of equality (or non-discrimination) on grounds of nationality (art.18 TFEU (ex 12); sex (art.157 TFEU (ex 141); equal pay (for equal work); and against producers or consumers under the CAP (art.40(3) TFEU ( 34(3)). Equality of treatment has been extended by secondary legislation into such areas as access to employment and housing (**Directive 2006/54** (repealing **Directive 76/207**). Equality of treatment is essential to secure the free movement of goods, persons, services and capital (e.g. art.34 TFEU: exception to the free movement of goods, provided there is no discrimination on grounds of nationality—see Ch.8). The ECJ has

applied the principle imaginatively to meet the demands of the single market. See e.g. *Cowan v Tresor Public* (Case 186/87) (p.155).

[2] For two recent examples of a breach of the principle of equality by the Italian government, see *Commission v Italy* (Case C-224/00) and *Commission v Italy* (Case C-388/01). In Case C-224/00 Italy was found to have infringed art.18 TFEU by maintaining in force a provision of the Italian Highway Code for different and disproportionate treatment of offenders according to the place of registration of their vehicle, effectively discriminating against nationals of other Member States not resident in Italy. In Case C-388/01 Italy was found to have infringed both arts 18 (non-discrimination) and 56 TFEU (ex 49) on services (see Ch.11) by applying differential rates for admission charges to museums, monuments, art galleries, etc. The rates favoured Italian nationals and persons resident in Italy aged 60, 65 or above, but excluded tourists and non-residents.

## Key Principle

The **Equal Treatment Directive** should be interpreted liberally and should not be limited in scope to discrimination on grounds of gender.

### P v S (Case C-13/94) 1996

P was employed as a manager by Cornwall County Council. He was taken on to work as a male employee, but informed his employers that he intended to undergo treatment for gender reassignment. After taking sick leave, P was not permitted to return to work in a female gender role. The final surgical operation took place after the expiry of notice of dismissal. P claimed for unfair dismissal before an industrial tribunal, claiming discrimination on grounds of sex. The tribunal made a request for an art.267 ruling to the ECJ to clarify the meaning of the **Equal Treatment Directive** in relation to transsexuals.

## Held

❖ (ECJ) Article 5(1) of the **Equal Treatment Directive 76/207** precludes the dismissal of a transsexual for a reason arising from the gender reassignment of the person concerned. [1996] ECR I-2143.

## Commentary

[1] Article 5(1) of **Directive 76/207** provided that application of the principle with regard to working conditions including the conditions governing dismissal means that men and women shall be guaranteed the same conditions

without discrimination on grounds of sex. This provision is now covered by **Directive 2006/54** (see Ch.14).

[2] The ECJ in *P v S* followed the submissions of Advocate General Tesauro that transsexuals do not constitute a third sex and were therefore protected by the directive against discrimination on the grounds of sex. He submitted that respect for fundamental rights is one of the general principles of EU law, and that the elimination of discrimination on grounds of sex forms part of those fundamental rights. The ECJ stated that dismissal of a person due to an intention to carry out treatment for gender reassignment is contrary to **Directive 76/207**.

[3] For an example of the application in the UK by the Employment Appeals Tribunal of the approach adopted in *P v S*, see *Chessington World of Adventures Ltd v Reed* (1997) (dismissal following gender reassignment surgery from male to female).

[4] For a more conservative approach after *P v S*, see *Grant v South West Trains* (Case C-249/96), in which the ECJ held that **Directive 76/207** does not cover issues of sexual orientation. The facts of this case concerned a claim in the UK for the special travel concessions to cover same sex partners prior to amendment of the Treaty to include art.19 TFEU (ex 13). Article 19 empowers the Council to take appropriate action to combat discrimination based on sex, racial or ethnic origin, religion or belief, disability, age or sexual orientation. Two directives based on art.13 were adopted in 2000: Directive 2000/43 on equal treatment between persons irrespective of racial or ethnic origin, and **Directive 2000/78** providing a general framework for equal treatment in employment and occupation (see Ch.14).

## PROCEDURAL RIGHTS

### Right to a hearing

**Key Principle**

A person whose interests are affected by a decision must be given the opportunity to be heard.

TRANSOCEAN MARINE PAINTS ASSOCIATION V COMMISSION (CASE 17/74) 1974
The Commission reached a competition decision concerning exemption under art.101(3) TFEU (ex 81(3)) of an agreement between the

## Held

❖ (ECJ) Interested parties have a right to be heard. The offending part of the decision was annulled (see p.66). [1974] E.C.R. 1063.

## Commentary

The principle of the right to a hearing was confirmed in the case of *Ismeri Europa Srl v Court of Auditors* (Case C-315/99P) in which the ECJ dismissed an appeal against a decision of the CFI arising from an application for damages allegedly suffered by the applicant as a result of criticisms made by the Court of Auditors in its report in 1996. The ECJ held that there was no breach of the principle by the Court of Auditors as it was not bound to submit drafts of its reports to third parties such as the applicant.

# RIGHT TO EFFECTIVE JUDICIAL CONTROL

## Key Principle

The individual is entitled to effective judicial control.

JOHNSTON V CHIEF CONSTABLE OF THE ROYAL ULSTER CONSTABULARY (CASE 222/84) 1986

Mrs Johnston, a member of the full-time reserve of the Royal Ulster Constabulary (RUC), brought an action before an industrial tribunal challenging the decision of the Chief Constable of the RUC not to renew her contract and to refuse her training in firearms. The Chief Constable had decided, in the light of the large number of police officers killed in Northern Ireland, that male police officers would carry firearms in future. Women would not be equipped with firearms and would not receive firearms training. In the industrial tribunal the Chief Constable produced a certificate issued by the Secretary of State for Northern Ireland, stating that Mrs Johnston's contract had not been renewed in order to safeguard national security and to protect public safety and public order. Under art.53 of the Northern Ireland Order the certificate was considered to be "conclusive evidence of purpose". Mrs Johnston claimed that the action contravened art.6 of **Directive 76/207** (obligation on Member States to introduce measures to enable applicants to pursue equal treatment claims before the courts). (See p.212)

**Held**

❖ (ECJ) The principle of judicial control in art.6 of **Directive 76/207** reflects arts 6 and 13 of the **ECHR**. It entitles all persons to an effective remedy in a competent court against measures which they consider contrary to the principle of equal treatment for men and women. The national courts were required to interpret a provision such as art.53 of the **Northern Ireland Order** in the light of **Directive 76/207**.

**Commentary**

Other procedural rights that have been recognised by the ECJ include the duty to give reasons: *UNECTEF v Heylens* (Case 222/86); and the right to protection against self-incrimination: *Orkem v Commission* (Case 374/87) and *Solvay v Commission* (Case 27/88) (in the context of criminal proceedings only, and therefore not applicable to the competition investigations in question).

# SUBSIDIARITY

**Key Principle**

The EU must act within the limits of the powers conferred on it by the Treaty. In areas outside the EU's exclusive competence, the EU must act in accordance with the principle of subsidiarity only if the proposed action cannot be sufficiently achieved by the Member States: art.5 TEU (ex 5 TEC).

UK v COUNCIL (THE WORKING TIME DIRECTIVE) (CASE C-84/94) 1996
The Council adopted **Directive 93/104** providing, inter alia, that average weekly working time should not exceed 48 hours, that there should be specified minimum rest periods and that workers should be entitled to four weeks' annual paid leave. The United Kingdom challenged the measure, claiming that it had been adopted on the wrong legal base, and that it contravened the principle of subsidiarity.

**Held**

❖ (ECJ) (1) The measure was properly adopted on the correct legal base (except for the second sentence of art.5, specifying Sunday for a rest day, which was annulled).
(2) The adoption of the directive was "not inconsistent" with the principle of subsidiarity. [1996] 3 C.M.L.R. 671.

**Commentary** ...........................................................................................................

[1] Subsidiarity was introduced into the by the **Maastricht Treaty**. It represents a check on the powers of the EU institutions by creating a presumption in favour of action by the Member States in areas where the EU does not possess exclusive powers (e.g. competition policy, environmental protection, education, transport). Article 5 TEU incorporates the principle of proportionality by stating that action by the EU shall not exceed what is necessary to achieve the objectives of the Treaty. Article 5 **TEU** (replacing art.5 TEC) after amendment by the **Treaty of Lisbon** covers the principles of subsidiarity, proportionality and conferral (the principle that the Union shall only act within the limits of the competences conferred on it by the Member States). National parliaments are required to scrutinise draft legislation for compliance with the principles of subsidiarity and proportionality.

[2] In *UK v Council* the need to improve the existing level of health and safety of workers through the imposition of minimum requirements presupposed EU-wide action. There was no breach of the principle of proportionality in the Council's view that improvements in the health and safety of workers could not be achieved by less restrictive measures.

[3] The principle of subsidiarity is increasingly invoked as a ground where annulment is sought. (See *UK v Council* (Case C-84/94); *Germany v EP and Council* (Case C-233/94) (the Deposit Guarantee Directive case); *Germany v EP and Council* (Case C-376/98) (the Tobacco Advertising case); and *Netherlands v EP and Council* (Case C-377/98) (the Biotechnology Patents Directive case).) In only one of these cases was the directive annulled (Tobacco Advertising), due to adoption on the wrong legal base. Thus breach of the principle of subsidiarity is yet to be successfully cited as a ground for annulment.

---

**THINK POINT**

..................................................................................................................

1. How did the ECJ in the early years approach the recognition of human rights, particularly those set out in the **ECHR**? What problem did the German courts experience in the protection of fundamental rights which caused a clash with EU law? How was this problem resolved by the ECJ?

..................................................................................................................
..................................................................................................................

2. Why do you think the ECJ is reluctant to annul measures for infringement of the principle of subsidiarity?

..................................................................................................................

# Enforcement of EU Law

## INTRODUCTION

Enforcement of EU law operates at a number of levels. This chapter is concerned with enforcement by the Commission under arts 258–260 TFEU (ex 226 and 228), as well as by the Member States under art.239 TFEU (ex 227). However, it should be remembered that the Commission is a relatively small organisation which is not in a position to pursue all breaches of EU law. Many important provisions of both primary and secondary law are directly effective (see Ch.1), providing scope for the individual to bring proceedings before the national courts which can give rise to a remedy such as damages, whereas actions under arts 258–260 provide no direct benefit to the individual.

## MEMBER STATES' OBLIGATIONS UNDER ART.4 TEU (EX 5 TEC)

**Key Principle**

Member States must take all appropriate measures to ensure fulfilment of the obligations arising from the Treaties or from secondary legislation. They must facilitate the EU's tasks and abstain from measures which could jeopardise the objectives of the Treaty: art.4 TEU.

> COMMISSION V GREECE (CASE 272/86) 1988
> The Commission requested information from the Greek government relating to cereal imports during enforcement proceedings under art.258. Greece failed to supply information at both the informal and formal stages.

**Held**

❖ (ECJ) Failure to supply the information amounted to a failure to facilitate the achievement of the EU's tasks under art.10 EEC (now art.4 TEU] [1988] E.C.R. 4875.

**Commentary**

Article 4 TEU lies at the heart of the Member States' obligations to implement and apply EC law. It is directly effective and is frequently cited by the ECJ. See e.g. *Von Colson* (Case 14/83) (see p.x) and *Francovich* (Joined Cases C-6 and 9/90). As the EU lacks the mechanisms necessary to enforce EU law (with the exception of the power to fine under art.260 (ex 228): see p.48 below) this obligation is transferred to the Member States under art.4 TEU.

## ACTIONS UNDER ART.258 TFEU

**Key Principle**
If the Commission considers that a Member State has failed to fulfil an obligation under the Treaty, it shall deliver a reasoned opinion on the matter after giving the state concerned the opportunity to submit its observations. If the state concerned does not comply with the opinion within the period laid down, the Commission may bring the matter before the ECJ: art.258.

**Key Principle**
As the reasoned opinion sets out the scope of the judicial proceedings under art.258, both sets of documents must be founded on the same grounds and submissions.

> COMMISSION V ITALY (CASE 31/69) 1970
> The Commission informed the Italian government by a letter dated July 12, 1986 that it had failed to comply with various regulations over refunds under the Common Agricultural Policy (CAP). In the reasoned opinion delivered in November 1968, the Commission found that Italy was in breach of the obligations under the regulations. When proceedings were issued in the ECJ they included references to infringement of two regulations of June 1968 which had not been set out in the reasoned opinion.

**Held**
❖ (ECJ) Even if the Member State concerned does not consider it necessary to avail itself of the opportunity to submit its observations, such an opportunity constitutes an essential guarantee under the Treaties and amounts to an essential procedural requirement in proceedings under art.258. The alleged failure deriving from the regulations of June 1968 must be excluded from the proceedings. [1970] E.C.R. 25.

**Commentary**
[1] Article 258 provides a two-stage mechanism (the administrative and judicial stages) for the Commission to bring proceedings against a Member State which has infringed an obligation under EU law. During the

administrative stage the Commission sends a letter setting out the breach and negotiates with the state in question. If the matter is unresolved the Commission may issue a reasoned opinion.

[2] The reasoned opinion must contain "a coherent statement of reasons which led the Commission to believe that the state in question has failed to fulfil an obligation under the Treaty": *Commission v Italy (Pigmeat)* (Case 7/61). It must also specify the action required to remedy the breach and any period for implementation.

[3] Non-compliance with the opinion entitles the Commission to start formal proceedings in the ECJ (the judicial stage). The decision to proceed is a matter for the discretion of the Commission: *Star Fruit v Commission* (Case 247/87).

**Key Principle**
In deciding to issue a reasoned opinion, the Commission acts as a college.

COMMISSION V GERMANY (CASE C-191/95)
The Commission brought enforcement proceedings against Germany under art.258 for a declaration that, by failing to impose penalties on companies which do not disclose their annual accounts (as required by various EU directives), Germany was in breach of EU law. At the time that the Commission decided to pursue proceedings in the ECJ, it had the facts of the case but not the text of the reasoned opinion before it.

**Held**
❖ (ECJ) The Commission's decision to issue a reasoned opinion and to bring an action for failure to fulfil obligations was the subject of collective deliberation by the college of commissioners. The college must be able to decide on the basis of the relevant information, though it need not decide on the final wording of the Act (normally an administrative step). The action was found to be admissible. [1998] E.C.R. I-000.

**Key Principle**
*Force majeure* (necessity) is no defence to an action under art.258.

COMMISSION V ITALY (CASE 101/84) 1986
Italy failed to submit statistical returns to the Commission from 1979 in relation to the carriage of goods contrary to Directive 78/546. The

Italian government put forward a defence of force majeure, claiming that it had been unable to comply following the destruction in a bomb blast of the vehicle register at the Data Processing Centre of the Ministry of Transport.

## Held

❖ (ECJ) While the bomb attack may originally have amounted to force majeure, the ensuing difficulties had only lasted for a certain time. The administration had failed to exercise due diligence to replace the equipment and collect the data. The Italian government could not, therefore, rely on the event to justify its continuing failure to comply. [1985] E.C.R. 1077.

## Commentary

Unless there has been a procedural flaw in the Commission's action, defences to actions in the ECJ under art.258 have rarely succeeded. This is due to the strength of the Commission's case when proceedings reach the judicial stage, as complaints that are not well founded are normally resolved at the administrative stage. One rare "success" in putting forward a defence arose in Case C-531/06 *Commission v Italy*. The Commission had brought enforcement proceedings against Italy in relation to its ban on unqualified pharmacists owing and operating pharmacies, which it argued infringed freedom of establishment and the free movement of capital. The ECJ, however, accepted that the measure was justified in order to protect the public in relation to the reliability and quality of medicinal products supplied.

## Key Principle

Failure to fulfil obligations may arise through administrative practice where national law is itself compatible with EU law.

### COMMISSION V FINLAND (CASE C-342/05) 2007

Directive 92/43 on the conservation of natural habitats and of wild flora and fauna provided for strict protection for certain species, of which the wolf was one. Member States could derogate from this protection under art.16 of the directive on the basis of decisions containing a clear and sufficient statement of reasons. A necessary precondition of such a derogation was the favourable conservation status of the species in question. Finland issued permits to hunt wolves on an annual basis. The ECJ held that a Member State which authorised wolf hunting on a preventative basis without establishing that such hunting would prevent serious damage was in breach of **Directive 92/43**.

## Key Principle

Practical difficulty in implementation is not a defence to enforcement proceedings.

COMMISSION V UK (CASE 128/78) 1979

Regulation 1463/70 provided for the installation of tachographs (to record rest periods and duration of driving) in vehicles used to carry passengers and goods on roads. It was due for implementation by January 1, 1976. The United Kingdom introduced a voluntary scheme to record the information and stated that it did not intend to implement the regulation fully for economic, industrial and practical considerations.

## Held

❖ (ECJ) Difficulties of implementation cannot be accepted as a justification. In permitting Member States to profit from membership of the EU, the Treaties places on them the obligation to observe its rules. For a state to break the rules unilaterally is a breach of the principle of solidarity under [4 TEU]. [1979] E.C.R. 419.

## Commentary

[1] Italy unsuccessfully argued that it should have a defence to proceedings arising out of non-implementation of a directive due to its frequent changes of government which prevented the adoption of national legislation: *Commission v Italy* (Case 28/81). Italy has been the most persistent offender in terms of art.258 actions. It has sought to remedy the problem by passing a statute that annually transposes all EU directives (verbatim) into national law.

[2] Ireland stated, in response to enforcement proceedings arising from its failure to transpose a directive on the inter-operability of the trans-European high-speed rail system, that no high-speed train was in operation at the time or would be in the foreseeable future. The ECJ considered the lack of a high-speed train to be irrelevant, pointing out the fact that if an activity referred to in a directive does not exist in a particular Member State, this cannot release the state from its obligation to ensure that the directive is properly transposed.

[3] If the ECJ finds that the state is in breach it will require the defaulting state to take the necessary steps to comply with the judgment: art.260. If the state concerned does not comply, the Commission may issue a reasoned opinion after following a repetition of the procedure under art.258 specifying the points of non-compliance. Non-compliance with the reasoned opinion

entitles the Commission to bring the case before the ECJ, which may impose a lump sum or penalty payment.

## Key Principle

If a Member State fails to comply with a judgment of the ECJ following enforcement proceedings it may impose a lump sum or periodical payment on it under art.260.

### COMMISSION V GREECE (CASE C-387/97) 2000

The Commission applied to the ECJ for a declaration under art.260 and for imposition of a daily periodical penalty, following Greece's failure to comply with a judgment against it of April 7, 1992 in Case C-45/91. The judgment required Greece to draw up and implement plans to dispose of toxic and dangerous waste under several environmental directives.

## Held

(1) By failing to take the necessary measures to dispose of waste, Greece had not implemented the judgment in Case C-45/91 and had failed to fulfil its obligations under art.260.

(2) The basic criteria which must be taken into account in order to ensure that penalty payments have coercive force and EU law is applied uniformly and effectively are: the duration of the infringement, its degree of seriousness, and the ability of the Member States to pay. In applying these criteria, regard should be made in particular to the effects which failure to comply has on public and private interests and to the urgency of getting the Member State to fulfil its obligations.

## Commentary

[1] Article 260 was amended by the **Maastricht Treaty** to allow for the imposition of a financial penalty where a Member State fails to comply with a judgment that they are in breach of. Previously, such judgments were often ignored.

[2] The ECJ considered that a periodical payment was best suited to the circumstances of the case and imposed a payment of €20,000 for each day of delay in implementing the necessary measures to comply with the judgment in Case C-45/91, from the date of the present judgment until full compliance.

[3] In *Commission v France* (Case C-304/02) the ECJ imposed both a lump sum and a penalty payment at the same time. The case arose out of an earlier judgment in 1991 against France (Case C-64/88) for infringement of fisheries conservation measures. The Court found that art.260 did not preclude the imposition of both types of penalties, in particular where the breach had continued for a long time and was inclined to persist. As a result, France was ordered to pay a lump sum of €20,000,000 and a penalty payment of €57,651,250 for each period of six months from delivery of the present judgment until full compliance with the judgment in Case C-64/88.

[4] Both a lump sum and periodic penalty were awarded in *Commission v Italy* Case C-469/04), following Italy's failure to recover unpaid state aid to promote employment. However, Italy did not suffer a double penalty in *Commission v Italy* (Case C-119/04) in relation to discrimination on grounds of nationality in foreign language posts in universities, due to its apparent compliance with an earlier judgment.

## Key Principle
The ECJ may prescribe the necessary interim measures in any cases before it: art.241.

> ### COMMISSION V UK (CASE 221/89R) 1989
> For facts, see p.5.

## Held
❖ (ECJ) The United Kingdom must suspend the offending provisions of the **Merchant Shipping Act 1988,** pending the determination of the proceedings under art.258.

## Commentary
Applications for interim relief are normally heard before the President of the ECJ, who has the discretion to refer cases to the full court if necessary.

# ACTIONS BETWEEN MEMBER STATES UNDER ART.259 TFEU

## Key Principle
Where a Member State considers that another Member State is in breach of EC law it may bring the matter before the ECJ if it has put the case before the

Commission which has not acted within three months of the reasoned opinion: art.259.

**FRANCE v UK (RE FISHING NET MESH SIZES) (CASE 141/78)**
France complained to the Commission about United Kingdom measures on fishing net mesh sizes. When the Commission did not proceed in the ECJ under art.258, France brought the matter before the ECJ under art.259.

**Held**

❖ (ECJ) The United Kingdom was in breach of [EU] law on fishing net mesh sizes. [1979] E.C.R. 2923.

**Commentary**

[1] Member States prefer to leave the resolution of their disputes with other states in the hands of the Commission, thus avoiding direct confrontation. Article 259 provides a mechanism for an aggrieved state to pursue its action directly against another state when the Commission has not acted on a reasoned opinion.

[2] Although proceedings have been commenced in a few other cases under art.259, *France v UK* is the only one resulting in an order against another state.

[3] The ECJ rejected an application by Belgium against Spain over a Spanish requirement that wine labelled "Rioja" must be bottled in the region of production: *Belgium v Spain* (Case C-388/95).

[4] An application by Spain against the United Kingdom over the voting rights of the residents of Gibraltar was also rejected. The United Kingdom had adopted the European Parliament (Representation) Act 2003 to implement the ruling of the European Court of Human Rights in *Matthews* (see Ch.3), to enable the residents of Gibraltar to vote in EP elections. Spain brought an action against the United Kingdom under art.259, claiming that the Act infringed art.20 TFEU (ex 17) on citizenship. Unusually, the Commission declined to issue a reasoned opinion, due to the sensitivity of the status of Gibraltar. The ECJ held that the United Kingdom could not be penalised for compliance with a judgment of the European Court of Human Rights: *Spain v UK* (Case C-145/04).

# SPECIFIC ENFORCEMENT PROCEEDINGS

## Actions under art.108 TFEU (ex 88) on illegal state aids

**Key Principle**

The Commission may issue a decision requiring a state to change or abolish illegal state aid within a specified time. Failure to comply entitles the Commission or any interested state to bring the matter before the ECJ: art.108 TFEU.

> BRITISH AEROSPACE AND ROVER GROUP HOLDINGS PLC V COMMISSION (CASE C-292/90) 1992
>
> The Commission had issued a decision requiring the United Kingdom government to recover payments considered to be illegal state aid made to the Rover Group before its takeover by British Aerospace. While the aid to Rover to absorb debts had been approved by the Commission, provided no further aid was granted, additional unauthorised financial concessions ("sweeteners" of £44.4 million) were made by the United Kingdom government to British Aerospace. British Aerospace and Rover sought annulment of part of the decision in the ECJ.

**Held**

❖ (ECJ) If the Commission considered that the United Kingdom had not complied with conditions in the decision and had paid further aid, it should have instituted proceedings directly against the United Kingdom under art.108, and given notice to the parties concerned to submit their comments. The decision was annulled in relation to the requirement to recover the additional payment of £44.4 million. [1992] E.C.R. I-493.

**Commentary**

After the judgment the Commission reopened proceedings on a proper basis under art.108, treating the payment as aid. An out-of-court settlement was reached with the United Kingdom government, as a result of which the sum was agreed to be repaid with interest.

## CHALLENGE UNDER ART.348 TFEU (EX 298) TO THE USE OF EXPEDITED PROCEDURES

**Key Principle**

Where it considers that a state is acting improperly, the Commission may challenge the action of a state which has brought expedited proceedings under art.346 TFEU (ex 296)or art.347 (ex 297) under art.348 (ex 298).

> COMMISSION V GREECE (CASE C-120/94R) 1994
>
> The Commission sought interim relief in relation to the closure by Greece of its border with the former Yugoslavian Republic of Macedonia, pending the hearing of the main action (Case C-120/94).

**Held**

❖ (ECJ) Interim relief was refused. The ECJ considered that the interpretation of arts 346-348 TFEU (ex 296–298) was uncertain and did not accept that there was an urgent prima facie case for relief. [1994] E.C.R. I-3037.

**Commentary**

Member States may derogate from the Treaty under arts. 346 and 347 TFEU (ex 296 and 297):

(a) to protect essential interests of their security connected with production and trade in arms, munitions and war material;

(b) where there is serious internal disturbance affecting the maintenance of law and order; and

(c) in the event of a serious balance of payments crisis. Member States must co-operate closely with the Commission to avoid improper use of these powers.

---

**THINK POINT**

Why do defences to actions under art.258 rarely, if ever, succeed?

How did the Maastricht and Lisbon Treaties strengthen the enforcement of judgments under art.260?

# Judicial Review of the Acts of the EU Institutions

## INTRODUCTION

The ECJ is empowered to examine the activities of the EU institutions to determine whether they are valid under art.263 TFEU (ex 230). Where an institution has failed to act where it is under a duty to do so, an action lies to the ECJ under art.265 TFEU (ex 232). Article 277 TFEU (ex 241) provides the means of indirect review, enabling an applicant to challenge the validity of a general act on which a later act or omission is based. Actions by individuals are brought in the General Court, with scope for appeal to the ECJ, whereas actions brought by the Member States or EU institutions are brought in the ECJ. The preliminary reference procedure under Art.267 TFEU (ex 234) provides another route by which the ECJ may review validity, but only where it arises from an action brought in the national courts (see Ch.7).

## ACTION FOR ANNULMENT UNDER ART.263 TFEU (EX 230)

Reviewable acts

**Key Principle**

The ECJ may review the legality of acts adopted jointly by the European Parliament (EP) and the Council, of acts of the Council, of the Commission and of the European Central Bank (ECB), and of the EP and European Council intended to produce legal effects vis-à-vis third parties: art.263(1).

> PARTI ECOLOGISTE ("LES VERTS") V EP (CASE 294/83) 1986
> Prior to amendment by the **Maastricht Treaty**, art.263 (then art.173 before renumbering by the **ToA**) did not expressly provide that acts of the EP may be challenged. Les Verts (the Green Party) sought under art.173 to challenge the allocation of funds by the Bureau of the EP to fight the 1984 European elections.

**Held** ..............................................................................................................

❖ (ECJ) An action for annulment may lie against measures adopted by the EP where they are intended to produce legal effects vis-à-vis third parties. The allocation was annulled. [1986] E.C.R. 1339.

**Commentary** ..................................................................................

[1] The decision in *"Les Verts"* has been incorporated verbatim in the amended version of art.67(1), reflecting the increased involvement of the EP in the decision-making process. See the pre-**TEU** decision in *Luxembourg v EP* (Case 230/81), [1983] E.C.R. 255, in which the ECJ annulled a resolution of the EP to move its seat from Luxembourg to Brussels, based on an action under the ECSC Treaty which recognised the power to review acts of the EP.

[2] The Treaty of Lisbon placed the acts of the European Council on a par with those of the EP in relation to annulment actions under art. 263(1) in terms of review.

**Key Principle** ..........................................................................

The ECJ will look at the substance rather than the form of a measure to determine whether it is intended to have legal effect.

CIMENTERIES V COMMISSION (NOORDWIJK'S CEMENT ACCORD) (CASES 8–11/66) 1967
Various undertakings enjoyed exemption from fines under a regulation in relation to competition. They were exposed to penalties when the Commission changed its practice in a notice sent out in a registered letter.

**Held** ..............................................................................................................

❖ (ECJ) (1) The measure affected the undertakings' interests by changing their legal position.
(2) It was not a mere opinion but a decision intended to produce legal effects and must be considered a reviewable act. [1967] E.C.R. 75.

**Commentary** ..................................................................................

[1] In *Cimenteries* and *"Les Verts"* the ECJ has recognised a category of reviewable acts known as "acts sui generis", not appearing in art.288 TFEU (ex 249) (which defines "regulations", "directives" and "decisions").

[2] Other examples of reviewable acts include:

(a) discussions of guidelines before the signing of the European Road Transport Agreement: *Commission v Council (Re European Road Transport Agreement)* (Case 22/70);

(b) a code of conduct issued by the Commission concerning the administration of the Structural Fund: *France v Commission* (Case C-303/90);

(c) a rejection by the Commission of a request for legal professional privilege in opposition to the seizure of a document, as such a decision has legal effects for the undertaking. The physical act of seizure of a document claimed to be confidential where no formal decision was taken amounts to a tacit decision which is also open to challenge: *Akzo Nobel Chemicals and Akros Chemicals v Commission* (Joined Cases T-125/03 and 253/03).

[3] Applicants, both privileged and non-privileged, must bring a claim for annulment within two months of publication of the measure, or of notification to the applicant, or of the day on which the applicant had knowledge of the measure (if not notified): art.263(3). Outside the time limit it may be easier to bring a challenge under art.277 (see p.68).

**Key Principle**

Certain "acts" may be so seriously affected by defects of form or procedure that they are non-existent and incapable of annulment.

> COMMISSION V BASF A.G. (CASE C-137/92P) 1992
> The original text of a decision imposing fines on various chemical companies had been altered after its adoption. Also, it had only been adopted in three of the official languages, leaving it to the Commissioner to adopt versions in the other languages. The CFI (now General Court) considered the decision to be so defective in form as to be non-existent. The Commission appealed to the ECJ.

**Held**

❖ (ECJ) The decision was defective but not sufficiently tainted by irregularity as to be non-existent. The original measure was annulled. A measure would be non-existent where it was "tainted by an irregularity whose gravity is so obvious that it cannot be tolerated by the Community legal order". [1994] E.C.R. I-2555.

**Commentary**

[1] Acts of the EU institutions are presumed to be lawful. Only in exceptional circumstances will an act be found to be non-existent.

[2] Other, less exceptional, examples of non-reviewable acts include:
  (a) a reasoned opinion under art.258: *Commission v Italy (Pigmeat)* (Case 7/61);
  (b) "comfort" letters issued by the Commission in competition cases, stating that an undertaking is not in breach of art.101(1) (ex 81(1)) or is exempt: *Lancôme v Etos B.V. (Perfumes)* (Case 99/79).

## LOCUS STANDI: THE RIGHT TO CHALLENGE

**Key Principle**

Member States, the European Parliament, the Council and the Commission may bring actions for annulment before the ECJ under art.263(2) TFEU without the need to demonstrate a legal interest in the proceedings.

> FRANCE AND OTHERS V COMMISSION (CASE T-425 ETC/04) 2010
> France sought to annul a Commission decision on state aid by France for France Télécom.

**Held**

❖ (General Court) As the act in question was a challengeable one creating binding legal effects, France, as a Member State, was entitled to bring an action for annulment without being required to show a legal interest in the proceedings (under appeal Case C-399/10P).

**Commentary**

The decision demonstrates that "privileged" applicants under art.263(2) are able to challenge any legally binding act of the EU institutions, unlike non-privileged applicants under art.263(4) who have to demonstrate that they are individually interested in an act which is not addressed to them.

**Key Principle**

The Court of Auditors, the Committee of the Regions and the ECB may bring actions on the same grounds for the purpose of protecting their prerogatives: art.263(3).

### EP v COUNCIL ("CHERNOBYL") (CASE C-70/88) 1990

The EP challenged the legal basis of a Council regulation on the permitted level of radioactive contamination in foodstuffs following the Chernobyl explosion.

**Held**

❖ (ECJ) The ECJ shall have jurisdiction in actions brought by the EP for the purpose of protecting its prerogatives. [1990] E.C.R. I-2041.

**Commentary**

[1] While Member States, the European Parliament, the Council and the Commission are all "privileged applicants" under art.263(2), the EP has only reached parity with the other institutions as a result of decisions of the ECJ followed by Treaty amendments.

[2] This change under the **Treaty of Lisbon** reflects the enhanced stature of the EP in the institutional structure of the EU. Before amendment by the **Maastricht Treaty**, art.263 (in its earlier form) did not recognise any entitlement by the EP to seek annulment. The **Maastricht Treaty** amended the Treaty to reflect the wording of the *"Chernobyl"* decision partly overruling its earlier decision in *EP v Council ("Comitology")* (Case 302/87 which had denied the EP the right to challenge under art.263.

[3] The *"Chernobyl"* decision illustrates what is meant by the phrase "protecting their prerogatives", which essentially refers to the protection of the institution's involvement in the legislative process. This is determined by the legal base on which the measure is adopted (see Ch.2 for more examples of challenges relating to choice of legal base). Where the "wrong" legal base is used, it may deprive an EU institution of participation in the legislative process.

[4] After amendment by the **Treaty of Lisbon**, the Court of Auditors, the Committee of the Regions and the ECB were permitted to bring a challenge in order to protect their prerogatives.

[5] It is more difficult for non-privileged applicants (natural or legal persons) to establish locus standi (standing). After amendment of art.263(4) by the **Treaty of Lisbon**, an individual may only challenge:

  (a) an act addressed to that person (e.g. a competition decision by the Commission);

  (b) an act which is of direct and individual concern to that person;

(c)  a regulatory act which is of direct concern to them and does not entail implementing measures.

## Key Principle
If the act is not addressed to the applicant, it must be of direct and individual concern to him.

### PLAUMANN & CO V COMMISSION (CASE 25/62) 1963
P, a major importer of clementines, sought to challenge a Commission decision addressed to the German government refusing to allow the government to reduce the duty on clementines imported from outside the EU.

## Held
To establish individual concern the applicant must show that he is affected by the decision as a result of factors particularly relevant to him, not because he is a member of a class affected by the measure. The application was inadmissible. [1963] E.C.R. 95.

### TOEPFER K.G. V COMMISSION (CASES 106 AND 107/63) 1965
The applicant, an importer of maize, sought an import licence from the German government. The German government refused, seeking authorisation from the Commission for the safeguard measures it had taken. A Commission decision addressed to Germany approved the safeguard measures and the government's refusal to grant all existing applicants a licence.

## Held
As the decision affected only existing applicants it was of individual concern to the applicant. The decision was annulled. [1965] E.C.R. 405.

## Commentary
[1] The difference between the locus standi of the applicants in *Toepfer* and *Plaumann* is that Toepfer could be identified as a member of a closed class of persons affected by the decision whereas Plaumann could not. (Anyone could import clementines.)

[2] See also *Spijker Kwasten B.V. v Commission* (Case 231/82): a Commission decision to allow a Dutch import ban on Chinese brushes could not be

challenged by a previous import licence holder. Note in addition *UPA* (Case C-50/00P) on p.xx.

[3] This restrictive approach was followed by the ECJ in *Greenpeace Council v Commission* (Case C-321/95P), upholding the decision of the CFI to refuse to recognise locus standi. The applicants were local residents and an environmental group opposed to the building of a power station. The basis of the ECJ's decision was that the applicants had only an indirect interest in the decision to provide financial assistance in the building of the power station.

[4] In a few cases the ECJ demonstrated a liberal approach to locus standi. In *Piraiki-Patraiki* (Case 11/82) Greek producers of cotton were found to be individually concerned in a Commission decision, due mainly to the obligation in the Greek **Act of Accession** to take such interests into account. See also *Sofrimport v Commission* (Case C-152/88): importers with goods in transit could challenge a regulation that had to take account of their interests. (They could be individually identified as having "goods in transit" on a particular date.)

[5] The *Plaumann* test for standing was upheld in *Unión de Pequeños Agricultores (UPA)* (Case C-50/00P) (see below, p.61).

## Key Principle

The fact that a general legislative measure applies to traders in a general way does not necessarily prevent individual traders from being individually concerned.

### CODORNIU V COUNCIL (CASE C-309/89) 1993

C sought to challenge a regulation reserving the word "crémant" for high-quality sparkling wines from specific regions in France and Luxembourg. C was a major producer of similar sparkling wines in Spain where it held a trade mark, and the largest producer of wines labelled "crémant" in the EU.

### Held

❖ (ECJ) The applicant was individually concerned because the reservation to producers in France and Luxembourg interfered with C's intellectual property rights. [1994] E.C.R. I-1853.

**Commentary**

[1] This decision departs from the previous case law of the ECJ in that there was no suggestion that the regulation had been adopted with the applicant in mind.

[2] In *Galileo Lebensmittel v Commission* (Case T-46/06, upheld in Case C-483/07P) the CFI held that the decisive factor in identifying the persons individually concerned by a measure of general application consists in the specific protection to which they are entitled under EU law. It also noted that membership of a restricted group must be combined with a specific duty on the part of the Commission to protect that group.

**Key Principle**

The requirement to establish individual concern in applications for annulment continues to be the *Plaumann* test.

UNIÓN DE PEQUEÑOS AGRICULTORES (UPA) (CASE C-50/00P) 2002

The applicant, UPA, a trade association in Spain, sought to challenge part of Regulation 1638/98 on the common organisation of the market in olive oil. The CFI refused to admit its application for annulment, on the basis that the trade association was not individually concerned. UPA appealed to the ECJ.

**Held**

UPA was not individually concerned in the regulation and so could not challenge it. The test for individual concern continues to be determined according to the rules in the *Plaumann* decision. Individuals who lack standing may plead invalidity before the ECJ under art.277. Alternatively, an action may be brought before the national courts who may be asked to make a reference to the ECJ under art.267.

The ECJ upheld the decision of the CFI.

**Commentary**

[1] The ECJ in *UPA* reverted to a traditional, restrictive view on standing, refusing to depart from the *Plaumann* formula, despite strong submissions supporting liberalisation of the criteria by Advocate General Jacobs that "[t]he only satisfactory solution [was] to recognise that the individual is individually concerned" where "the measure has, or is liable to have, a substantial adverse effect on his interests".

[2] In *Plaumann* the ECJ emphasised that responsibility for ensuring effective judicial protection rests with the Member States. It refused to intervene if such protection was absent, stating that any change to the rules on standing may only come through amendment to the wording of art.263.

[3] For a few months in 2002 before the ruling in *UPA* it looked as if a new and more liberal approach to standing was developing. The CFI departed from the *Plaumann* formula in *Jégo Quéré* (Case T-177/01), an action under art.263 brought by a French fishing company which had fished for some time off Ireland using nets with a mesh size which was prohibited as a result of Commission Regulation 1162/2001. The applicant sought to annul the regulation (clearly a measure of general application). The CFI held the action to be admissible, referring to the need to avoid depriving the applicant of the right to an effective remedy under arts 6 and 13 of the **ECHR**. It proposed that a non-privileged individual applicant should be regarded as individually concerned by a measure of general application if it "affects his legal position in a manner which is both definite and immediate, by restricting his rights or by imposing obligations on him". However, the CFI decision was overturned by the ECJ following its own decision in *UPA*, thus denying the applicant standing.

[4] Jurisdiction to hear art.263 applications by non-privileged applicants passed to the General Court (then the CFI) in August 1993. The General Court has followed the pre-*Codorniu*, restrictive approach of the ECJ in refusing to accept that a claim to locus standi could be based on a disadvantageous competitive position. See *Campo Edro Industrial v Council* (Case T-472/93) in which a regulation gave aid in sugar pricing to producers of sugar from cane and beet but not to isoglucose producers. Despite being the sole Spanish producers of isoglucose, the applicants were denied locus standi to challenge the regulation. A similarly restrictive approach was taken in *CSR Pampryl v Commission* (Case T-114/99). Here a long-standing cider producer who had sold cider under various names including the indication "Pays d'Auge" sought to challenge a regulation which registered "Pays d'Auge" as a protected designation. The applicant failed to establish that the use of the geographical name over which it claimed a right stemmed from a specific right granted at national or EC law before the regulation and which had been adversely affected by that regulation.

[5] In *Regione Autonoma Friuli-Venezia Giulia v Commission* (Case T-417/04) the applicant sought unsuccessfully to annul a provision in a regulation limiting the right to use "Tocai friuliano". The CFI found that the applicant, unlike the applicant in *Codorniu*, was not prevented by a measure of general

application from using an intellectual property right which it had relied on long before the adoption of the measure. The general interest of a region in securing prosperity was insufficient to establish individual standing.

[6] The ECJ upheld the ruling of the CFI in *Rothley* declaring inadmissible an application by 70 MEPs to annul a decision by the EP on amendments to its Rules of Procedure following the Inter-institutional Agreement of May 1999 between the EP, the Council and the Commission on internal investigations by the European Anti-Fraud Office. The CFI considered that there were no factors enabling individual MEPs to be distinguished individually. As the measure affected the applicants in the same way as all other MEPs, the inadmissibility of the action did not create inequality between the applicants and other MEPs: *Rothley and others v EP* (Case C-167/02P).

[7] The hard line on standing was maintained in 2003 against tobacco companies from the Philip Morris and Reynolds Groups: *Philip Morris International* (Joined Cases T-377/00, T-379/00, etc.). The cases involved decisions to bring proceedings before the US courts in connection with allegations that the cigarette companies were involved in smuggling cigarettes into the EU for distribution. The applicants sought to challenge the decisions to proceed. The CFI ruled that the applications were inadmissible, repeating the formula in *UPA* that it was not the function of the Court to usurp the authority of the EU deriving from the Treaty.

[8] In *Alrosa v Commission* (Case T-170/06) the applicant sought to annul a decision by the Commission to accept binding commitments from De Beers, an undertaking in a dominant position under art.102 TFEU (ex 82) (see Ch.13) to limit and cease production of rough diamonds. The applicant was held to be individually concerned in the decision which had been reached at the end of proceedings in which the applicant had played a decisive part. The proceedings were intended to end a long-standing business relationship between De Beers and the applicant, with a significant effect on the applicant's market position (on appeal, Case C-441/07P—application rejected on the merits).

## Key Principle

Any natural or legal person may challenge a regulatory act which is of direct concern to him or her and which does not entail implementing measures: art.263(4) TFEU

## Inuit Tapiriit Kanatami and others v EP and Council (CaseT-18/10) 2011

The case concerned a challenge under art.263 to an EU regulation harmonising the rules placing seal products on the market. While some of the applicants were seal hunters and trappers, and so individually concerned, others were not. (One, for example, was a doctor undertaking research on seal valves.)

### Held

❖ (General Court) (1) "Regulatory acts" under art.263(4) cover all acts of general application other than legislative acts.

(2) The act in question was adopted under the co-decision (now ordinary) procedure. As art.289(1) and (3) TFEU define legislative acts as those adopted under the ordinary procedure, it follows that the regulation was a legislative act. The test for whether an act is legislative or regulatory depends on the procedure for its adoption. There was thus no need to consider whether the measure required implementing measures, so art.263(4) did not apply. It was therefore necessary for the applicants to demonstrate individual (as well as direct concern) under the *Plaumann* formula. They were unable to do so and the action was declared inadmissible.

### Commentary

[1] The **Treaty of Lisbon** amended the wording of art.263(4) to enable non-privileged applicants to challenge a regulatory act of direct concern to them without the need for individual concern. This change does not go as far as the reform sought by Advocate-General Jacobs in *UPA*, although it indicates a slight softening of the criteria for access.

[2] The General Court in *Inuit* found the measure to be legislative rather than regulatory because it had been adopted under the ordinary legislative process. This follows from the (somewhat circular) wording of art.289(3) which provides that "[l]egal acts adopted by legislative procedure shall constitute legislative acts".

[3] The General Court held in Case T-532/08 *Norilsk Nickel Harjavalta and Umicore v Commission* and Case T-539/09 *Etamine v Commission* that the change to the rules under art.263(4) does not apply retrospectively, i.e. before the entry into force of the **Treaty of Lisbon**.

**Key Principle** ..................................................................................................................
An individual is only directly concerned in a measure where its implementation leaves no discretion to the addressees.

> REGIONE SICILIANA V COMMISSION (CASE T-341/02) 2004
> The Commission provided financial assistance to Italy from the Regional Development Fund for the construction of a motorway in Sicily between Messina and Palermo. It issued a decision addressed to Italy ending the assistance. The authority responsible for implementing the project, the Region of Sicily, sought to challenge the decision under art.263.

**Held** ...........................................................................................................................
❖ (CFI) As the national authorities had discretion in implementing the contested measure, the Region of Sicily lacked direct interest in the proceedings and so lacked standing to bring a challenge.

**Commentary** ...............................................................................................................
An applicant will only be able to establish that a measure is of direct and individual concern where it affects his legal position and where its implementation flows automatically from the EU measure without the need for the adoption of further rules. The decision was upheld by the ECJ in Case C-417/04P.

## Grounds for challenge

**Key Principle** ...............................................................................................................
A measure may be challenged under art.263 if an essential procedural requirement is infringed.

> ROQUETTE FRÈRES S.A. v COUNCIL (CASE 138/79) 1980
> The Council sent the EP a draft regulation fixing a quota for isoglucose producers for consultation in March 1979, asking for its views during April, so that the measure could be adopted by July. This would only have been possible if the EP had convened a special session but no such request was made by the Council or Commission. The measure was adopted by the Council in June 1979, with reference in the Preamble to the fact that the EP had been "consulted". R, a member of a closed group of isoglucose producers, sought to challenge the regulation.

## Held

❖ (ECJ) Failure to consult the EP, as required under the Treaty, was a breach of an essential procedural requirement. The regulation was annulled. [1980] E.C.R. 3333.

## Commentary

[1] Failure to specify the legal basis of a measure may also be regarded as breach of an essential procedural requirement: *Commission v Council* (Case 45/86), as may failure to state the reasons for a decision: *Germany v Commission (Re Tariff Quotas on Wine)* (Case 24/62).

[2] A measure may also be challenged under art.263 on grounds of lack of competence (similar to ultra vires in English law) (See e.g. *Germany v EP and Council* (Case C-380/03), the Tobacco Advertising case. In this case the ECJ annulled a decision of the CFI due to the Commission's lack of competence to impose a general ban on tobacco advertising under art.114 TFEU (ex 95) and other articles, as well as infringement of the Treaty or any rule relating to its application, or misuse of power.)

[3] There is a time limit of two months from the date of the decision within which to bring a challenge under art.120. In *Pitsiorlas v Council and ECB* (Case C-193/01P) the ECJ held that, in exceptional circumstances, an excusable error may have the effect of making the applicant not out of time. It overturned the previous decision of the CFI that there were no such circumstances in this case which had led it to hold the application inadmissible.

## Key Principle

A measure may be annulled where it is in breach of a general principle of EU law.

TRANSOCEAN MARINE PAINT ASSOCIATION V EC COMMISSION (CASE 17/74) 1974
The Commission issued a measure in relation to the renewal of an exemption from the competition rules policy without providing an opportunity for the members of the Association to be heard. The Association argued that the measure should be annulled because it had been denied a hearing.

## Held

❖ (ECJ) A person whose interests are affected by a decision by a public authority such as the Commission considering an exemption must be given an opportunity to submit his observations. The offending part of the measure was annulled. [1974] E.C.R. 1063.

## Commentary

[1] This case provides an example of the ECJ's adoption of a general principle from the domestic law of the Member States: in this case, the United Kingdom (audi alterem partem). Infringement of a rule to the Treaty's application is interpreted liberally by the ECJ to cover any general principle of law, whether in international law, in the domestic legal systems of the Member States or in the general principles recognised by the ECJ (see Ch.3).

[2] It should be remembered that it is open to the national courts, where there are proceedings, to refer a question to the ECJ for a ruling on validity under art.267 (see Ch.7), as well as to clarify the meaning of the measure in question.

## ACTION FOR INACTIVITY UNDER ART.232

### Key Principle

If the EP, Council or Commission fails to act on an infringement of the Treaty, the Member States and other institutions of the EU may bring an action before the ECJ to have the failure established: art.265 (ex 232).

> EP v COUNCIL (CASE 13/83) 1985
> The EP sought to challenge the failure of the Council to implement a common transport policy under art.90 TFEU (ex 70) and to reach a decision on 16 Commission proposals on transport.

### Held

❖ (ECJ) While there was no enforceable obligation to implement a common transport policy under art.264 TFEU (ex 231), the Council was required to act to implement the freedoms expressed in art. 91 TFEU (ex 71), and other Treaty provisions within the transitional period (end of 1961). To be enforceable, obligations must be sufficiently defined to allow the ECJ to establish whether failure to adopt them is lawful.

**Commentary**

This obligation in art.265 mirrors that in art.263. Rules on locus standi are similar, with the EU institutions in a privileged position relative to individuals.

**Key Principle**

An individual may bring proceedings under art.265 where an institution has failed to address to him or her an act other than a recommendation or opinion.

> BETHELL V COMMISSION (CASE 246/81) 1982
>
> Lord Bethell sought to force the Commission to apply the competition rules against various European airlines. As this sector was outside Reg.17 (which provided the main rules on competition at the time), Lord Bethell had no entitlement to insist that the Commission carry out an investigation.

**Held**

The applicant was not directly and individually concerned and could not challenge the Commission's inaction under art.265, nor its refusal to act under art.263. [1982] E.C.R. 2277.

**Commentary**

No action may be brought under art.265 unless the institution has first been called upon to act. It has two months in which to act or define its position, after which the applicant has a further two months in which to bring an action. A successful action under either art.265 or 263 requires the institution to take the necessary steps to implement the judgment: art.266 TFEU (ex 233). There are no sanctions for non-compliance.

## INDIRECT CHALLENGE UNDER ART.277 (EX 241)

**Key Principle**

Despite the expiry of the time limit under art. 263(6) (that is, two months from the date of adoption), any party may under art.277 TFEU (ex 241) plead that an act of general application is inapplicable on the same grounds as set out in art.263(2).

## ITALY V COUNCIL AND COMMISSION (CASE 32/65) 1966

Italy brought proceedings under art.263 to annul a regulation and indirectly challenged two further regulations under art.277. The Commission raised the issue of whether a Member State may make an indirect challenge.

**Held**

❖ (ECJ) As the regulations were not relevant to the issue in question the challenge under art.277 was dismissed. [1966] E.C.R. 389.

**Commentary**

[1] The ECJ did not rule on the entitlement of a Member State to make an indirect challenge under art.277.

[2] Article 277 applies only to acts of general application. These will usually be classed as regulations. However, it is substance not form that indicates the true character of a measure. (See *Simmenthal v Commission* (Case 92/78) in which the ECJ held that a general notice of invitation to tender was normative in character and thus capable of indirect challenge under art.277.)

[3] The effect of a successful challenge under art.277 will lead to the regulation in question being declared inapplicable and any subsequent measure void.

### THINK POINT

Do you think the case law of the ECJ in relation to the standing of individuals to challenge a measure of EU law is too restrictive? If the scope for mounting a challenge were widened in line with Advocate General Jacobs' submissions in *UPA*, what would be the risks?

When may a challenge be brought under art.277? How does the position differ from art.263?

# Liability of the EU Institutions

## Non-contractual liability

### INTRODUCTION

The ECJ has jurisdiction under art. 268 TFEU (ex 235) over actions against the EU institutions or its servants for compensation under art.340 TFEU (ex 288) arising out of its wrongful acts or omissions. Unlike the rules on standing under art.263, any person may bring an action under art.340. Actions by individuals are brought in the General Court with an appeal to the ECJ.

**Key Principle**

The EU must, in accordance with the general principles common to the laws of the Member States, make good any damage caused by its institutions or by its servants in performance of their duties (art.340(2)).

> LÜTTICKE V COMMISSION (CASE 4/69) 1966
> Lütticke sued the Commission for damages under art.340(2), claiming that it had failed to require the German government to change a disputed provision of national law. Under the German measure in question, he was obliged to pay taxes, which he alleged contravened EU law.

**Held**

❖ (ECJ) There was no wrongful act or omission. The Commission had done all that it could in negotiating with the German government. Non-contractual (tortious) liability is established under art.340 where there is:

(a) a wrongful act or omission by an EU institution or its servants;

(b) damage to the applicant;

(c) a causal connection between the wrongful act or omission and the damage. [1971] E.C.R. 325.

**Commentary**

[1] *Lütticke* establishes that a claim for damages under art. 340(2) is an independent action. It departed from the previous approach of the ECJ in *Plaumann* (see Ch.5) that annulment proceedings must be brought (e.g. under art.263) before a claim may be pursued under art.340(2).

[2] In *New Europe Consulting and Brown v Commission* (Case T-231/97) a claim arose out of the sending of a fax by the Commission to a number of co-ordinators under the EC PHARE programme alleging irregularities by the applicants. The applicants, a consultancy chosen to implement a programme, claimed that the Commission should compensate them for the harm suffered as a result of sending the fax. The CFI considered that the Commission should have held an enquiry into the alleged irregularities. It held that the three requirements of *Lütticke* were established: a wrongful act by the Commission, damage (in the form of harm to the image of the applicants) and a causal link between the breach and the damage. The Commission was ordered to pay compensation of €125,000.

[3] *Schneider Electric v Commission* (Case C-440/07P) (see Ch.13) concerned a damages claim against the Commission in the context of the merger control. The ECJ seems to have been willing, in principle, to award damages where a company, Schneider, had been unable to proceed with its take-over of another, Legrand. The CFI had previously overruled a Commission refusal to clear the merger of the two companies on the basis of the Commission's inadequate economic analysis. Schneider sought damages for the loss claimed to have been suffered from the Commission's actions. The ECJ (reversing the CFI decision), however, found that the infringement had not caused the loss alleged to have been suffered to Schneider's assets.

**Key Principle**
Unusual and special damage must be established before the EU may incur liability for a lawful act.

Dorsch Consult Ingenieurgesellschaft mbH (Case C-2337/98P) 2000

The applicant entered into a contract in 1975 with the government of Iraq to organise and supervise the construction of a highway in Iraq. In August 1990, following the invasion of Kuwait by Iraq, the Security Council of the UN adopted a series of resolutions, including Resolution 661 (1990) which ordered an embargo to be placed on trade with Iraq. The Council of the EU responded immediately by adopting Regulation 2340/90 to that effect. The Iraqi government froze all assets and rights of companies trading with Iraq where those companies were based in countries covered by the embargo. The applicant, not having received payment from the Iraqi authorities for sums previously acknowledged, sought damages from the Council of the EU in the CFI in Case T-184/95.

The claim was based on the submission that the loss was caused by the adoption of **Regulation 2340/90** by the EU which in turn had led to the Iraqi action against companies such as the applicant. The application was dismissed. The applicant appealed to the ECJ.

**Held**

❖ (ECJ) (upholding the decision of the CFI) (1) It is necessary, where damages are claimed for a lawful or unlawful act by the EU institutions, to prove that the alleged damage is real and that a causal link exists between that act and the alleged damage. The damage could not be attributed to **Regulation 2340/90,** but to UN Resolution 661 (1990) imposing sanctions on Iraq.
(2) Where damages are claimed for a lawful act of the EU institutions, it is a precondition of liability that there is unusual and special damage. Iraq had to be regarded as a "high-risk" country even before the invasion of Kuwait. As a result the damage suffered by the applicant did not exceed the economic risks inherent in the sector concerned.

**Commentary**
[1] The ECJ noted that an applicant must produce evidence to show that it has exhausted all avenues and legal remedies open to it in order to recover its claim before the Court.

[2] A similar approach was taken by the ECJ in *FIAMM v Council and Commission* (Cases C-120 &121/06P), which arose out from a long-running dispute between the EU and the World Trade Organisation. The ECJ held that liability without fault was not an established principle of EU law. It did not rule out such a principle but found that, if it existed, it would be subject to the requirement for unusual and special damage (as in *Dorsch Consult*).

**Key Principle**
Failure of administration ("faute de service") is a wrongful act or omission for which the EU is vicariously liable under art.288(2).

RICHEZ-PARISE V COMMISSION (CASE 19/69, ETC.) 1969
Some members of staff of the Commission were given wrong information about pensions, as a result of which they decided to take early retirement. Although the Commission discovered the mistake it did not seek to correct the information. The officials sued the Commission under art.340(2).

**Held**

❖ (ECJ) Even though the giving of the advice originally was not wrongful, failure to correct the information was a "faute de service". The Commission was liable to compensate members of staff who had relied on its advice. [1970] E.C.R. 325.

**Key Principle**

A negligent act by a servant is a wrongful act for which the EU will be vicariously liable provided it is performed in the course of his duties ("faute de personne").

> SAYAG V LEDUC (CASE 5/68) 1968
> Sayag was an engineer employed by Euratom. While driving to visit an atomic plant in Belgium he injured someone in a road accident. The Belgian court made an art.267 reference to the ECJ.

**Held**

❖ (ECJ) Driving a motor vehicle is not an act performed in the course of duty unless it is necessary in an emergency or other exceptional circumstances. Euratom was not vicariously liable. [1969] E.C.R. 329.

**Commentary**

The distinction between "faute de service" (a fault in the operation of the system) and "faute personnelle" (a personal fault by an individual) reflects French administrative law. Thus in EU law vicarious liability attaches to "faute de service" and to "faute personnelle" where the wrongful act is closely connected to the individual's duties (i.e. not a "frolic of one's own"). As in French law, the EU institutions may be vicariously liable for matters that would be considered maladministration in English law.

# LIABILITY FOR LEGISLATION: THE "SCHÖPPENSTEDT FORMULA"

**Key Principle**

The EU is not liable in relation to a legislative measure involving choices of economic policy unless a sufficiently serious breach of a superior rule of law for the protection of the individual has occurred.

> ZUCKERFABRIK SCHÖPPENSTEDT V COUNCIL (CASE 5/71) 1971
> The applicant, a sugar trader, sought compensation under art.340(2) for damage suffered as a result of a regulation, claiming that the measure

infringed another regulation and art.40(3) TFEU (ex 34(3)) (the principle of non-discrimination under the CAP). The Council objected, claiming that the action would undermine the system of judicial review under art.263.

## Held

❖ (ECJ) The ruling of the ECJ in *Lütticke* (see above) was approved and the application was declared admissible. However, the breach was not found to be "sufficiently flagrant". As a result the application failed. [1971] E.C.R. 975.

## Commentary

[1] Most EU law involves choices of economic policy. It is the ECJ's responsibility to examine the acts of the institutions to determine when those acts should give rise to compensation to individuals. It is not intended that individuals should be protected from variations in the market.

[2] Although known as the "Schöppenstedt Formula", the principle stated above represents a reformulation by the ECJ in *Bayerische HNL v Council and Commission* (Joined Cases 83/76, etc.), approving the decision in *Schöppenstedt*. (See below.)

[3] The ECJ confirmed its adherence to the "Schöppenstedt Formula" in *Bergaderm* (below), where it restated the formula using slightly different wording.

## Key Principle

There must be a breach of a superior principle of law.

CNTA v COMMISSION (CASE 74/74)
This case concerns the system for monetary compensation amounts (MCAs) payable to exporters under the CAP to compensate for fluctuations in exchange rates. CNTA entered into various export contracts before the system was abolished in France by the Commission, claiming to have based the contractual prices on the MCAs. CNTA claimed damages for the losses arising from the ending of the scheme from the Commission.

## Held

❖ (ECJ) The regulation infringed the principle of legal certainty, in particular the principle of legitimate expectations. In the absence of overriding public interest the Commission had violated a superior rule of law by not taking transitional measures to protect the trader. However, as no actual loss had been suffered, no damages were awarded. [1975] E.C.R. 533.

## Commentary

The wrongful act was the failure to give reasonable notice, not the adoption of the regulation (which was not declared invalid). Other general principles which have been invoked in damages claims include proportionality and equality. (See Ch.3.)

## Key Principle

The rules on liability of the EU institutions are the same as those applying to the Member States.

LABORATOIRES PHARMACEUTIQUES BERGADERM AND GOUPIL V COMMISSION (CASE C-352/98P) 2000

The applicant, in an appeal against a decision of the CFI, sought damages against the Commission for losses suffered as a result of a Commission directive on cosmetics. The directive prohibited the use of various substances thought to be possibly carcinogenic, one of which was used by the applicant (the only company to do so) in its suntan lotions. As a result, the applicant went into liquidation. The CFI dismissed the action and rejected the applicant's claim that the directive was an administrative rather than legislative act. The applicants appealed to the ECJ which upheld the decision of the CFI.

## Held

❖ (ECJ) EU law confers a right to damages where three conditions are met:
  (1) the rule of law infringed must be intended to confer rights on individuals;
  (2) the breach must be sufficiently serious;
  (3) there must be a direct causal link between the breach of the obligation resting on the state and the damages sustained by the injured parties.

## Commentary

[1] It is clear from the judgment of the ECJ in *Bergaderm* that it is not the nature of the measure which is significant but the degree of discretion enjoyed by the EU institution. Thus it makes no difference to an action in damages whether the act in question is legislative or administrative.

[2] The test under *Bergaderm* to establish a sufficiently serious breach involving wide discretion is whether the EU institution manifestly and gravely disregarded the limits on its discretion.

[3] These are the same rules as applied by the ECJ to the Member States in *Brasserie du Pêcheur/Factortame III* (see Ch.1).

### Key Principle

The rule of law must be intended for the protection of the individual.

> KAMPFFMEYER V COMMISSION (JOINED CASES 5/66, ETC.) 1967
> The applicants, German grain importers, applied to the German authorities for a licence to import grain from France. The German authorities refused, suspending imports. The Commission confirmed the decision. Under Regulation 19 such applications could only be refused if a serious disturbance of the market was threatened. The applicants challenged the Commission decision under art.263 in the ECJ and also sued the German government in the national courts.

### Held

❖ (ECJ) Although the rules of law in question were not of direct and individual concern to the applicant (under art.263), the protection of individual interests such as the applicant's was intended. The application was admissible. As there was no serious threat to the market, the Commission decision was unjustified ("faute de service") and was annulled. [1967] E.C.R. 245.

### Commentary

[1] A rule intended to benefit a class of persons may be found to benefit an individual.

[2] The ECJ deferred a decision on damages until the concurrent proceedings before the German courts were completed.

[3] The EU may not be liable where there is an overriding public interest. In *Mülder v Commission* (Joined Cases C-104/89 and 37/90) milk producers who had no quota due to lack of production in the year preceding their application were given a quota based on 60 per cent of production in the year before that. The ECJ held that although the quota decision was illegal because it infringed the principle of legitimate expectations, the Council had taken account of a higher public interest in fixing the rate, without gravely and

manifestly disregarding the limits of its discretionary power. [1992] E.C.R. I-3061.

## Key Principle
The breach must be sufficiently serious.

> BAYERISCHE HNL V COUNCIL AND COMMISSION (CASES 83/76, ETC.) 1978
> In order to use up the skimmed milk powder "mountain" the Council
> adopted a regulation requiring animal feed producers to buy skimmed
> milk powder from EC intervention agencies. This was more expensive
> than soya, which had previously been used as feed. Some farmers
> brought actions in the national courts, leading to art.267 references to
> the ECJ. Others claimed damages in the ECJ.

## Held
❖ (ECJ) (1) (Under art.267) The regulation was invalid because it infringed the
principles of non-discrimination and proportionality.
(2) (Under art.340) There was a breach of a superior rule of law which was
intended to protect the individual. However, the breach was not sufficiently
serious; in a legislative field involving wide discretion, the EU is not liable
unless there has been a manifest and grave breach. Thus damages were not
available to the farmers. [1978] E.C.R. 1209.

## Commentary
[1] Despite the invalidity ruling under art.267 it did not follow that the breach
was serious enough to satisfy the Schöppenstedt Formula under art.340.

[2] In *Cantina Sociale di Dolianova v Commission* (Case T-166/98) the loss
arose as a result of the Commission's failure to provide a scheme to pay
compensation to the applicants for the preventive distillation for the wine.
The CFI decided that the principle of non-discrimination and prohibition of
unjustified enrichment had been infringed. Such breaches were seen as
sufficiently serious and led to a rare finding against the Commission. However the ECJ annulled the decision in Case C-51/05P on the basis of the expiry
of the five-year period of limitation.

[3] In *Citymo v Commission* (Case T-271/04) the CFI found that the Commission's continuing pursuit for two months of pre-contractual negotiations with
a body tendering for a contract when it knew these negotiations were

doomed to fail was a sufficiently serious breach of the principle of good faith, despite the Commission's wide discretion under the regulation in question.

[4] *MyTravel v Commission* (Case T-212/03) concerned a damages claim arising from a Commission refusal to clear a merger in *Airtours v Commission* (Case T-342/99—see Ch.13). The CFI held that the errors of assessment in the Commission's economic analysis did not amount to a sufficiently serious breach of a rule of law and dismissed the action.

[5] *Schneider v Commission (Case C-440/07P)* (see p.187), the ECJ held that a procedural defect in a competition case (denial by the Commission of the parties' right of defence) was a sufficiently serious breach of a rule intended for the protection of the individual. Note that the CFI decision was overruled on the basis of failure to establish that the breach caused the damage.

## DAMAGES

**Key Principle**
Damages for loss of profits may be available against the EU institutions.

> CNTA v COMMISSION (CASE 74/74) 1975
> See p.74.

**Held**
❖ (ECJ) A firm is entitled to compensation for losses caused by currency speculation where this has been caused by the EU. [1975] E.C.R. 533.

**Commentary**
The applicant was not in fact exposed to risk because its purchaser could pay in either French francs or American dollars. As the purchaser had paid in francs (with no exchange rate consequences) there was no actual loss. Traders cannot rely on the EU for protection against the operation of the market.

**Key Principle**
An award of damages may be reduced by the contributory negligence of the applicant.

Stanley Adams was employed in Switzerland by the pharmaceutical company, Hoffman-La Roche. He handed over documents to the Commission, as a result of which the company was found to have infringed art.86 and was fined. Adams had requested confidentiality from the Commission, which failed to ensure that he was not identified from the documents. On returning to Switzerland from Italy where he had set up a business, Adams was arrested and charged with industrial espionage under Swiss law. Adams' wife committed suicide while her husband was in custody awaiting trial. Adams was convicted of industrial espionage and given a one-year suspended sentence. He claimed that his credit-worthiness had been destroyed, leading to the failure of his business in Italy.

**Held**

❖ (ECJ) The Commission was liable for breach of the principle of confidentiality and for failing to warn Adams of the risk of prosecution in Switzerland. The damages were reduced by one half due to Adams' carelessness in failing to inform the Commission of his whereabouts and in returning to Switzerland despite the risk of prosecution. [1985] E.C.R. 3539.

**Commentary**

As there have been relatively few awards of damages under art.340 made by the ECJ or General Court, it is difficult to identify a set of principles from individual decisions, beyond stating that damages should not be too remote (*Lütticke*) and must be a sufficiently direct result of an unlawful act or omission by an EU institution *Dumortier Fils S.A. v Council* (Joined Cases 64/76, etc.)). Note the liberal limitation period (five years) for bringing a claim under art.340(2) (art.43 of the Statute of the Court), unlike the two-month period for an annulment action under art.263.

# CONCURRENT LIABILITY

**Key Principle**

Where the national authority is primarily at fault the action should be brought in the national courts.

KAMPFFMEYER V COMMISSION (JOINED CASES 5/66, ETC.) 1967
See p.76.

**Held**

❖ (ECJ) The amount of damages awarded against the Commission could not be finalised until K had completed proceedings before the German courts.

**Commentary**

[1] The requirement to pursue a remedy in the national courts has been upheld in *Haegeman v Commission* (Case 96/71). There are problems arising from this approach as the scope or availability of a remedy may vary between Member States.

[2] The ECJ has not been consistent on the need to exhaust national remedies before proceeding in the ECJ (now in the General Court).

In *Krohn v Commission* (Case 175/84) it was held to be appropriate to bring an action in the ECJ rather than the national courts where the national authorities, on Commission instructions, had refused an import licence.

---

**THINK POINT**

Why do you think the ECJ and CFI/General Court have adopted such a strict approach to claims for damages against the EU institutions, particularly where the measure is one of general application? Do you think it should be made easier to sue the EU institutions in damages?

How has the case law on the liability of the EU institutions influenced the development of the ECJ's approach to the liability of the Member States?

# Preliminary Rulings

## Preliminary rulings under art.267

### INTRODUCTION

The preliminary reference procedure under art.267 (ex 234) is extremely important. It provides a mechanism enabling national courts to seek clarification on the meaning or validity of a provision of EU law. The ECJ has used the art.267 procedure to develop essential principles such as direct effect, supremacy and state liability. Rulings under art.267 bind all the Member States, regardless of the state from which they originated.

**Key Principle**
Article 267 is essential for the uniform character of the law established by the Treaty and has the object of ensuring that in all circumstances EU law is given the same interpretation in all states of the Union.

> RHEINMÜHLEN-DÜSSELDORF V EINFUHR- UND VORRATSSTELLE GETREIDE (JOINED CASES 146 AND 166/73) 1974
> R, a German cereal exporter, unsuccessfully sought to rely on [EU] law in the Hessian Tax Court to obtain an export rebate. He appealed to the Federal Tax Court (Bundesfinanzhof) which quashed the decision of the lower court, holding that R was entitled to a rebate. The case was sent back to the Hessian Tax Court to decide certain points of fact. The Hessian Tax Court, although bound under German law by the decisions of the Federal Tax Court, refused to follow the decision of the higher court and referred several questions to the ECJ under art.267. R appealed to the Federal Tax Court against the lower court's decision to make a reference. The Federal Tax Court then referred further questions to the ECJ to determine the extent of a lower court's powers to make a reference in such circumstances.

**Held**
❖ (ECJ) The power of a lower court to make a reference cannot be abrogated by national law; the lower court must be free to refer if it considers that the higher court's ruling could lead to it giving a judgment contrary to [EU] law. [1974] E.C.R. 33.

**Commentary** ....................................................................................

[1] Article 267 provides a mechanism which enables the ECJ to give preliminary rulings on:

(a) the interpretation of the Treaties;

(b) the validity and interpretation of acts of the institutions, bodies offices or agencies of the Union.

[2] Article 267(4) provides that if a question is raised in a case pending before a court or tribunal of a Member State with regard to a person in custody, the ECJ shall act with the minimum of delay.

[3] The procedure has been of great importance in the development of EU law. As the Treaties represent a framework (or "traité cadre") with little detail or definition, the ECJ has used the procedure to explain and clarify their provisions. The task of interpreting EU law has been described by Bingham J. in the UK High Court as involving the "creative process of supplying flesh to a spare and loosely constructed skeleton", *Customs and Excise v Samex*, 1983.

[4] The interpretations apply equally to all Member States, irrespective of the origin of any individual reference, thus ensuring uniformity of interpretation throughout the EC. Article 267 rulings are interlocutory (interim) rulings provided by the ECJ. After the question has been formulated by the national court, proceedings should be suspended pending the ruling, which may take up to two years. The national court should then apply the ruling to the issues in question.

[5] The General Court (then known as the CFI) was given the power to hear questions referred for a preliminary ruling under art.267 by the **Treaty of Nice** in specific areas laid down by the Statute of the Court. Where the General Court considers that the case requires a decision of principle likely to affect the unity or consistency of EU law, it may refer the case to the ECJ for hearing. Decisions of the General under art.267 may (exceptionally) be reviewed by the ECJ under conditions and limits laid down by the Statute where there is a serious risk of the unity or consistency of EU law being affected.

## Court or Tribunal

**Key Principle**

Any court or tribunal of a Member State has the power to make a reference under art.267 to the ECJ.

---

> BROEKMEULEN V HUISARTS REGISTRATIE COMMISSIE (CASE 246/80) 1981
>
> A Dutch Appeals Committee for General Medicine (not regarded as a court or tribunal under Dutch law) refused B's application to practise as a doctor in the Netherlands. During the course of a reference the ECJ considered whether the Committee was a court or tribunal for the purpose of art.267.

**Held**

❖ (ECJ) Where there is no right of appeal to the ordinary courts, the Appeals Committee, which operates with the consent of the public authorities and with their co-operation and which delivers decisions which are final after an adversarial procedure, must be regarded as a court or tribunal for the purpose of art.267. [1981] E.C.R. 2311.

**Commentary**

[1] For a body to be considered a court or tribunal under art.267 it is essential that the body in question exercises a judicial function (by making legally binding decisions), is competent to make a reference and is subject to control by public authorities. These elements were found by the ECJ to be lacking in *Nordsee Deutsch Hochseefischerei GmbH* (Case 102/81) where an arbitrator was appointed without participation of public authorities, under a contract in which recourse to arbitration was voluntary.

[2] A body exercising a purely administrative function is not covered by art.267. See, for example, *Victoria Film* (Case C-134/97) (body acting in administrative capacity making binding decisions on matters of individual tax planning), and *Standesamt Stadt Niebüll* (Case C-96/04) (body exercising administrative authority to determine a child's surname). The ECJ refused in both cases to hear applications under art.267.

[3] Where a body exercises both judicial and administrative functions, it will not be treated as a court or tribunal for the purpose of art.267 when exercising an administrative function: *Radiotelevisione Italiana (RAI)* (Case C-440/

98), in this case a retrospective review by the Corte dei Conti involving the assessing and checking of the results of administrative activity was considered by the ECJ to be an administrative function.

[4] The characteristics required of a court or tribunal were listed in *Dorsch Consult* (Case C-54/96) as including whether the body is established by law, its jurisdiction is compulsory, its procedure adversarial, whether it applies rules of law and whether it is independent. The last factor, "independence", was the subject of a ruling in Joined Cases C-110/98 *Gabalfrisa* and C-147/98 *Abrahamson*. In *Gabalfrisa* the ECJ found that there was a separation of functions between the tax authorities and a Spanish tax tribunal which heard complaints against the decisions of those authorities within the framework of internal administrative action. In *Abrahamson* an appeals committee with independent power to examine appeals against appointments in universities in Sweden was found to have the character of a third party and to be functionally separate. In both cases, the bodies were found to be courts or tribunals under art.267. In *Cartesio Oktató és Szolgáltató bt* (Case C-210/06) an appellate court hearing an appeal from a lower court responsible for maintaining a commercial register was considered to be a court.

## NECESSITY

**Key Principle**
Where a question of interpretation or validity of EU law is raised before a court or tribunal of a Member State, that court or tribunal may, if it considers that a question is necessary to enable it to give judgment, request the ECJ to give a ruling on it (art.267(2)).

> CILFIT SRL. AND LANIFICIO DI GAVARDO SPA. V MINISTRY OF HEALTH (CASE 283/81) 1982
> Wool importers disputed a health inspection levy imposed by the Italian government on wool imported from outside the EC (now EU), arguing that wool is an animal product (for which charges could not be imposed by regulation) and therefore not subject to such a charge. The Italian government claimed that the interpretation of "animal product" was obvious under the *acte clair* principle, in which case no reference under art.267 was necessary. The Italian Supreme Court referred the question to the ECJ.

**Held**
❖ (ECJ) A reference to the ECJ is not necessary where:

(1) the question of EU law is irrelevant;

(2) the question has already been decided by the ECJ; and

(3) the correct interpretation is so obvious as to leave no scope for doubt.

[1982] E.C.R. 3415.

## Commentary

[1] While the ruling in *CILFIT* was formulated in response to a question concerning mandatory references under art.267 (see below), it applies also to discretionary references. The *acte clair* doctrine derives from French administrative law: international treaties need not be referred to the government for interpretation if the meaning is clear.

[2] In *Bulmer v Bollinger* (CA, 1974) [1974] 2 All E.R. 1226, Lord Denning drew up guidelines for the United Kingdom courts in making referrals to the ECJ. The guidelines, though not binding, were treated as influential. Factors to be taken into account were stated to include the existence of a previous ECJ ruling, the conclusiveness of the reference to the judgment, the need to establish the facts, delay, the wishes of the parties and costs. Lord Denning's guidelines have been criticised as unduly restrictive, and should not be followed where they conflict with *CILFIT*.

[3] The Court of Appeal ruled that three factors must be present if a reference is to be made: the facts must be clear, the provision of EU law must be conclusive to the determination of the case, and the judge must consider whether he himself can resolve the question of EU law with complete confidence (*R. v International Stock Exchange of the UK and the Republic of Ireland Ex p. Else* [1993] 1 All E.R. 420.

## MANDATORY REFERENCES

### Key Principle

Where a question of interpretation or validity of EU law is raised before any court or tribunal of a Member State against whose decisions there is no judicial remedy, that court or tribunal shall bring the matter before the ECJ (art.267(3)).

> ### COSTA V ENEL (CASE 6/64) 1964
> Several questions were referred to the ECJ by the Italian small claims court (see p.3). As the sum claimed was very low there was no right of appeal to a higher national court.

**Held** ............................................................................................................

❖ (ECJ) "National courts against whose decisions, as in the present case, there is no judicial remedy must refer the matter" to the ECJ. [1964] E.C.R. 585.

**Commentary** ........................................................................................

[1] Identification of the courts covered by the obligation to refer under art.267(3) was controversial for many years. The decision in *Costa* was seen as support for the "concrete" theory in relation to the decision to refer. States following the concrete theory accepted that courts from which there was no prospect of appeal in the case in question were obliged to refer cases under art.267(3). By contrast, states following the "abstract" theory considered that only courts of last resort were required to refer.

[2] Doubts over whether to apply the concrete or abstract theory were resolved by the Court's decision in *Lyckeskog* (Case C-99/00) in favour of the concrete theory.

**Key Principle** ......................................................................................

In every case, there should be a point where a national court would be covered by the obligation to refer to the ECJ under art.267(3).

> LYCKESKOG (CASE C-99/00) 2002
>
> Lyckeskog (L) had been found guilty by the Tingsrätt (district court in Sweden) of attempting to smuggle 500kg of rice from Norway into Sweden. (Individuals were permitted to import up to 20kg for personal use.) He appealed against his conviction to the Hovrätt för Västra Sverige, against whose decisions a right of appeal lay to the Högstra domstol (supreme court). The Högstra domstol may issue a declaration of admissibility if it is important for guidance as to the application of the law that the appeal be examined by the court. The Hovrätt referred questions to the ECJ under art.267 to determine, to clarify the status under art.267(3) of courts issuing a declaration of admissibility.

**Held** ............................................................................................................

❖ (ECJ) Where the decisions of a national court or tribunal may be appealed to the national supreme court only if that supreme court declares that the appeal is admissible, such a court is not regarded as a court of last resort under art.267(3), and so is not under an obligation to refer. [2002] ECR I-4839.

## Commentary

[1] The decision in *Lyckeskog* means that a national supreme court will be obliged to refer questions to the ECJ under art.267(3) either when it considers an application for admissibility or when it hears the case itself.

[2] The only exceptions to the obligation to refer arise under the doctrines of *acte clair* (i.e. where the meaning is clear) and "acte éclairé" (i.e. where a materially identical matter has already been decided by the ECJ): see *CILFIT* (p.xx). The ECJ held in *Köbler v Austria* (Case C-224/01) that a national court's failure to refer under art.267(3) where it was manifestly apparent that it should do so could give rise to state liability under *Francovich* (see Ch.1). However, in this case, the failure was found not to be manifestly apparent as Austria had acted in good faith in the belief that the matter was covered by a previous decision of the ECJ.

## Key Principle

References under art.267 may still be made where there is a prior ruling of the ECJ on a similar point.

> DA COSTA EN SCHAKE N.V. V NEDERLANDSE
> BELASTAGINGENADMINISTRATIE (CASES 28–30/62) 1963
> A Dutch court of last resort referred questions identical to those in *Van Gend en Loos* (see p.2) on which judgment had recently been given by the ECJ. The Commission argued that the reference should be dismissed for lack of cause, as no questions remained for interpretation.

## Held

❖ (ECJ) Where an authoritative ruling has been made on an identical point, a national court need not refer. However, no national court may be deprived of the opportunity to refer a provision that has already been interpreted. [1963] E.C.R. 31.

## Commentary

[1] The ECJ does not operate a formal doctrine of binding precedent. Nevertheless, it does tend in most cases to follow its own previous decisions. In *Da Costa* the Court stated that making a reference on a point materially identical to a previous ruling may "deprive the obligation [to refer under art.234] of its purpose and thus empty it of its substance". The national court was directed to the judgment in *Van Gend en Loos*. Where the ECJ intends to depart from its

own previous decision it normally makes the change of direction very clear. (See e.g. *Keck and Mithouard* (Joined Cases C-267 and 268/91) (p.101).)

[2] Where a question referred to the ECJ is manifestly identical to a question on which the Court has ruled earlier, it may, under art.104 of its Rules of Procedure, give its decision by reasoned order in which reference is made to the previous judgment. This rule was invoked for the first time in relation to interpretation in *Beton Express v Direction Regionale des Douanes de la Reunion* (Case C-405/96) and in relation to validity in *Conata and Agrindustria v Aimaa* (Cases C-332 and 333/96).

## MISUSE OF THE ART.267 PROCEDURE

### Key Principle
Questions referred by national courts must involve genuine issues of EU law or they will not be considered by the ECJ.

> FOGLIA V NOVELLA (No.1) (CASE 104/79) 1980
> F and N, wine dealers in France and Italy, inserted a clause in their contract of sale not to pay any tax that contravened EC law. F sought to recover from N the tax incurred by a carrier of the goods in France. It appeared that the parties might have artificially concocted the contractual terms and the litigation in order to obtain a ruling on the validity of the French law.

### Held
❖ (ECJ) It is the duty of the ECJ to supply rulings in genuine disputes. To rule in circumstances such as the present case would jeopardise the system by which individuals can protect themselves against tax provisions contrary to the Treaty. [1980] E.C.R. 745.

### Commentary
[1] The ECJ refused to rule in *Foglia v Novella (No.1)* and remitted the case to the national court. Undeterred, the Italian court made a further attempt to refer the same questions to the ECJ in *Foglia v Novella (No.2)* (Case 244/80). Again the ECJ refused to answer, stating that the Court must be especially vigilant when asked to consider the validity of the national laws of another Member State. The decision has been criticised as unhelpful to the national court faced with a real, not a hypothetical, problem (the validity of the tax under EU law). See also *Meilicke* (Case C-83/91) (refusal to rule on academic issue regarded by the ECJ as an artificial question).

[2] The ECJ has declined to rule in a number of cases. See, for example, *SPUC v Grogan* (Case C-159/90) in which no ruling was made in relation to public policy and the availability of information about abortion services because the information was available without charge and so was outside the scope of art.66 TFEU (ex 59).

[3] Compare with *Dzodzi v Belgium* (Joined Cases C-297/88 and 197/89) (application of EU social security rules outside the EU where national law made reference to EU rules). The ECJ was prepared to make a ruling in order to ensure the uniform application of EC law.

[4] *Andersson v Sweden* (Case C-321/97) concerned a question of inter-pretation of the EEA Agreement (an agreement between various EFTA states and the EU). As the agreement involved the application of the agreement in the EFTA states and arose prior to Sweden's accession to the EU, the ECJ ruled that it had no jurisdiction to consider the question.

## RULINGS ON VALIDITY

**Key Principle**
While national courts may declare that a provision of EU law is valid, only the ECJ may declare a provision of EU law invalid.

> FOTO-FROST V HAUPTZOLLAMT LUBECK-OST (CASE 314/85) 1987
> A German court referred to the ECJ the question of whether a national court could declare invalid a provision of EU law (in this case, a decision which appeared to conflict with a regulation).

**Held**
❖ (ECJ) National courts have no jurisdiction to declare that acts of EU institutions are invalid. [1987] E.C.R. 4199.

**Commentary**
In *Foto-Frost* the ECJ stated that an exception to the rule might arise in the event of an applicant seeking an interim injunction (although no question had been referred on this point). The issue was taken up in *Zuckerfabrik* (see p.90).

## Key Principle

The national courts are not precluded by art.267 of the Treaty from suspending enforcement of a national administrative measure adopted on the basis of an EU regulation.

ZUCKERFABRIK SUDERDITHMARSCHEN A.G. V HAUPTZOLLAMT ITZEHOE (CASE C-143/88) 1991

Z, a sugar producer, complained that a German decision imposing a levy based on an EU regulation was invalid. The German court referred a number of questions to the ECJ, including the possible basis for the suspension of a national measure based on a regulation that may be invalid.

## Held

❖ (ECJ) A national court may suspend a national measure adopted to implement an EU regulation if:

(1) the national court entertains serious doubts as to the validity of the EC measure and itself refers the question of validity to the ECJ (if this has not already been done);

(2) there is urgency and a threat of serious and irreparable damage to the applicant;

(3) the national court takes due account of the EC's interests. [1991] E.C.R. I-415.

## Commentary

[1] Due to the time needed to obtain an art.267 reference from the ECJ the need for an interim remedy pending final resolution of the issues has become great in a number of cases. In *R. v Secretary of State for Transport Ex p. Factortame* the House of Lords applied the ruling of the ECJ in Case 213/89 (see Ch.1) and suspended the offending parts of the **Merchant Shipping Act 1988**. The House of Lords held that interim relief was necessary to protect the rights of individuals under EU law.

[2] The ECJ introduced a simplified procedure in 2000. This may be involved in three circumstances:

• where the question referred is identical to one referred earlier;

• where the answer to the question may clearly be deduced from existing case law; or

• where the answer to the question admits of no reasonable doubt.

Using the procedure enables the ECJ to provide a response within five months.

# Free Movement of Goods

## 8

## INTRODUCTION

The single or internal market is central to the rationale of the EU. Article 26 TFEU (ex 14) provides for an internal market comprising an area within which the free movement of goods, persons, services and capital is ensured in accordance with the Treaty. The main Treaty provisions on the free movement of goods are art.34 TFEU (ex 28) which prohibits quantitative restrictions and all measures having equivalent effect on imports, art.35 TFEU (ex 29) which makes a similar provision in relation to restrictions on exports, and art.36 TFEU (ex 30) which provides for derogations (exceptions) from arts 34 and 35 on specific grounds. The EU is also a customs union, with no duties payable on the importation and exportation of goods between Member States under art.28 TFEU (ex 23). Discriminatory taxation is prohibited under art.110 TFEU (ex 90).

## THE CUSTOMS UNION

### Key Principle
Member States are required under art.28 TFEU (ex 23) to form a customs union. Customs duties on imports and exports and charges having equivalent effect are prohibited under art.30 TFEU (ex 25).

> VAN GEND EN LOOS V NEDERLANDSE ADMINISTRATIE DER BELASTINGEN (CASE 26/62) 1963
> For facts, see p.2.

### Held
❖ (ECJ) Article 30 is directly effective. [1963] E.C.R. 1.

### Commentary
The customs union involves the prohibition between Member States of customs duties on imports and exports and of charges having equivalent effect, and the adoption of a customs tariff in relation to third countries (non-Member States) (art.30).

*Van Gend en Loos* illustrates the importance attached by the ECJ to the customs union by recognising that individuals may enforce their rights under art.30 before the national courts.

## Key Principle

A charge having equivalent effect which is disguised as a tax or levy is illegal under art.30.

### Sociaal Fonds voor de Diamantarbeiders v S.A.C. Brachfeld (Cases 2 and 3/69) 1969

The Belgian government imposed a levy on imported diamonds in order to provide social security benefits for diamond workers. An art.267 reference was made to the ECJ.

## Held

❖ (ECJ) The imposition of a charge on goods crossing a frontier is an obstacle to the free movement of goods. Such a levy is prohibited under art.30 independently of its destination or purpose. [1969] E.C.R. 211.

## Commentary

If the diamond workers' welfare scheme had been funded through a non-discriminatory system of taxation without reference to imports it would have been permissible under art.110 (see below).

# DISCRIMINATORY TAXATION

## Key Principle

No Member State may impose a tax directly or indirectly on products from another Member State greater than that applied to similar domestic products. Indirect protection through taxation of domestic products is also illegal: art.110.

### Commission v UK (Re Excise Duties on Wine) (No.1) (Case 170/78) 1980

The Commission sought a declaration under art.260 TFEU (ex 228) that the United Kingdom had infringed art.110 by imposing a higher excise duty on light wines than on beers.

**Held** ...................................................................................................................

❖ (ECJ) Allowing for changing drinking habits and the increasing popularity of wine in the United Kingdom it is possible to regard wine and beer as similar products in competition with each other and to compare the taxation of each. No ruling was made pending further investigation. [1980] E.C.R. 417.

**Held** ...................................................................................................................

❖ (ECJ) (No.2) (Case 170/78A) 1983 (Following the investigation by the Commission) The United Kingdom tax system discriminated against imported wine so as to afford a protection to domestically produced beer, contrary to art.110. [1983] E.C.R. 2265.

**Commentary** ...................................................................................................

[1] Article 110 allows Member States freedom to create their own internal systems of taxation provided there is no discrimination between Member States. Similar products may be taxed differently only where the distinction is objectively justified. In *Commission v France* (Case 196/85) there was no breach when traditional sweet wines were taxed at a lower rate than ordinary wines to provide economic assistance to rural areas dependent on wine production.

[2] In *Humblot v Directeur des Services Fiscaux* (Case 112/84) road tax was payable to the French government at a higher rate on cars of more than 16c-v, the highest engine capacity for cars made in France. A French taxpayer sought to recover the additional tax paid on a 36c-v car imported from Germany. The ECJ held the system to be a breach of art.110. An amended tax system was later found still to breach art.110.

[3] In *Stadtgemeindebetriebe Frohnleiten GmbH v Bundesminister für Länd- und Forstwirtschaft, Umwelt und Wasserwirtschaft* (Case C-221/06) a levy was imposed on the long-term depositing of waste at a waste-disposal site in Austria. Whereas contaminated waste from Austria was exempted from the levy, no such exemption was applied to the deposit of waste from other Member States. The ECJ found that such a system of internal taxation discriminated against other Member States contrary to art.110.

# QUANTITATIVE RESTRICTIONS AND MEASURES HAVING EQUIVALENT EFFECT

## Key Principle

Quantitative restrictions and all measures having equivalent effect are prohibited under art.34.

> ### R. v Henn and Darby (Case 34/79) 1980
> The United Kingdom seized pornographic goods imported from the Netherlands. The importers were prosecuted and an art.267 reference was made to the ECJ by the House of Lords.

## Held

❖ (ECJ) A total ban is a quantitative restriction under art.34. (The measure was in fact found to be justified under art.36: see p.105.) [1979] E.C.R. 3795.

## Commentary

[1] Anything which restricts importation by reference to quantity (e.g. a quota system) is a quantitative restriction.

[2] Inactions as well as actions may be a breach of art.34. In *Commission v France* (Case C-265/95) the Commission brought enforcement proceedings against France under art.258 for failing to act to prevent disruption to the free movement of agricultural goods such as Spanish strawberries. The problems arose from protest action by French farmers and others, intercepting lorries, destroying their loads and threatening their drivers. The ECJ held that the French government's failure to adopt necessary and proportionate measures was a breach of (old) art.10 EC (now art.4 TEU).

[3] The ECJ reached a different decision in *Schmidberger v Austria* (Case C-112/00), highlighting the need to assess the use of discretion. In this case, the Austrian government decided not to ban a demonstration by an environmental group. As a result, the Brenner motorway was closed for 30 hours, disrupting the transportation of goods between Germany and Italy. The ECJ held that, although the decision was an MEQR, it was within the Member State's discretion, proportionate and in accordance with fundamental rights. There was no breach of art.34.

## Key Principle

All trading rules enacted by Member States which are capable of hindering, directly or indirectly, actually or potentially, intra-EU trade are to be considered as measures having an effect equivalent to quantitative restrictions.

> **PROCUREUR DU ROI V DASSONVILLE (CASE 8/74) 1974**
> Dassonville, a trader, imported Scotch whisky into Belgium from France without a certificate of origin, contrary to Belgian law. He was charged with a criminal offence but pleaded that the Belgian requirement contravened art.34. An art.267 reference was made.

## Held

❖ (ECJ) In the absence of harmonisation, a Member State may take measures to prevent unfair practices provided they are reasonable and do not hinder inter-member trade. It was more difficult for a trader importing goods in circulation in another Member State to obtain a certificate than for an importer to do so when importing the goods directly from the state of production. Thus the requirement to obtain a certificate was a measure having equivalent effect and was illegal under art.34. [1974] E.C.R. 837.

## Commentary

[1] *Dassonville* is important in that it defines what is meant by a "measure having equivalent effect" (MEQR). Further examples of MEQRs include inspection fees at frontiers and charges for storage pending inspections. Following the decision in *Keck and Mithouard* (see p.xx) a more restrictive approach has been taken by the ECJ to measures regarded as MEQRs.

[2] Directive 70/50 divides measures into distinctly effective measures (which do not apply equally to domestic and imported goods) and indistinctly effective measures (which apply alike to both domestic and imported goods).

[3] Under art.3 of **Directive 70/50** indistinctly applicable measures only infringe art.34 when they are disproportionate (i.e. more restrictive than necessary to achieve their objective).

[4] The ECJ in *Commission v Netherlands* (Case C-297/05) considered the compatibility of national rules relating to the import of vehicles from another Member State. The rules required such vehicles to undergo an identification and a roadworthiness test before registration in the Netherlands. The Court found that the identification test was little more than an administrative formality, with no deterrent effect on imports. The roadworthiness test, however, was not proportionate to the legitimate aims of road safety and

protection of the environment. A less restrictive approach such as recognition of proof issued in another Member State would have been enough. The Netherlands was found to be in breach of art.34.

## Key Principle
Member States may not promote national products where this involves discrimination against imports.

> COMMISSION V IRELAND (CASE 249/81) 1982
> A scheme was operated ("Buy Irish") to promote the sales of Irish goods to shoppers in Ireland. A symbol indicating Irish origin was attached to goods and an information service was available. According to the Irish government the scheme was not particularly successful as the sale of imported products actually rose during the promotion period. The Commission brought an action against the Irish government under art.258.

## Held
❖ (ECJ) If a measure is capable of restricting imports it is illegal under art.34. [1982] E.C.R. 4005.

## Commentary
Contrast the "Buy Irish" case with *Apple and Pear Council v Lewis* (Case 222/82) in which a Council funded by a levy on apple and pear growers in England and Wales was created to promote the consumption of English and Welsh varieties. Some growers refused to pay, claiming that the scheme infringed art.34. The ECJ (under art.267) held that it was permissible to promote a product by reference to its qualities, even where those qualities are typical of national production.

## Key Principle
There is no valid reason why goods which have been lawfully produced and marketed in one Member State should not be introduced into any other Member State (the principle of mutual recognition).

> REWE-ZENTRAL A.G. V BUNDESMONOPOLVERWALTUNG FUR BRANNTWEIN ("CASSIS DE DIJON") (CASE 120/78) 1979
> Cassis de Dijon is a blackcurrant liqueur originating in France where it contains 15–20 per cent alcohol by volume. German law required fruit

liqueurs to have a minimum alcohol content of 25 per cent. While the measure was not discriminatory it clearly excluded French cassis from the German market. German importers challenged the measure in the national court which made an art.267 reference.

**Held**

In the absence of EU rules, the Member States may regulate the production and marketing of alcoholic drinks. Obstacles to movement within the EU arising from disparities between national laws relating to the marketing of the products must be accepted in so far as they may be necessary to satisfy mandatory requirements relating in particular to the effectiveness of fiscal supervision, the protection of public health, fairness of commercial transactions and the defence of the consumer. [1979] E.C.R. 649.

**Commentary**

[1] The ECJ rejected German government claims that a requirement for a higher alcohol content discouraged alcoholism and that it protected consumers against unfair commercial practices. The requirement infringed the principle of proportionality and, while mandatory, was not necessary. Consumers could be protected by being given information about the alcoholic content on the label.

[2] The mandatory requirements in *Cassis* have provided a basis for departing from art.34 in cases involving indistinctly applicable measures. They were not satisfied in *Commission v Germany* (Case 178/84) in which a long-standing ban on additives in beer was found to be unjustifiable on health grounds. Other unjustifiable measures have included a restriction on the shape of bottles containing traditional alcoholic drinks and a requirement to sell margarine in cubes.

[3] Note that distinctly applicable measures may only be justified under art.36 (see p.104).

[4] The principle of mutual recognition represents a widening of the *Cassis* principle to cover all goods, not merely alcoholic beverages. It has provided the basis for the single market (1992) programme of directives to harmonise standards.

**Key Principle**

National strategies to protect the environment may infringe art.34.

Danish law required that beer and soft drinks could be sold only in reusable containers, as part of a deposit-and-return scheme on grounds of environmental protection. The scheme was later modified to allow producers to market a limited quantity of drinks in non-approved containers. The Commission brought an action under art.258 in the ECJ, claiming that the measure infringed art.34.

## Held

❖ (ECJ) Although protection of the environment is an important objective, the quantitative restriction on beverages that could be sold in non-approved containers had a disproportionate effect on importers from other EU states. Denmark was in breach of art.34. [1988] E.C.R. 4607.

## Commentary

[1] This case illustrates the difficult position of a Member State introducing a measure that can affect imports, in the absence of common EU rules. Contrast the decision with *Oebel* (Case 155/80) in which a Belgian law forbidding night working in bakeries was held not to infringe art.34 because it did not affect imports.

[2] In another case concerned with the environmental problems associated with drinks packaging, this time where common EU rules have been adopted, the court found that problems can still occur where harmonisation is not complete. *Commission v Germany* (Case C-463/01) concerned enforcement proceedings brought against Germany which required the producers and distributors of drinks in non-reusable packaging to charge a deposit and take back the packaging. As Directive 94/62 on packaging and packaging waste (requiring producers of mineral water to bottle at source) did not fully harmonise the law, the German legislation had to be assessed for compatibility with art.34. While the German rules could be justified as necessary to protect the environment, they infringed the principle of proportionality as the transition period for producers and distributors to adopt was only six months.

[3] Other mandatory requirements recognised since *Cassis* include the protection of fundamental rights (*Schmidberger* (Case C-112/00): see above) and the pluralism of the press (*Vereinigte Familiapress Zeitungsverlags under vertriebs GmbH v Heinrich Bauer Verlag* (Case C-368/95), in which the ECJ found that prizes offered in magazines could eliminate competition from smaller papers unable to afford to offer prizes).

**Key Principle** ................................................................................................

The regulation of Sunday trading falls within the discretion of Member States to make political and economic choices to accord with national or regional socio-cultural characteristics.

TORFAEN BOROUGH COUNCIL V B&Q PLC (CASE 145/88) 1989
The defendant was charged with trading on a Sunday contrary to the Shops Act 1950. The magistrates' court referred to the ECJ the question of whether such a measure breached art.34.

**Held** ................................................................................................

❖ (ECJ) It is a legitimate part of socio-economic policy for Member States to regulate opening hours. Such rules do not infringe art.34 provided they are not disproportionate and do not affect inter-member trade. [1989] E.C.R. 3851.

**Commentary** ................................................................................................

[1] *Torfaen* left many shops and local authorities in confusion over Sunday trading. Later decisions clarified the position. The ECJ stated unequivocally in *Stoke on Trent and Norwich City Council v B&Q* (Case C-169/91) that the prohibition in art.34 does not apply to national legislation prohibiting retailers from opening their premises on Sundays. The Sunday trading laws did not discriminate against imports. Their legitimacy turned on proportionality (weighing national interests in achieving the objective against EU interests in the free movement of goods).

[2] A ban on the employment of labour in France and Belgium on Sundays was also outside art.34: *Marchandise* (Case C-332/89) and *Conforama* (Case C-312/89).

[3] The Sunday Trading Act 1994 now permits shops in England and Wales below a certain floor area to trade freely on Sundays. Larger shops may trade for six hours between 10am and 6pm.

**Key Principle** ................................................................................................

Article 34 does not apply to selling arrangements by Member States which do not affect inter-member trade.

K and M had resold goods at a loss contrary to French law. They claimed that the prohibition restricted the volume of sales of imported goods and so infringed art.34. An art.267 reference was made.

## Held

❖ (ECJ) Contrary to what had previously been decided, the application to products from other Member States of national provisions restricting or partitioning certain selling arrangements does not hinder directly or indirectly, actually or potentially, trade between Member States within the meaning of the *Dassonville* judgment. [1993] E.C.R. I-6097.

## Commentary

[1] *Keck and Mithouard* signals a departure from the previous line of case law developed by the ECJ since *Cassis*. Traders had relied too heavily on art.34 to challenge national measures restricting commercial freedom where there was no effect on imports. Member States should be free to adopt measures that do not affect inter-member trade, provided these conform to the principle of proportionality.

[2] Later cases have confirmed this approach. See also *Belgapom v Itm Belgium and Vocarex S.A.* (Case C-63/94), in which potatoes were sold at a loss contrary to Belgian law. The ECJ held that art.34 does not apply to national legislation prohibiting sales at a very low profit margin. In *Tankstation't Heukste vof and Boermans* (Case C-401/92) Dutch rules on opening hours of shops in petrol stations were also found to be outside art.34. A similar finding was made in *Hunermund v Landesapothekerkammer Baden-Wurttemberg* (Case C-292/92) involving a prohibition on the promotion of para-pharmaceutical products outside pharmacies. In *Société d'Importation Edouard Leclerc-Siplec v TFI Publicité S.A. and M6 Publicité S.A.* (Case C-412/93) a French ban on televised advertising of the distribution sector was held to be a selling arrangement outside art.34 as it prohibited a particular form of promotion and marketing, but was not discriminatory.

[3] Where a measure is not considered to be a selling arrangement, it infringes art.34, but may be legitimate if it satisfies one of the exceptions in *Cassis*. In *Konsumentombudsmannen (KO) v Gourmet International Products AB (GIP)* (Case C-405/98) Swedish legislation prohibiting the advertising of alcoholic drinks was found not to be a selling arrangement as it made market access more difficult. However, it was justified in the interests of public health provided it was proportionate. Assessing proportionality was left to the national courts.

[4] *Åklagaren v Mikkelson and Ross* (Case C-142/05) arose from another prohibition under Swedish law, this time on the use of personal pleasure craft on waters which were not designated waterways. The ECJ found the restriction to be contrary to art.34 as it impeded access to the market. However, it was justified on environmental grounds subject to the satisfaction of various conditions on "navigable waterways" which were left to the national courts to determine.

**Key Principle**

National requirements placing a dual burden of regulation by the state of production and the state of sale are not selling arrangements, but infringe art.34.

> **VERBAND SOZIALER WETTBEWERB EV V CLINIQUE LABORATOIRES SNCF (CASE C-315/92)**
>
> German law banned the use of the name "Clinique" for cosmetics. The effect of this requirement was to require the repackaging of imported cosmetics to be sold in Germany.

**Held**

❖ (ECJ) The measure was not a selling arrangement. It infringed art.34 and was not justified in order to avoid confusing customers.

**Commentary**

[1] *Verband* provides an example of a "product requirement", placing a dual burden on the importer to satisfy the requirements of the state of sale to repackage the goods before they can be sold in another Member State, despite the fact that the goods have already satisfied the state of production. Such a requirement is not a selling arrangement as it represents a restriction on the free movement of goods.

[2] Similar reasoning was employed in another case of German origin, this time involving national restrictions on unfair competition: *Verein gegen Unwesen in Handel und Gewerbe Köln v Mars GmbH* (Case C-470/93) (Requirement to repackage Mars bars with the words "plus ten per cent" on the wrapping for sale in Germany infringed art.35).

[3] In *Georg Schwarz v Bürgermeister der Landeshaupstadt Salzburg* (Case C-366/04) the ECJ found that a ban by Austria on the sale of unwrapped

chewing gum from automatic vending machines imposed an additional burden on importers, but was justified on grounds of public health.

[4] A German rule requiring image storage media such as photographs to be subject to inspection and classification to protect young persons was held not be a selling arrangement. However, such a rule was legitimate under art.34 if the procedure was transparent and open to challenge: *Dynamic Media Vetriebs GmBH* (Case C-244/06).

## Key Principle
Each case should be assessed on its merits to determine the actual or potential effect of national legislation in relation to art.34.

### HOUTWIPPER (CASE C-293/93) 1994
Dutch law required all precious metals to be hallmarked according to certain specifications before being offered for sale. Thus imported goods would require re-hallmarking on entering the Netherlands.

### Held
❖ (ECJ) While the hallmarking requirement was a mandatory measure to protect consumers and promote fair trading, it infringes art.34 by requiring the fixing of a fresh hallmark where an equivalent hallmark has already been affixed in another Member State. [1994] E.C.R. I-4249.

### Commentary
[1] Unlike *Keck and Mithouard*, the measure in *Houtwipper* (which pre-dated the *Keck* ruling) discriminated against imports.

[2] In *Deutscher Apotekverband v DocMorris and Waterval* (Case C-322/01) the ECJ held that a national restriction limiting the sale of medicinal products to pharmacies infringed art.34. It found that the national rule, which prohibited the advertising of such products by mail order, was justified under art.36 in relation to medicinal products sold on prescription, but not in relation to products which are not subject to prescription.

[3] In *Ker-Optika* (Case C-108/09) similar issues arose in relation to national legislation in Hungary limiting the sale of contact lenses to opticians' shops which had the effect of prohibiting the sale of contact lenses from other Member States via the internet. The ECJ found that the restriction infringed art.34 as it was disproportionate. While the measure served to protect the

health of consumers, this objective could be achieved by less restrictive means.

## QUANTITATIVE RESTRICTIONS ON EXPORTS AND MEASURES HAVING EQUIVALENT EFFECT

### Key Principle
Restrictions on exports will only breach art.35 if they have as their object or effect the restriction of patterns of exports, providing an advantage to the home product or market.

> GROENVELD V PRODUKTSCHAP VOOR VEE EN VLEES (CASE 15/79) 1979
> Dutch law prohibited all meat processors from stocking or processing horsemeat, in order to prevent the export of horsemeat to countries prohibiting its sale. Groenveld decided to make horsemeat sausages, contrary to Dutch law, claiming that the law infringed art.35 by prohibiting the processing and exporting of horsemeat.

### Held
❖ (ECJ) Article 35 did not apply to a rule which did not discriminate between goods for the home market and for export. [1989] E.C.R. 3967.

### Commentary
[1] The *Cassis* justifications for restrictions on imports do not apply to exports. Whereas importers face a "dual burden", namely the requirements of the home state and of the importing state, exporters need only satisfy the requirements of the home state. Thus export restrictions may only be justified under art.36.

[2] "Quantitative restrictions" and "measures having equivalent effect" have the same meanings for art.35 as for art.34.

## DEROGATIONS FROM ARTS 34 AND 35

### Key Principle
Articles 34 and 35 do not preclude prohibitions on imports, exports or goods in transit justified on grounds of public morality, public policy or public security; the protection of life or health of humans, animals or plants; the protection of national treasures possessing artistic, historic or archaeological value; or the protection of industrial or commercial property. Such

prohibitions must not constitute a means of arbitrary discrimination or a disguised restriction on trade between Member States: art.36.

**Key Principle** ..........................................................................................
Restrictions on imports or exports may be justified on grounds of public morality.

> R. v HENN AND DARBY (CASE 34/79) 1979
> See p.95. The United Kingdom seized films and publications being imported from the Netherlands into the United Kingdom. The importers were prosecuted under customs and excise legislation with importing indecent and obscene arts. In their defence the importers claimed that the prohibition contravened art.34 in that a stricter standard was being applied to imported than to domestic goods. An art.267 reference was made.

**Held** ..........................................................................................
❖ (ECJ) A Member State may lawfully prohibit on grounds of public morality the importation from another Member State of indecent or obscene materials as understood by its domestic laws. A prohibition on imports that is stricter than the domestic prohibition is not a measure designed to give indirect protection to a national product or aimed at creating arbitrary discrimination depending on where the goods are produced. [1979] E.C.R. 3795.

**Commentary** ..........................................................................................
*Henn and Darby* illustrates the general requirement of art.36 that a measure must be necessary, but must not involve arbitrary discrimination or a disguised restriction on inter-member trade. Contrast *Conegate Ltd v HM Customs and Excise* (Case 121/85) in which there was a lawful domestic trade in the goods in question (inflatable dolls). Seizure of dolls being imported from Germany into the United Kingdom on grounds that they were indecent and obscene was a breach of art.34, being discriminatory on grounds of nationality.

**Key Principle** ..........................................................................................
Restrictions on imports or exports may be justified on grounds of public policy.

### R. v THOMPSON (CASE 7/78) 1978

United Kingdom law in force at the time prohibited the importation of gold coins and export of silver-alloy coins minted before 1947. The case turned on the distinction between whether the coins were "goods" or "means of payment". Under United Kingdom law it was illegal to melt down or destroy coins, even if they were no longer legal tender.

### Held

❖ (ECJ) As the coins were not legal tender they were goods under art.34. A ban on destroying such coins with a view to preventing their being melted down or destroyed in another Member State was justified on grounds of public policy under art.36, because it stemmed from the need to protect the right to mint coinage which is traditionally regarded as involving the fundamental interests of the state. [1978] E.C.R. 2247.

### Commentary

[1] "Public policy" is a translation of the French term "ordre public". *R. v Thompson* is a rare example of a successful invocation of the exception. Public policy does not cover consumer protection (*Kohl v Ringelhan* (Case 177/83)) or economic considerations (*Cullet v Centre Leclerc* (Case 231/81)).

[2] For a House of Lords ruling on public policy under art.36 in the context of a restriction on exports, see *R. v Chief Constable of Sussex Ex p. Trader's Ferry* [1998] 3 W.L.R. 1260. This case concerned a decision by the Chief Constable of Sussex to reduce the level of policing at the port of Shoreham where there had been a prolonged campaign of protest against the export of live animals to the Continent. (The Chief Constable had justified his decision on the basis that policing the prolonged campaign reduced his capacity to carry out other policing responsibilities.) International Trader's Ferry, the exporter, sought judicial review of the Chief Constable's decision. The HL held that the Chief Constable had not acted unreasonably in English law. Without making a reference to the ECJ, the HL held that, assuming the decision to be a measure equivalent to a quantitative restriction on exports under art.35, it was justified on grounds of public policy. Such grounds could arise where the broader requirements of public policy justified steps being taken. The Chief Constable's actions were proportionate and reasonable in the light of available resources.

### Key Principle

Restrictions on imports or exports may be justified by public security.

Irish law required importers of petroleum products to buy up to 35 per cent of their needs from the Irish National Petroleum Company at fixed prices. Ireland sought to justify this requirement on both public policy and public security grounds, claiming that this was the only method by which the national refining capacity could be maintained and the products sold.

**Held**

❖ (ECJ) The measure was justified on grounds of public security rather than public policy. Maintaining a refinery enabled Ireland to enter into long-term contracts with oil producers who would ensure greater continuity of oil supplies during a crisis. [1983] E.C.R. 2727.

**Commentary**

The ECJ accepted that a measure justified on grounds of public security might also achieve economic objectives without taking it outside art.36.

**Key Principle**

Restrictions on imports and exports may be justified on grounds of protection of life and health of humans, animals or plants.

OFFICIER VAN JUSTITIE V KAASFABRIK EYSSEN B.V. (CASE 53/80) 1981
A cheese producer was prosecuted in the Netherlands for using nisin, a preservative prohibited under Dutch law, in processed cheese. Nisin was a permitted ingredient in other Member States. Scientific research was divided as to the harmfulness of the additive. The cheese producer argued that the ban infringed art.34 as it impeded imports.

**Held**

❖ (ECJ) In the absence of harmonisation, a state may protect the public by banning additives where there is genuine scientific doubt about their safety. [1981] E.C.R. 409.

**Commentary**

[1] This decision forms part of a series of cases on the use of additives (cf. *Commission v Germany* (Case 178/84) on p.90). In *Ministre Public v Claude Muller* (Case 304/84) it was held that the requirement for authorisation for specific additives is subject to the principle of proportionality; thus the process of application must be rapid and straightforward. Prior national

authorisation may also be required for medical products (*Lucien Ortscheit GmbH v Eurim-Pharm GmbH* (Case C-320/93)).

[2] Note that the protection of public health is a consideration that outweighs all others, especially economic considerations: *Boehringer v Council* (Joined Cases T-125 and 126/96).

[3] In *Rosengren and others* (Case C-170/04) the ECJ considered the validity of a prohibition under Swedish law on the importation of alcoholic drinks, the sale of which in Sweden is subject to a state-controlled monopoly. The ECJ found that the prohibition should be assessed under art.34 and not art.37 TFEU (ex 31) on state monopolies of a commercial character. The measure was found to be a quantitative restriction, which was not justified on grounds of health under art.36. (The Swedish law had only a marginal effect on limiting the consumption of alcohol and was disproportionate as it applied to all persons, not just the young.)

**Key Principle**

The risk to health must be real and form part of a seriously considered health policy.

### COMMISSION V UK (CASE 40/82) 1982

The United Kingdom unilaterally and hastily introduced a ban on the importation of poultry meat and eggs after extensive lobbying by United Kingdom poultry producers just before Christmas 1981. The United Kingdom government claimed that the measure was necessary under art.36 to prevent British flocks catching a form of poultry disease known as Newcastle Disease. Enforcement proceedings were brought against the United Kingdom.

**Held**

❖ (ECJ) The ban was not part of a health policy but was a disguised restriction on trade. Less restrictive methods would have been sufficient. The measure could not be justified on grounds of animal health under art.36. [1982] E.C.R. 2793.

**Commentary**

The measure appeared to be an attempt to protect United Kingdom producers from French competition. French turkey farmers later sought to recover their losses from the United Kingdom government in *Bourgoin SA v MAFF* (CA).

Although the claim was struck out they won an out-of-court settlement of £3.5 million.

## Key Principle
Where there is uncertainty as to the existence or extent of risks to human health, the institutions may take protective measures without having to wait until the illegality and seriousness of those risks becomes fully apparent.

NATIONAL FARMERS' UNION AND OTHERS (CASE C-157/96); UNITED KINGDOM V COMMISSION (CASE C-180/96)
The Commission adopted emergency measures in 1996 to counteract the threat to health posed by BSE ("mad cow disease"), prohibiting the UK from exporting beef worldwide. The UK contested the decision under art.263. The ECJ considered that the Commission was entitled to react to the publication of new information about the disease, and that the confinement of animals and products within a particular territory was an appropriate measure, even in relation to exports to third countries.

## Held
❖ (ECJ) (1) The measures were not disproportionate: there was no need to wait until the full extent of the risks became apparent.
(2) The measures were not illegal, and were properly based on art.43 TFEU (ex 37) on the Common Agricultural Policy. [1998] E.C.R. I-2211; [1998] E.C.R. I-2265.

## Commentary
[1] In *Commission v France* (Case C-1/00) the Commission brought enforcement proceedings against France for unilaterally maintaining the export ban on British beef after the ban was lifted in August 1999 for certain meats and meat products. While declaring that France had acted unlawfully in refusing to adopt the necessary measure to implement the lifting of the ban, the ECJ found that its failure was not as extensive as the Commission had claimed, in view (partly) of the difficulty in interpreting and implementing the relevant Commission decision.

[2] The precautionary principle has been followed in a number of later cases. In *Pfizer Animal Health S.A. v Council* and *Alpharma Inc v Council* (Cases T-13/99 and T-70/99) the CFI upheld the Council's decision to ban certain antibiotics as additives in animal feed, confirming that preventive measures may

be taken before the reality and seriousness of the risk is fully apparent. There must, however, be a real risk. The CFI acknowledged that the degree of risk cannot be set at zero. Before taking any preventive measure, public authorities must carry out a risk assessment involving both a scientific component (as thorough a scientific assessment as possible taking account of the degree of urgency) and a political component ("risk management" involving a decision by the authorities on the measures deemed appropriate according to the degree of risk) (CFI ruling upheld by ECJ in Case C-329/99).

[3] In *Artegodan GmbH v Commission* (Cases T-74/00 etc.) the CFI annulled Commission decisions ordering the withdrawal of marketing authorisation for anti-obesity drugs. After finding that the Commission was not competent to adopt the decisions as competence remained with the Member States, it went on to consider validity. The CFI held that the conditions for withdrawal of marketing authorisation must be interpreted in accordance with the general principle of protection of public health. Applying the precautionary principle where there is scientific uncertainty, the Court found that mere changes in scientific criteria for assessing the efficacy of a medical product justify withdrawal of a marketing authorisation only if those changes are supported by new data (under appeal—Case C-221/10P).

**Key Principle**
Restrictions on imports and exports may be justified on grounds of the protection of national treasures possessing artistic, historic or archaeological value.

COMMISSION V ITALY (RE EXPORT TAX ON ART TREASURES) (CASE 7/68)
The Italian government imposed a tax on the export of art treasures from Italy, claiming that such a tax would be less restrictive than an export ban. The Commission brought an action in the ECJ under art.258.

**Held**
❖ (ECJ) The measure was illegal under art.30 (prohibition on customs duties and measures equivalent to customs duties). It could not therefore be justified under art.36. [1968] E.C.R. 423.

**Key Principle**
Restrictions on imports and exports may be justified on grounds of the protection of industrial and commercial property.

## EMI Electrola v Patricia (Case 341/87) 1989

Patricia and other record companies sought to take advantage of the fact that the copyright to the records of Cliff Richard had expired in Denmark but not in Germany by buying recordings in Denmark and importing them for resale in Germany.

**Held**

❖ (ECJ) The recordings had not been marketed by the holder of the copyright (EMI) or with his consent, even though they had been lawfully placed on the market. EMI could rely on the copyright to keep out the recordings. [1989] E.C.R. 79.

**Commentary**

[1] Intellectual property rights (as industrial property rights are now usually known) take forms such as trade marks, copyright, patents and design rights. They usually operate at national level to provide protection for the holder of the right on a territorial basis. It follows that such rights may impede the free movement of goods under arts 34 and 35. They may also infringe the competition rules under arts 101 TFEU (ex 81) and 102 TFEU (ex 82). While art.36 provides an express exception for industrial property rights, it states that such prohibitions must not constitute a means of arbitrary discrimination or disguised restriction on trade between Member States. Harmonisation of intellectual property rights is proceeding steadily.

[2] There is an extensive body of case law on intellectual property in the ECJ and General Court. Space in this text does not permit a full treatment. Many cases, particularly on trade marks, concern pharmaceutical products. One example of a particularly significant decision in which the ECJ reconsidered its earlier decisions was *Bristol-Myers Squibb v Paranova* (Joined Cases C-427, 429 and 436/93). Paranova, a parallel importer (i.e. an importer acting without the consent of the trade mark holder) bought pharmaceutical products outside Denmark, repackaged them and resold them in Denmark, undercutting the trade mark holder. The ECJ accepted that the trade mark holder may oppose marketing of the product where there is a risk of damage to the contents as a result of inappropriate repackaging, as this might damage the reputation of the trade mark holder. However, the trade mark must not artificially partition the market. The trade mark holder's rights may be limited only to the extent that the repackaging undertaken by the importer was necessary to market the product in the state of import, an objective test.

[3] A number of cases on luxury goods concern international exhaustion, the principle that once goods have been put on the market by the trade mark

holder or with his consent outside the area of territorial protection for the trade mark, the trade mark holder may not rely on his rights to prevent re-importation. In *Silhouette International v Hartlauer* (Case C-355/96) S, a company registered in Austria (then a member of the EEA prior to accession), made high-cost spectacles and H was a cut-price distributor not permitted to distribute S's products. S sought an injunction to prevent H, who had obtained a consignment of S's spectacles in Bulgaria, from re-importing them into Austria. The ECJ held, under art.267, that national rules on international exhaustion in respect of products put on the market outside the EEA under that mark by the trade mark holder, or with his consent, are contrary to art.7(1) of the Trade Marks Directive. While the ECJ reaffirmed its stance in *Sebago and Ancienne Maison Dubois v G.B. Unie* (Case C-173/98), the *Silhouette* decision was heavily criticised.

**Key Principle**

The consent of a trade mark proprietor to marketing within the EEA goods placed on the market outside the EEA must be expressed unequivocally.

ZINO DAVIDOFF S.A. V A&G IMPORTS; LEVI STRAUSS & CO, LEVI STRAUSS (UK) LTD V TESCO STORES; TESCO PLC V COSTCO WHOLESALE UK LTD (JOINED CASES C-414, 415 AND 416/99) 2001

Zino Davidoff was the proprietor of two trade marks registered in the UK and used for toiletries and cosmetic products. The goods were sold by Davidoff within and outside the EEA. A&G acquired stocks originally placed on the market in Singapore by Davidoff or with the company's consent and imported the goods into the UK for resale.

Levi Strauss, the proprietor of the trade marks "Levi's" and "Levi 501" registered in the UK, always refused to sell its jeans to Tesco or Costco. When Tesco and Costco sold in the UK genuine Levi products obtained outside the EEA, Levi Strauss began proceedings in the UK courts for trade mark infringement. Davidoff brought a similar claim. The High Court referred questions from the various proceedings under art.267, to elicit clarification of the exhaustion principle in the context of the **Trade Marks Directive**, where goods have been placed on the market within the EEA by the proprietor or with his consent.

**Held**

(1) Consent constitutes the decisive factor in the extinction of the proprietor's exclusive right to prevent third parties from importing goods bearing his trade mark.

(2) Intention to renounce the proprietor's rights must be unequivocally demonstrated. Consent must be expressed positively. Implied consent cannot be inferred from mere silence.

**Commentary**

*Davidoff* and *Silhouette* demonstrate the continuing power of the trade mark holder to exert rights which make it difficult for the consumer to obtain cheaply priced imports from parallel traders.

---

**THINK POINT**

Why was the decision in *Cassis de Dijon* so important in terms of the mutual recognition of the standards under which goods were produced and marketed?

Why are the requirements for derogation under art.36 TFEU more difficult to satisfy than the exceptions under *Cassis de Dijon*?

# Free Movement of Capital

## 9

## INTRODUCTION

The free movement of capital is one of the four freedoms under art.26 TFEU (ex 14). However, it lagged behind the other freedoms (goods, persons and services) until the completion of the internal market in 1992. Some Member States used exchange control restrictions as a tool of economic policy until Directive 88/361 was adopted as part of the single market programme (see below). The **TFEU** (at the time, the **EC Treaty**) was amended by the **Treaty of Maastricht** to reflect the wording of the directive.

### Key Principle

All restrictions on the free movement of capital between Member States are prohibited: art.63(1) TFEU (ex 56(1)).

> **MINISTERIO FISCAL V ALDO BORDESSA (CASES C-358 AND 416/93) 1995**
> Various Spanish and Italian nationals were charged with attempting to take out of Spain more money than was permitted under exchange control laws without prior authorisation. The Spanish court made an art.267 reference to the ECJ.

### Held

❖ (ECJ) Article 1 of **Directive 88/361** prohibiting all restrictions on the free movement of capital is directly effective from July 1, 1990. Member States may require persons crossing borders to declare their assets but may not require a prior administrative authorisation, such a requirement being disproportionate. [1995] E.C.R. I-361.

### Commentary

The original provision in the **Treaty of Rome** for the free movement of capital was not directly effective. **The Maastricht Treaty** incorporated the wording of **Directive 88/361** into the Treaty, so that the revised provision is also directly effective: see *Sanz de Lera* (below). The provisions on free movement of capital may be found in arts.63–66 TFEU (ex 56–59).

## Key Principle
National laws prohibiting the export of currency without prior authorisation are illegal under EU law.

> **MINISTERIO FISCALO V SANZ DE LERA AND OTHERS (CASES C-163, 164 AND 250/94) 1995**
> Various individuals took money in excess of the permitted limits out of Spain to Turkey and Switzerland. They were prosecuted under Spanish law. An art.267 reference was made to clarify the legal status of [what is now] art.63 TFEU.

## Held
❖ (ECJ) Member States may not require prior authorisation before currency is exported, but may require a declaration of assets. [1995] E.C.R. I-4821.

## Commentary
[1] The ECJ also held that art.63 which provides for the free movement of capital between the EU and third states, is directly effective.

[2]*Sanz de Lera* was decided after the Maastricht amendments to the Treaty. It upholds the decision in *Bordessa*. The decision extends the principle of the free movement of capital to third countries (i.e. non-Member States).

[3] The ECJ recognised that the free movement of capital under art.56 is a fundamental principle of the Treaty which may only be restricted in accordance with art.65(1) or by "overriding requirements of the general interest": *Commission v Spain* (Case C-463/00). Any restrictions must comply with the principle of proportionality.

## Key Principle
"Golden shares" (i.e. shares held by the governments of Member States in recently nationalised companies) may constitute a restriction on the free movement of capital contrary to art.63.

> **COMMISSION V PORTUGAL (CASE C-171/08) 2010**
> The government of Portugal held shares providing special rights relating to the election of one third of the directors in the recently nationalised company, Portugal Telecom.

**Held**

❖ (ECJ) (1) The regime governing the shareholding infringed art.63, in view of the influence conferred on the management of the company, which was not justified by the size of the shareholding. It was not justified by the exception under art.65(2) on grounds of public security (here the need to maintain the security of the telecommunications network in a time of crisis), as this could only be invoked where there was a genuine and sufficiently serious threat to a fundamental interest of society.

(2) The restriction infringed the principle of proportionality as it allowed the Member State too wide a discretionary power relative to the objectives pursued.

**Commentary**

The case is one of a series of similar rulings on cases involving "golden shares" by the ECJ against Member States including the UK and France, which were found to infringe art.63. These decisions may be contrasted with the ruling in *Commission v Belgium* (Case C-503/99) relating to "golden shares" in two energy companies which entitled the Belgian government to oppose the sale or transfer of the companies' strategic assets and to be involved in key management decisions. The ECJ held in this case that although the rules were a restriction on the free movement of capital, they were justified under art.65(1)(b) in order to maintain energy supplies, and were not disproportionate.

**Key Principle**

The free movement of capital is subject to the right of Member States to take measures in the field of taxation and in the prudent supervision of financial institutions: art.65(1)(b) TFEU (ex 58(1)(b)).

COMMISSION V BELGIUM (CASE C-478/98) 2000

In 1995 the Belgian government adopted a law prohibiting Belgian residents from subscribing to securities of a loan on the eurobond market, claiming that the measure ensured effective fiscal supervision by preventing tax evasion. The Commission brought enforcement proceedings under art.258.

**Held**

(1) The prohibition contravened the principle of proportionality.

(2) A general presumption of tax evasion does not justify a measure which infringes the Treaty.

## Commentary

Member States are also permitted under art.65(1)(a) TFEU to apply their tax laws so as to distinguish between taxpayers on the basis of their residence or where their capital is invested, provided the measures do not constitute arbitrary discrimination or a disguised restriction on the free movement of capital and payments.

## Key Principle

The free movement of capital is subject to the right of Member States to take measures which are justified on grounds of public policy or public security: art.65(1)(b).

ASSOCIATION EGLISE DE SCIENTOLOGIE DE PARIS, SCIENTOLOGY INTERNATIONAL RESERVES TRUST v THE PRIME MINISTER (CASE C-54/99) 2000

The applicants asked the Prime Minister of France on February 1, 1996 to repeal various legislative provisions laying down a system of prior authorisation for direct foreign investments. Having found that legislative amendments on February 14, 1996 amounted to a system of prior authorisation, they interpreted this as a refusal by the Prime Minister to comply with their request and mounted a challenge in the Conseil d'Etat. A reference was made to the ECJ under art.267 to clarify the meaning of art.65(1)(b) in such circumstances.

## Held

Article 65(1)(b) precludes a system of prior authorisation for direct foreign investments which confines itself to defining in general terms the affected investments as those which represent a threat to public policy and public security, with the result that the persons concerned cannot identify the circumstances in which prior authorisation is required.

## Commentary

The derogation in art.65(1)(b) is interpreted strictly and is subject to the requirement that the measures do not amount to arbitrary discrimination or a disguised restriction on the free movement of capital between Member States: art.65(3).

# ECONOMIC AND MONETARY UNION

The euro was introduced as the single currency of states participating in Economic and Monetary Union on January 1, 1999, under the control of the European Central Bank. 17 states have so far adopted the euro (Austria, Belgium, Cyprus, Estonia, Finland, France, Germany, Greece, Ireland, Italy, Luxembourg, Malta, the Netherlands, Portugal, Slovakia, Slovenia and Spain). The UK, Denmark and Sweden remain outside the Eurozone. The future of the Eurozone remains uncertain in the light of the financial crises in 2011–12 in several Member States.

The provisions for the free movement of capital in arts 63–66 TFEU apply to all Member States, regardless of whether they belong to the Eurozone.

## Key Principle
Member States must not raise the amount of a tax when effecting its conversion into the euro.

> ESTAGER (CASE C-359/05) [2007] ECR I-581 (2007)
> The French government adopted a law to convert a tax which was previously payable into euros. In so doing, it effected a conversion at a rate higher than EU regulations provided. Estager claimed repayment of a portion of tax which it considered it had overpaid. A reference was made to the ECJ under art.267.

## Held
The Council regulations on the introduction of the euro preclude legislation which, on effecting the conversion into euros, raised it to an amount higher than provided in the regulations unless such an increase meets the requirements of legal certainty and transparency.

## Commentary
The need to satisfy the requirements of legal certainty and transparency protected the confidence of economic agents in relation to the introduction of the euro. The national legislation under consideration must make it possible to distinguish clearly the decision of the national authorities to increase the amount of the tax from the process of conversion of the sum due into euros.

### THINK POINT

To what extent has the free movement of capital been recognised under the TFEU?

# Citizenship and Free Movement of Workers

10

## INTRODUCTION

The **Maastricht Treaty** introduced the concept of Union citizenship under arts 20 and 21 TFEU (ex 17 and 18) as part of the move to political union. Individuals holding the nationality of one of the Member States were given residence rights throughout the EU. This was a very important development, as previously the main categories of free movement and residence rights within the EU depended on economic status, as workers, individuals exercising the right of establishment, the providers of services or their families.

This chapter covers citizenship, as well as the free movement of workers under arts 45–48 TFEU (ex 39–42). The right of establishment under arts 49–55 TFEU (ex 43–48) and the freedom to provide services under arts 56–62 TFEU (ex 49–55) are covered in Ch.11.

Directive 2004/38 provides detailed rights for Union citizens and their families, which are covered in this chapter, as well as in Ch.11 in relation to restrictions on rights.

## CITIZENSHIP

**Key Principle**

Every person holding the nationality of a Member State is a citizen of the Union (art.20(1) TFEU (ex 17(1)).

Every citizen shall have the right to move and reside freely within the territories of the Member States, subject to the limitations and conditions laid down in the Treaty and by the measures adopted to give it effect (art.21(1) TFEU (ex 18(1)).

> MARTÍNEZ SALA (CASE C-85/96) ECR I-2691 1998
> Martínez Sala was a Spanish national and long-term resident in Germany where she had worked from time to time. She was refused child-rearing allowance by the German authorities after she gave birth, on the basis that her residence permit had expired (although she had applied for a new one).

## Held

Where a Union citizen is lawfully resident in the territory of the host state, he or she may rely on the principle of non-discrimination in art.18 TFEU (ex 12) in all areas within the scope and application of the Treaties.

## Commentary

[1] The ruling was of great importance, as it enabled Union citizens to claim rights on a par with the nationals of the host state where they were lawfully resident. In Sala's case, it meant that any lawfully resident Union citizen would be able to claim the child-rearing allowance on the same basis as a German national. This approach enabled the ECJ to develop its case law on citizenship, strengthening the basis on which residence rights could be claimed for Union citizens who were not necessarily economically active.

[2] In *Bickel and Franz* (Case C-274/96) the ECJ held that the right to have criminal proceedings conducted in a language other than the principal language of the state concerned was covered by the principle of non-discrimination in art.18 TFEU. A national rule providing for such an entitlement which was not extended to the residents of other areas infringed art.18.

[3] Article 20 TFEU was implemented in part by Directive 93/109 (right to vote in EP and local elections). For a decision by the European Court of Human Rights on the question of voting rights, in the EP, see *Matthews* (Ch.3). In *Commission v Belgium*, the ECJ found that Belgium had infringed **Directive 93/109** when it refused to allow nationals other than Belgian nationals to stand and vote in local elections.

## Key Principle

A Member State may withdraw nationality from a Union citizen who has acquired it by deception.

JANKE ROTTMAN V FREIESTADT BAYERN (CASE 135/08) 2010
Rottman was an Austrian national who moved to Germany after being investigated for fraud in Austria which led to the issuing of a European arrest warrant against him. He applied successfully for naturalisation in Germany without disclosing the criminal proceedings. When the German authorities became aware of the proceedings, they withdrew his German nationality from him, by which time he had also lost his Austrian nationality.

**Held** ...............................................................................................

❖ (ECJ) (art.267) A Member State may withdraw from a Union citizen the nationality of that State when that nationality was acquired by deception, provided the decision is subject to the principle of proportionality.

**Commentary** ..........................................................................................

The Member State of origin was required to interpret its own law so as to ensure that the Union citizen was not rendered stateless.

**Key Principle** ......................................................................................

Children of Union citizens must be admitted to the host state's educational, apprenticeship and vocational training under the same conditions as the nationals of the host state.

> CASAGRANDE V LANDESHAUPTSTADT MUNCHEN (CASE 9/74) 1974
> C was the child of a deceased Italian national who had been working in Germany. His application for a monthly educational grant was rejected by the Munich authorities because the grant was payable only to German nationals, stateless persons and aliens with asylum.

**Held** ...............................................................................................

❖ (ECJ) (art.267) In providing that the children of migrant workers must be admitted to educational courses under the same conditions as the nationals of the host state, art.12 of Regulation 1612/68 covers not only admission but also general measures to facilitate admission (i.e. grants and loans). [1974] E.C.R. 773.

**Commentary** ..........................................................................................

[1] The decision in *Casagrande* was expressed in terms of the rights of the children of migrant workers, rather than Union citizens, as it was decided prior to the introduction of Union citizenship.

[2] Article 24(1) of **Directive 2004/38** provides for the equal treatment of Union citizens and their families, including family members who are not nationals of a Member State. While art.12 and other provisions of **Regulation 1612/68** were retained until 2011, arts 10 and 11 were repealed. The remaining sections of **Regulation 1612/68** were repealed in 2011 by Regulation 492/11, which consolidated the law.

## Key Principle

Article 21 TFEU (ex 18) is directly effective.

### BAUMBAST V R. (CASE C-413/99) 2002

B, a German national married to a Bolivian woman, worked in the UK where the family lived. When B's business failed, he worked outside the UK, though the family remained behind, travelling to Germany from time to time for medical treatment. The UK government refused to renew the residence permits for B and his family.

## Held

❖ (ECJ) (art.267) A Union citizen who has ceased to be a migrant worker may rely on art.21(1) to provide a right of residence. While the exercise of the right is subject to terms and conditions, they must be applied in accordance with the general principles of EU law, particularly the principle of proportionality.

## Commentary

[1] Proportionality was an important element in the Court's reasoning in *Collins* (Case C-138/02), enabling it to recognise the rights of economically inactive jobseekers. The case arose from the refusal of a jobseeker's allowance to an Irish national who had entered the UK to look for work. The Court held that Union citizens were entitled to claim this allowance, which was intended to facilitate access to the labour market. The UK's residence requirement had to be interpreted subject to the principle of proportionality. A claim for social assistance by a Union citizen who was not economically active was upheld in *Trojani* (Case C-456/02) by application of the principle of non-discrimination.

[2] In *Chen and Zhu* (Case C-200/02) the Court recognised the residence rights of the Chinese parents of a child born in Northern Ireland to a mother who then moved to Wales. The parents, seeking to avoid China's "one child" policy, had originally moved to Northern Ireland for the birth, to enable the child to acquire Irish nationality. The ECJ held that a third-country national with sufficient resources who is the parent or carer of a minor who is an EU national and covered by sickness insurance has indefinite residence rights.

[3] **Directive 2004/38** provides for three categories of residence rights. Firstly, Union citizens are entitled to residence of up to three months on production of a valid passport or ID card under art.6(1), provided the individual does not become a burden on the state. Secondly, residence rights for more than three months are provided by art.7(1) for citizens who are workers or self-employed in the host state, if they have sufficient resources to avoid becoming a

burden on the host state and comprehensive medical insurance. Union citizens who are following a course of study in the host state may reside, subject to a declaration that they have sufficient resources to avoid becoming a burden on the host state and have comprehensive medical insurance. Family members accompanying or joining Union citizens are also entitled to residence. Thirdly, permanent residence rights apply where citizens have resided lawfully for five years or more under art.16.

[4] Free movement of Union citizens would be meaningless if workers could not install their families with them. Prior to repeal by **Directive 2004/38**, **Regulation 1612/68** recognised the right of installation for workers' families under art.10(1). See, for example, *R. v Immigration Appeal Tribunal Ex p. Surinder Singh* (Case C-370/90), in which the ECJ held that art.10(1) applied to family members of a worker returning to his home state.

[5] **Directive 2004/38** gives Union citizens and their family members the right to move freely and to reside throughout the territories of the Member States. It amended **Regulation 1612/68**, repeals most previous relevant secondary legislation (including Directives 68/360, 90/364 and 365, 93/96) and replaced Directive 64/221.

[6] Workers and their families may remain permanently in the state of residence, even after the death of the worker, under art.12 of **Directive 2004/38**.

## SPOUSES AND PARTNERS

**Key Principle**
Residence rights may arise from applying the principle of non-discrimination, where provision is made under national law in some cases. The spouse of the worker is entitled to install himself or herself with the worker in the territory of the state where the Union citizen is resident.

### NETHERLANDS V REED (CASE 59/85) 1986
Ms Reed lived with her partner in the Netherlands. Both were United Kingdom nationals but only Ms Reed's partner was employed. After living in the Netherlands for a year, Ms Reed sought a residence permit. She claimed that social developments in the Netherlands had reached the stage where an unmarried couple living together in a stable relationship should be treated as husband and wife for EU immigration purposes. The Dutch court made an art.267 reference to the ECJ.

**Held**

❖ (ECJ) Social developments in a single Member State cannot affect the - development of EU law; thus relationships outside marriage cannot entitle the individual concerned to be treated as a spouse. However, under Dutch law an alien who had a stable relationship with a Dutch national was permitted to reside in the country under certain conditions. Applying the principle of non-discrimination, an alien should be granted the same rights of residence whether cohabiting with a Dutch national or an EU national. [1986] E.C.R. 1283.

**Commentary**

[1] Ms Reed gained the right to reside in the Netherlands because there was a Dutch law giving residence rights to aliens in specific circumstances which, under art.18 (the principle of non-discrimination), was extended to her.

[2] **Directive 2004/38** redefines "spouse" to include the partner with whom the Union citizen has a registered partnership where the legislation of the Member States treats registered partnerships as equivalent to marriage.

[3] Other individuals not covered by the definition of "family members" may benefit from art.3(2) of the directive. This provision requires Member States to facilitate the entry and residence of family members where serious health grounds require the personal care of the family member by the Union citizen and of partners with whom the Union citizen has a duly attested durable relationship.

**Key Principle**

Separation does not dissolve the marital relationship for the purpose of EU residence rights.

DIATTA V LAND BERLIN (CASE 267/83) 1985

A woman of Senegalese nationality married a French national. The couple lived in Germany where the husband was employed. After a year they separated with the intention of becoming divorced. After Mrs Diatta's temporary residence permit expired she applied for an extension. The application was refused on the ground that, as she no longer lived with her husband, she was not a family member of an EU national.

## Held

❖ (ECJ) Article 10(3) of **Regulation 1612/68** (repealed by **Directive 2004/38**) does not imply that the family must live under the same roof permanently. The marital relationship cannot be regarded as dissolved so long as it has not been terminated by the competent authority. [1985] E.C.R. 567.

## Commentary

The residence rights of separated spouses are now covered by art.13(2) of **Directive 2004/38** (see below).

## Key Principle

Third-country nationals married to Union citizens may rely on art.3(1) of **Directive 2004/38** to accompany or join the Union citizen in another Member State.

METOCK AND OTHERS V MINISTER FOR JUSTICE, EQUALITY AND LAW REFORM (CASE C-127/08) 2008

Metock and the other applicants were third-country (i.e. non-EU) nationals who had arrived in Ireland where they had claimed asylum. In each case, they then married Union citizens who were not Irish nationals after their arrival in the country. The Irish government refused their applications for residence cards on the basis that they were not lawfully resident, as Irish law required third-country nationals in such circumstances to have been resident in another Member State before arriving in Ireland. The Irish High Court made an art.267 reference to the ECJ.

## Held

(1) **Directive 2004/38** precludes legislation which requires residence in another Member State prior to arrival in the host state in the case of third-country nationals married to Union citizens who are not nationals of the host state.

(2) Third-country nationals married to Union citizens who are not nationals of the host state may rely on art.3(1) of **Directive 2004/38** to join or accompany the Union citizen, regardless of when and where the marriage took place.

## Commentary

[1] *Metock* clarified the rights of third-country nationals after the decision in *Akrich* (Case C-109/01) under art.10 of **Regulation 1612/68** (now repealed) that a third-country national could not benefit from a right of residence

unless he was lawfully-resident. *Metock* follows the ruling in *Jia v Migrationsverket* (Case C-1/05), that third-country nationals may acquire residence rights under EU law without having been previously resident in another Member State, enabling such individuals to move directly to the host state from outside the EU.

[2] The directive improved the rights of separated and divorced spouses. It provides in art.13(2) that divorce, annulment or termination of a registered partnership does not result in loss of residence rights of family members who are not Union citizens, where the marriage or registered partnership has lasted for at least three years including one year in the host state or, by agreement, where the spouse or partner who is not a Union national has custody of the children. The position before the directive was unclear, although the ECJ had ruled in *Diatta* (Case 267/83) that separation did not end a marital relationship where divorce had not taken place.

[3] A Member State is entitled under art.35 of the Directive to question whether a marriage is real. Where it finds that the marriage is one of convenience or has been forced, it may refuse or withdraw rights under the directive.

## EDUCATION AND VOCATIONAL TRAINING

**Key Principle**
Discrimination in access to vocational training on grounds of nationality infringes art.18 TFEU.

> GRAVIER V CITY OF LIÈGE (CASE 293/83) 1985
> Gravier, a French national, had been offered a place by the Académie Royale des Beaux-arts in Liège on a four-year course to study the art of the strip cartoon. She objected to paying the "minerval", an enrolment fee payable by students who were not Belgian nationals, claiming that the payment infringed art.56 (receipt of services—see Ch.11). An art.267 reference was made.

**Held**
❖ (ECJ) (1) Conditions of access to vocational training are covered by the Treaty. The imposition of a fee such as the "minerval" on students who are not nationals of the host state constitutes discrimination contrary to art.18. (2) Any form of education which prepares for a qualification or particular profession, trade or employment, or which provides the necessary training

and skills for such a profession, trade or employment is vocational training, even if the programme includes an element of general education. [1985] E.C.R. 593.

## Commentary

The ECJ has interpreted "vocational training" widely, to cover almost all undergraduate degrees except those intended to benefit general knowledge rather than to prepare for a profession: *Barra v Belgium and City of Liège* (Case 309/85). In *Blaizot v University of Liège* (Case 24/86) the ECJ held that a six-year veterinary course, the first half of which was academic and the second half vocational, should be regarded as a single course of vocational training. The consequence of *Gravier* and subsequent decisions has been that Union citizens attending undergraduate degree courses in EU states other than their own can no longer be charged higher fees than home students. While the Court found that there is no entitlement to a grant from the host state in *Brown v Secretary of State for Scotland* (Case 197/86) and *Lair v University of Hanover* (Case 39/86), the decision in *Bidar* (Case C-209/03) (below) casts doubt on these decisions.

## Key Principle

The entitlement of students who are studying in another Member State to access to non-contributory benefits should not be made subject to a condition which is not applied to the nationals of the host state.

### Grzelczyk v Centre Public d'Aide Sociale d'Ottignies-Louvain-la-Neuve (CPAS) (Case C-184/99) 2001

G, a French national, was a student of physical education at a university in Belgium where he was resident. For the first three years of his course he supplemented his income through part-time work and credit. In his fourth and final year he applied to the CPAS for payment of the "minimex", the minimum subsistence allowance. The CPAS was denied reimbursement of the allowance by the Belgian state authorities on the ground that G did not satisfy the nationality requirement. G challenged the decision before the Labour Tribunal which made a reference to the ECJ under art.267 to clarify the meaning of **Regulation 1612/68** and the relevance of the concepts of European citizenship and non-discrimination.

## Held

(1) The case is concerned solely with discrimination on grounds of nationality.

(2) A Union citizen lawfully resident in another Member State may rely on art.18 in all areas covered by EU law (*Martínez Sala*).

(3) Articles 18 and 20 TFEU preclude entitlement to a non-contributory benefit such as the "minimex" from being made conditional, in relation to nationals from Member States other than the host state where they are legally resident, on falling within **Regulation 1612/68** (see now art.7(2) of Regulation 492/ 2011) where no such condition applies to nationals of the host state.

## Commentary

[1] The ECJ stated in *Grzelczyk* that "Union citizenship is destined to be the fundamental status of nationals of Member States, enabling those who find themselves in the same situation to enjoy the same treatment in law irrespective of their nationality, subject to such exceptions as are expressly provided for". It commented that pursuit by a Union citizen of university studies in a Member State other than the state of which he is a national cannot, of itself, deprive him of the possibility of relying on the prohibition of all discrimination on grounds of nationality laid down in art.18 TFEU.

[2] The ECJ found that national legislation limiting the number of students on university medical and paramedical courses regarded as non-resident while being Union citizens was contrary to arts 18 and 21 TFEU, as it amounts to discrimination on grounds of nationality: *Bressol, Chavaret and others v France* (Case C-73/08). Such a restriction could be justified to protect public health, however, if it was proportionate.

## Key Principle

Students may be required to demonstrate a sufficient degree of integration into the society of the Member State before being granted a subsidised loan or grant.

### DANY BIDAR (CASE C-209/03) 2005

The applicant was a French national, resident in the UK since he arrived in 1998 with his mother, who required medical treatment. He attended school in London and then began a degree in Economics at University College London. Although he received a maintenance grant, he was refused a student loan on the grounds that he was not settled in the UK. The UK court referred questions to the ECJ for interpretation.

## Held

❖ (ECJ) EU citizens lawfully resident in another Member State were covered by the principle of non-discrimination in art.18 TFEU for the purpose of assistance for students, whether as a subsidised loan or as a grant to cover maintenance costs, provided the students have demonstrated "a certain degree of integration into the society of that State". This may be satisfied by showing that the student in question had lived in the Member State for "a certain length of time".

## Commentary

[1] Although the ECJ referred to *Brown* and *Lair* in its ruling, it found that the position had changed with the introduction of Union citizenship, enabling the application of the principle of non-discrimination to apply.

[2] The ECJ held in *Morgan and Bucher* (Joined Cases C11 and 12/06) that while a Member State may, in principle, limit its financial assistance to students who have demonstrated a sufficient degree of integration, it must ensure that its detailed rules for the award of grants do not impose an unjustified restriction on free movement and that they are proportionate.

[3] In *Förster v Hoofddirectie van de Informatie Beheer Groep* (Case C-158/07) the ECJ held that a requirement for five years' uninterrupted residence was appropriate to guarantee that an applicant for a maintenance grant was sufficiently integrated into the society of the host Member State.

## WORKERS

## Key Principle

Freedom of movement for workers shall be secured within the Union: art.45 (ex 39).

## Key Principle

A worker is someone who performs services for and under the direction of another in return for remuneration during a certain period of time.

> LAWRIE-BLUM V LAND BADEN WURTTEMBERG (CASE 66/85) 1986
> Lawrie-Blum, a United Kingdom national, passed the first examination to qualify as a teacher in Germany. However, she was refused admission to the period of probationary service which must be undertaken before the second examination because she was not a German national. While Lawrie-Blum claimed that the refusal on nationality grounds infringed art.45(2), the Land argued that a probationary teacher was not a "worker" under art.45.

**Held**

❖ (ECJ) A trainee teacher who, under the direction and supervision of the school authorities, is undergoing a period of service in preparation for the teaching profession, during which he provides services by giving lessons and receives remuneration, must be regarded as a worker under art.45(1), irrespective of the legal nature of the employment relationship. [1986] E.C.R. 2121.

**Commentary**

[1] The meaning of "worker" must be defined in EU, not national, terms. The ECJ clarified the expression "migrant worker" under **Regulation 1612/68** (now repealed) in *Hartmann* (Case C-212/05) to include a national of a Member State who, while maintaining his employment in that state, has transferred his residence to another state and has since worked as a frontier worker.

[2] Article 45 does not give rights to EU nationals working in their own countries. This is regarded as a purely internal situation and so is not covered by EU law. Thus a Surinamese mother was not entitled to join her son, a Dutch national, in the Netherlands where he was working: *Morson v The Netherlands* (Cases 35 and 36/82) 1982. Similarly, in *Macarthy v Secretary of State for the Home Department* (Case C-434/09) the ECJ held that a Union citizen who has never exercised free movement rights and has always resided in the state of which he or she is a national is not covered by art. 21 TFEU or art.3(1) of **Directive 2004/38**.

# WORK AND ECONOMIC ACTIVITY

**Key Principle**

The rules governing the free movement of workers only apply to individuals who pursue or wish to pursue an economic activity.

LEVIN V STAATSSECRETARIS VAN JUSTITIE (CASE 53/81) 1982
Mrs Levin, a United Kingdom national married to a non-EU national, sought a permit to reside in the Netherlands. She was refused on the ground that, as she was not gainfully employed, she could not be considered as a "favoured EEC citizen". She appealed against the decision through the Dutch courts, meanwhile working part-time as a waitress. An art.267 reference was made.

## Held

❖ (ECJ) The expression "worker" covers those who undertake part-time work, even where they are paid at a lower rate than the national guaranteed minimum, provided the work is genuine and not marginal or ancillary. [1982] E.C.R. 1035.

## Commentary

Part-time employment supplemented by public assistance was considered to be "work" in *Kempf v Staatssecretaris van Justitie* (Case 139/85) 1986. In *Steymann v Staatssecretaris van Justitie* (Case 196/87) 1988, a member of a religious community who received pocket money and keep was a worker because commercial activity was a genuine and inherent part of membership. Contrast with *Bettray v Staatssecretaris van Justitie* (Case 344/87) 1989 where subsidised work carried out by a former drug addict at a rehabilitation centre was not work as it was not a genuine economic activity.

# RIGHTS OF ENTRY

## Key Principle

Workers who are EU nationals and their families are entitled, on production of a passport or valid identity card, to enter the territory of other Member States in order to work.

> PROCUREUR DU ROI V ROYER (CASE 48/75)
> R, a French national with a conviction for procuring, was prosecuted with (and later convicted of) illegal entry into Belgium. R had not complied with administrative formalities on entry into Belgium where his wife ran a dance hall. He was expelled on the grounds that his personal conduct showed that he was a danger to public policy and that he had not observed the conditions for aliens. An art.267 reference was made.

## Held

❖ (ECJ) The right for EU nationals to enter the territory of another Member State covers the right to enter in search of work or to rejoin a spouse or family. Failure by a national of a Member State to complete the legal formalities on access, movement and residence does not justify expulsion. [1976] E.C.R. 497.

**Commentary**

[1] In *R. v Immigration Appeal Tribunal Ex p. Antonissen* (Case C-292/89) 1991 the ECJ found that deportation of a convicted drug dealer after six months' residence in the UK without finding work did not contravene EU law, unless the individual concerned could provide evidence that he was continuing to seek employment and had a genuine chance of finding work.

[2] Involuntary unemployment is not a ground for deportation.

[3] In *MRAX v Belgium* (Case C-459/99) the ECJ held that third-country nationals who are married to EU nationals should possess a visa when crossing the border into other Member States. However, in view of the principle of proportionality, a Member State may not send back such an individual who has not got a passport, visa or identity card, provided he can prove his identity and married status, and he does not represent a threat to public policy, public security or public health.

[4] See arts 4 and 5 of **Directive 2004/38** for the rules on exit and entry.

[5] Workers from the accession states (i.e. those states joining the EU in 2004 and 2007) have been subject to transitional measures by some Member States restricting their access to the labour market of the EU. These restrictions expired in April 2011 for those joining in 2004, and will expire in December 2013 for Bulgaria and Romania, who joined in 2007. Until the expiry of the transitional period, workers from the accession states must be given priority over third-country nationals. When they are entitled to gain access to the labour market, they should be treated equally with the nationals of the host state.

## EQUALITY OF TREATMENT

**Key Principle**

Freedom of movement entails the abolition of discrimination based on nationality between workers of Member States as regards employment, remuneration and other conditions of work and employment: art.45(2).

## ELIGIBILITY FOR EMPLOYMENT

**Key Principle** .............................................................................
EU nationals are entitled to take up and pursue employment in the territory of another Member State under the same conditions as the nationals of the host state: art.1, **Regulation 492/2011.**

> COMMISSION v FRANCE (CASE 167/73) 1974
> The French Code du Travail Maritime specified that a proportion of the crew of merchant ships must be French nationals. While this proportion had been set at three French crew members to one non-French crew member, the French government claimed that it had not in practice been applied against EC nationals. The Commission brought enforcement proceedings against France under art.258 for breach of art.45 TFEU and art.4 of **Regulation 1612/68** (now repealed) (prohibition on restriction by number of percentage of EU nationals in a particular activity or area).

**Held** ...........................................................................................
❖ (ECJ) In failing to amend the Code in relation to EU nationals from other Member States, France was in breach of art.45 TFEU and art.4 of the regulation. [1974] E.C.R. 359.

**Commentary** .................................................................................
While a state may not prescribe special recruitment procedures, limit advertising or otherwise hinder the recruitment of non-nationals, it may impose conditions relating to linguistic competence: *Groener v Minister for Education* (Case 379/87) (requirement for teachers in vocational schools in Ireland to be proficient in the Irish language permissible in the light of national policy on promotion of the Irish language).

**Key Principle** ...............................................................................
The regulation of professional sporting activities is subject to the principle of equality.

> UNION DES ASSOCIATIONS EUROPÉENNES DE FOOTBALL v JEAN-MARC BOSMAN (CASE C-415/93) 1995
> UEFA, which regulates national football associations, had adopted two rules for implementation nationally. The first rule, incorporated into players' contracts, allowed national football clubs to impose a transfer fee when a player moved to a new club. Without a fee players could not

change clubs. The second rule restricted the number of non-national players in a national club to three. Bosman, a Belgian footballer, was unable to move from a Belgian to a French club because the transfer fee was rejected. He sued the Belgian club, the Belgian national football association and UEFA, claiming that the rules infringed art.45(2).

## Held

❖ (ECJ) Transfer rules such as those adopted by UEFA directly affect players' access to the employment markets in other Member States and constitute an obstacle to the free movement of workers under art.45. Rules restricting the rights of EC (now EU) nationals to take part in professional football matches also amount to an obstacle to free movement. Such rules are covered by art.45(2) and by art.4 of **Regulation 1612/68** (now repealed) (prohibition of quotas based on nationality) implementing art.45(2). [1996] All E.R. (EC) 97.

## Commentary

[1] Discrimination on grounds of nationality in professional and semi-professional sport contravenes both art.45 and art.18 TFEU, the principle of non-discrimination: *Dona v Mantero* (Case 13/76) 1976. See also *UNECTEF v Heylens* (Case 222/86) 1987.

[2] It is, however, legitimate to restrict membership of a team on grounds of nationality for non-economic reasons (e.g. to represent a particular country in an international match). See also *Deliège* (Cases C-51/96 and C-191/97).

[3] The ECJ held in *Olympique Lyonnais SASP v Oliver Bernard and Newcastle United* (Case C-325/08) that a rule requiring trainee players to pay damages greater than the cost of training of they signed to another club when their training period ended was discriminatory and not objectively justified.

## EQUALITY IN EMPLOYMENT

### Key Principle

Workers who are nationals of other Member States may not be treated differently from national workers on account of nationality in relation to conditions of employment, dismissal, reinstatement or re-employment.

### SOTGIU V DEUTSCHE BUNDESPOST (CASE 152/73) 1974

Sotgiu was an Italian national living in Germany where he was employed by the Federal Post Office. His family remained in Italy. Under a collective wages agreement he was entitled to a separation allowance. However, the allowance was payable at a lower rate for workers whose normal residence was abroad than for those whose home was in Germany. He challenged the rate in the German courts, which made an art.267 reference.

**Held**
❖ (ECJ) A separation allowance falls within the concept of "conditions of employment and work" under art.7(1) of **Regulation 1612/68** (now repealed). [1974] E.C.R. 153.

**Commentary**
[1] Equal treatment is now governed by art.24 of **Directive 2004/38** for Union citizens. The equal treatment of workers is covered by art.7 of **Regulation 492/2011**.

[2] The ECJ considered in *Sotgiu* that it made no difference whether the payment was voluntary or compulsory. Once the state had decided to pay the allowance to its own nationals, it must extend the same benefit to EU nationals from other Member States.

## SOCIAL AND TAX ADVANTAGES

**Key Principle**
Non-national EU workers are entitled to the same social and tax advantages as national workers.

FIORINI (CRISTINI) v SNCF (CASE 32/75) 1976
An Italian widow living in France claimed for a special fare reduction card which the French railways (SNCF) provided to the parents of large families, this concession having previously been claimed by her husband. The claim was refused because Mrs Fiorini was not a French national. She challenged the refusal in the French courts, which made an art.267 reference.

**Held**
❖ (ECJ) Article 7(2) of **Regulation 1612/68** (now repealed) applied to all social or tax advantages, irrespective of whether they derive from the contract of employment. As the family were entitled to remain in France (under Regulation 1251/70) they were also entitled under art.7(2) to equal "social advantage". [1975] E.C.R. 1085.

**Commentary**

[1] See now art.24 of **Directive 2004/38** and art.7 of **Regulation 492/2011**.

[2] In *Castelli v ONPTS* (Case 261/83) 1984 a guaranteed minimum income for old people, paid to an Italian widow living with her retired son in Belgium, was held to be a "social advantage". See also *Reina v Landeskreditbank Baden-Wurttenberg* (Case 65/81) (interest-free loan granted on childbirth by a credit institution incorporated under public law to low-income families in order to stimulate the birth rate is a social advantage).

## MAINTENANCE GRANTS AND EDUCATION

**Key Principle**

A maintenance grant to cover education is a social advantage.

> LAIR V UNIVERSITY OF HANOVER (CASE 39/86) 1988
> Mrs Lair was a French national living in Germany for five years, during which time she had worked but had also been involuntarily unemployed from time to time. Having enrolled on a language course at the University of Hanover, she applied for a maintenance grant (an interest-free loan) from the German authorities. Her application was refused on the ground that she had not been employed in Germany for five years, a requirement only applied to foreign applicants. She challenged the refusal in the German courts, which made an art.267 reference.

**Held**

❖ (ECJ) (1) While art.18 TFEU applies to grants for access to education (e.g. tuition fees), it does not apply to maintenance grants. A maintenance grant is a "social advantage" under art.7(2) of Regulation 449/2011, provided the course in question is vocational.

(2) For an immigrant to retain the status of "worker" there must be a connection between his previous career and choice of study. Member States may not lay down minimum periods of residence or employment, as the concept of "worker" is an EU one, which cannot be limited by national law. [1988] E.C.R. 3161.

**Commentary**

[1] Similar issues were raised in *Brown* (Case 197/86), decided by the ECJ on the same day as *Lair*. In *Brown* the applicant was a student with dual British-French nationality. Having been brought up in France he had been offered a place to study electrical engineering at Cambridge. To gain practical

experience, Brown undertook pre-university industrial training with a firm in Scotland, such training being open only to students holding the offer of a degree place. Brown's application to the United Kingdom government for a grant for fees and maintenance was refused, as he had not lived in the United Kingdom for the required three years. The ECJ held under art.267 that while the applicant's pre-university industrial experience gave him the status of worker, he had obtained the work only because of his university place. He was not, therefore, entitled to a grant under **Regulation 1612/68** (now repealed).

[2] The rulings in *Brown* and *Lair* should be read subject to the recent decision of the ECJ in *Bidar* (Case C-209/03) (above).

## EMPLOYMENT IN THE PUBLIC SERVICE

**Key Principle**
The principle of free movement in art.45 does not apply to employment in the public service: art.45(4).

> COMMISSION V BELGIUM (RE PUBLIC EMPLOYEES) (CASE 149/79) 1980
> A wide range of posts in the public service in Belgium was advertised as reserved for Belgian nationals: posts in the National Railway Company, the National Local Railway Company, the City of Brussels and the Commune of Auderghem. The Commission brought art.226 proceedings against Belgium which sought to invoke art.45(4) as a defence.

**Held**
❖ (ECJ) To be covered by art.45(4) employment must involve direct or indirect participation in the exercise of powers conferred by public law and duties designed to safeguard the general interests of the state or other public authorities. [1982] E.C.R. 1845.

**Commentary**
[1] The distinction between posts outside and posts within the exception does not seem entirely logical. Posts outside art.45(4) have been held by the ECJ to include nurses in public hospitals, local authority gardeners and teachers in public educational institutions, in contrast with local authority nightwatchmen and architects who are within the exception.

[2] In 1988 the Commission issued a notice listing occupations which should not normally be covered by the exception: public health services, teaching in

state educational establishments, non-military research in public establishments and public bodies responsible for administering commercial services. Arguably, only high-level posts with a particular allegiance to the state should be covered (e.g. the police and the judiciary).

[3] In *Commission v Luxembourg* (Case C-473/93) 1996 the ECJ found that Luxembourg was in breach of art.45 by restricting civil service and public sector employment in relation to teaching, health, inland transport, telecommunications, water, gas and electricity, regardless of the level of responsibility.

## DEROGATION FROM THE PRINCIPLE OF FREE MOVEMENT

**Key Principle**
Freedom of movement of workers may be restricted on grounds of public policy, public health and public security: art.45(3).

**Key Principle**
Measures taken on grounds of public policy of public security shall be based exclusively on the personal conduct of the individual concerned: art.27(2), **Directive 2004/38**.

> VAN DUYN V HOME OFFICE (NO.2) (CASE 41/74) 1974
> Ms Van Duyn, a Dutch national, sought to take up employment for the Church of Scientology in the United Kingdom. At the time the Church of Scientology was not illegal in the United Kingdom but was considered by the government to be socially harmful. She was refused entry to take up the post on grounds that it was undesirable for anyone to enter the country to work for the Church of Scientology. Ms Van Duyn sought judicial review in the High Court, which made an art.267 reference.

**Held**
❖ (ECJ) (1) Articles 45(1) and (2) are directly effective in the national courts from the end of the transitional period (1961).
(2) **Directive 64/221** (see now **Directive 2004/38**) was found to be directly effective.
(3) A Member State, in imposing restrictions on grounds of public policy, is entitled to take account, as personal conduct, of an individual's association with an organisation which the Member State considers socially harmful, even where no equivalent restriction is placed on the nationals of the host state. [1974] E.C.R. 1337.

## Commentary

[1] **Directive 64/221** was repealed and replaced by **Directive 2004/38**.

[2] The derogations in **Directive 64/221** applied not only to workers but also to all categories of EU nationals including those exercising the right of establishment or provision of services in another Member State. "Public policy" is a translation of the French expression "ordre public" and is closer to the United Kingdom legal concept of "public order". The derogation must be strictly interpreted, although national authorities have discretion within the limits of the Treaty and secondary legislation. "Public security" is rarely invoked, but overlaps with the concept of public policy. Diseases that might endanger public health, public policy or public security were listed in an annex to the directive.

[3] *Van Duyn* appears to allow a dual standard whereby Member States may impose stricter requirements on EC nationals entering the country than on their own nationals. In *Adoui and Cornuaille v Belgian State* (Joined Cases 115 and 116/81) the ECJ upheld the ruling in *Van Duyn* in the context of a refusal to grant two French prostitutes residence permits in Belgium where prostitution is not illegal. However, the Court added that in such circumstances a state must not base the exercise of its powers on assessments of conduct that would have the effect of applying an arbitrary distinction to the nationals of other Member States.

## Key Principle

The public policy proviso may only be invoked where there is a genuine and sufficiently serious threat to one of the fundamental interests of society.

> ### R. v Bouchereau (Case 30/77) 1977
>
> B, a French national working in the United Kingdom, was convicted of the unlawful possession of drugs in 1976. Six months earlier he had been convicted of another offence of possession and had been conditionally discharged for 12 months. The magistrates' court, before recommending deportation, made an art.267 reference to clarify the meaning of "public policy".

## Held

❖ (ECJ) (1) A recommendation to deport is a measure under art.3 of **Directive 64/221**.

(2) Previous criminal convictions may only be taken into account where they provide evidence of personal conduct amounting to a present threat.

(3) Recourse to the concept of public policy presupposes the existence of a genuine and sufficiently serious threat to the requirements of public policy affecting one of the fundamental interests of society. [1977] E.C.R. 1999.

## Commentary

[1] The threat must derive from the conduct of the individual in question and is not to discourage others. In *Bonsignore v Oberstadtdirektor der Stadt Koln* (Case 67/74) 1975, an Italian national living in Germany accidentally shot dead his brother. He was convicted but no sentence was imposed. B appealed against his deportation order to the local administrative court which made an art.267 reference. Held: (ECJ) deportation may not be ordered for reasons of a general preventive nature. Failure to observe administrative formalities does not provide grounds for deportation: *Royer* (Case 48/75) (see p.xx).

[2] Procedural rights covering the right of re-entry, the requirement to specify the grounds for decision and entitlement to remedies are also provided by **Directive 64/221.**

[3] The provisions in **Directive 2004/38** are similar to those in **Directive 64/221** but specify (in art.27(2)) that measures taken on grounds of public policy or public security shall comply with the principle of proportionality and shall be based exclusively on the personal conduct of the individual concerned. Criminal convictions are not automatically grounds for taking such measures.

## Key Principle

Automatic expulsion from the territory of a Member State for possession of illegal drugs for personal use is not justified.

### DONATELLA CALFA (CASE C-348/96) 1999

Mrs Calfa, an Italian national on holiday in Crete, had been charged by the Greek authorities with possession of prohibited drugs for her personal use. As the recipient of services under art.56 (see Ch.11) she would have been entitled to move around the EU on holiday, subject to the derogations in **Directive 64/221.** If convicted, she faced an automatic life ban from re-entering Greece under Greek law. The Greek court referred questions to the ECJ under art.267 to clarify the meaning of the directive in such circumstances.

## Held

❖ (ECJ) The ECJ ruled that automatic expulsion following a criminal conviction infringed **Directive 64/221** (now repealed) because it took no account of the personal conduct of the offender or the extent to which he or she posed a threat to public policy. [1999] E.C.R. I-11.

## Commentary

*Calfa* reaffirms the principle in earlier decisions such as *Bouchereau* and *Bonsignore* that the personal conduct of the individual and the nature of the threat must be considered before any expulsion may be justified under the **Directive**.

## Key Principle

A Member State may not expel a Union citizen unless there are imperative grounds of public security where the individual has resided in the host Member States for the previous ten years: art.28(3), **Directive 2004/38**.

> ### LAND BADEN-WÜRTTEMBOURG V TSAKOURIDES(CASE C-145/09) 2010
>
> T was born in Germany where he had an unlimited residence permit. He spent a short time in 2004 running a pancake stall in Greece, returning to Germany to work for a few months before resuming work on the pancake stall in 2005 in Greece. He had a criminal record in Germany which included convictions for assault. After an international arrest warrant was issued, he was returned to Germany where he was convicted in 2007 of illegal dealing in narcotic drugs as part of an organised group and sentenced to six and a half years' imprisonment. The German authorities sought to expel him to Greece in 2008 for an unlimited period, on the basis that the measures were justified under art.28(3) on "imperative grounds of public security". The national court referred questions to the ECJ under art.267.

## Held

v (ECJ) A decision to expel must be based on an individual examination of the situation of the person concerned, taking into account factors including age, health, centre of family or occupational interests, duration of absences from the host state and links with the country of origin. The decisive criterion for enhanced protection is ten years' residence before the measure. Expulsion may be justified on "imperative grounds of public security" under art.28(3) or "serious grounds of public policy" under art.28(2) only if it is necessary and proportionate with regard to the exceptional seriousness of the threat, to protect the interests it aims to secure. Regard must be had to the length of residence in the host state.

## Commentary

[1] The ECJ found that the fight against crime in relation to dealing with narcotics is capable of being covered by the concept of "imperative grounds of public security" or "serious grounds of public policy".

[2] Legal residence in the host state before the entry into force of **Directive 2004/38** in April 2006 may count towards the continuous period of five years' residence, to enable the individual to acquire permanent residence rights: *Secretary of State for Work and Pensions v Lassal* (Case C-162/09). It should follow that the 10-year period for enhanced rights would be similarly viewed.

## Key Principle

A Member State may not impose territorial restrictions on residence on a national from another Member State except in circumstances where such prohibitions may be imposed on its own nationals.

### RUTILI V MINISTER OF THE INTERIOR (CASE 36/75) 1975

R, an Italian national and trade union activist, was required by the French authorities to reside in specified regions in France. He sought annulment of the decision on residence before the French courts which made an art.267 reference to the ECJ.

## Held

❖ (ECJ) Measures restricting the right of residence which are limited to part of the national territory may not be imposed on EU nationals from other Member States except where they could also be applied to nationals of the state concerned. [1975] E.C.R. 1219.

## Commentary

The ECJ in *Rutili* describes **Directive 64/221** (arts 2 and 3) as a manifestation of the principle in the **European Convention on Human Rights** that no restrictions in the interest of national security or public safety shall be placed on rights secured by the Convention other than those which are necessary to protect those interests in a democratic society.

**Key Principle** ...........................................................................................................

Where there is no right of appeal to a court of law, a decision refusing renewal of a residence permit ordering expulsion of an EU national from another Member State shall not normally be taken without an opinion from a competent authority of the host country: art.9, **Directive 64/221** (now repealed).

> R. v SECRETARY OF STATE FOR THE HOME DEPARTMENT EX P. GALLAGHER (CASE C-175/94) 1996
>
> G, an Irish national, had a previous conviction for a firearm offence. He was deported from the United Kingdom on grounds of suspicion of involvement with terrorist activities.

**Held** ...........................................................................................................

Article 9 requires an opinion to be obtained from a competent, independent body before deportation. [1995] E.C.R. I-4253.

**Commentary** ...........................................................................................................

[1] Gallagher later brought a claim for state liability against the UK government arising from his deportation. The Court of Appeal considered that waiting for G to make his representations and for the independent monitor to report before deportation would not have been in G's interests as he would have been detained in custody. G was able to make representations to the UK government after deportation. A report was obtained retrospectively from the independent monitor, supporting the decision to deport. The CA held that the breach was not sufficiently serious for G to succeed; while the breach was "manifest" it was not "grave" (see Ch.1).

[2] Article 31 of **Directive 2004/38** provides for procedural safeguards on expulsion decisions.

[3] Some relaxation of border controls has occurred as a result of the Schengen Convention, though the Convention was not adopted by the United Kingdom, Denmark and Ireland. The Convention allows free movement of Union citizens without passport inspections at borders. It was incorporated into the Treaties by the **Treaty of Amsterdam**, subject to an "opt out" by non-participating states. In *Wijsenbeek* (Case C-378/97), prior to the **Treaty of Amsterdam**, the Dutch court sought a preliminary ruling on the question following W's refusal to allow inspection of his passport when travelling from Strasbourg to Rotterdam. The ECJ held that, in the absence of harmonisation measures, Member States remain free to carry out identity checks at borders provided penalties for breach are not disproportionate.

[4] The free movement of persons has also been affected by the changes under Title V on visas, asylum, immigration and other policies on the free movement of persons, which is based on an area of security and justice within which the free movement of persons is assured. Title V TFEU provides in art.67 (ex 61 TEC and 29 TEU) that "[t]he Union shall constitute an area of freedom, security and justice with respect for fundamental rights and the different legal systems and traditions of the Member States". In addition, Member States are required under art.8 TEU to develop a "special relationship with neighbouring countries, aiming to establish an area of peace and prosperity and good neighbourliness, founded on the values of the Union and characterised by close and peaceful relations based on co-operation."

## THINK POINT

How did the ECJ use the concept of lawful residence in *Martínez Sala* to develop the rights of residence of Union citizens? What is the relevance of the principle of non-discrimination?

Is the decision of the ECJ in *Van Duyn* consistent with *Adoui*? Which decision do you think better represents the current position?

# Right of Establishment and Freedom to Provide Services

## 11

## INTRODUCTION

The right of establishment is protected by arts 49–55 TFEU (ex 43–48). It is a permanent right, recognising the rights of EU nationals (either individuals or companies) to set up in business other than in the home state. It is complemented by arts 56–62 TFEU (ex 49–55) on the provision of services. The provision of services, unlike establishment, is a temporary right, lasting for the duration of the services and does not necessarily require residence. Both the right of establishment and the provision of services are subject to the limitations in **Directive 2004/38** on grounds of public policy, public health and public morality. The directive repealed and replaced previous secondary legislation which also provides rights for the self-employed and their families, including the right to stay on after the period of self-employment. In addition, Directive 2006/123 the Services Directive, was adopted for implementation by December 2009. While the aim of the directive is to simplify the law on the provision of services, it has been criticised for its complexity, particularly in relation to derogations.

## THE RIGHT OF ESTABLISHMENT

### Key Principle
Restrictions on the freedom of establishment of nationals of a Member State in the territory of another Member State shall be prohibited: art.49(1) TFEU (ex 43(1).

> REYNERS V BELGIAN STATE (CASE 2/74) 1974
> Reyners was a Dutch national living in Belgium where he wished to be admitted to practise the profession of "avocat", having gained the appropriate academic qualification. He was prevented by a requirement that only Belgian nationals could be admitted. He challenged the Belgian law in the Conseil d'Etat which made an art.267 reference to the ECJ.

**Held**  ........................................................................................................

❖ (ECJ) (1) Article 49 became directly effective by the end of the transitional period (1961) and was not dependent on the adoption of further directives. [1974] E.C.R. 631.

(2) The profession of advocate is not an activity connected with state authority under art.51 TFEU (ex45) and is thus not excluded from art.49.

**Commentary**  ....................................................................................

[1] The right of establishment under art.49 entitles an EU national who is established in one Member State to set up a business in another state on the same conditions as a national of the state concerned. EU nationals may take up and pursue activities as self-employed persons and set up and manage undertakings. They may also establish an agency, branch or subsidiary in another state. The right applies both to natural and legal persons (companies incorporated in a Member State). There is considerable overlap between the right of establishment and the provision of services: see below.

[2] In *Commission v UK* (Case C-246/89) (see p.x) United Kingdom requirements based on nationality and domicile for registration of fishing vessels were discriminatory. They infringed arts 49 and 56 and resulted in an order against the United Kingdom government in *Factortame III* (Case C-48/93) to compensate the Spanish fishermen who suffered financial loss.

[3] Directive 96/71 on the posting of workers in the framework of the provision of services was adopted to protect the rights of workers posted from one Member State to another for a limited time in order to carry out work. Member States are required to guarantee posted workers certain basic employment protection rights in the state where the work is carried out. The ECJ has adopted a series of recent decisions (including *International Transport Workers' Federation v Finnish Seamen's Union* (Case C-438/05)) on the directive. The Commission concluded in June 2007 that many Member States were in breach of the directive. Luxembourg was found to be in breach in having failed to transpose the directive in *Commission v Luxembourg* (Case C-319/06).

[4] A Spanish requirement for prior authorisation before opening a new pharmacy in a specific area tied to conditions of population density and distance between pharmacies was found not to infringe art.49 in principle, unless the requirement prevents a sufficient number of pharmacies from being established in an area with special demographic features: *Blanco Perez and Chao Gómez* (Case C-570/07).

## Key Principle

Even where there is no discrimination on grounds of nationality, national requirements on qualifications may hinder the right of establishment under art.49.

VLASSOPOULOU V MINISTERIUM FOR JUSTIZ, BUNDES- UND
EUROPAANGELEGENHEITEN BADEN-WURTTEMBERG (CASE C-340/89)
V, a Greek lawyer and member of the Athens Bar, sought admission as a lawyer in Germany. She challenged the German demand to examine her qualifications for comparison with national requirements.

## Held

❖ (ECJ) A Member State may require the examination of an individual's qualifications from another Member State before admission to the legal profession to determine the extent to which the knowledge and qualification attested by the diploma correspond to those of the host state. [1993] 2 C.M.L.R. 221.

## Commentary

Where a diploma corresponds only partially, the individual may be required to prove that he or she has acquired the necessary knowledge and qualifications. Contrast *Vlassopoulou* with *Thieffry v Conseil de L'Ordre des Avocats à la Cour de Paris* (Case 71/76) in which a Belgian lawyer with academic qualifications recognised as equivalent was refused admission to the Paris Bar because he lacked a French diploma.

## Held

❖ (ECJ) Such a requirement breached art.49. See also *Patrick v Ministre des Affaires Culturelles* (Case 11/77) where a United Kingdom trained architect could not be prevented from practising in France where his qualifications were recognised as equivalent.

## Key Principle

Rights of establishment and the provision of services may be restricted where the limitation is objectively justified in the general interest.

COMMISSION V GERMANY (CASE 205/84) 1986
German law required the providers of insurance services in the territory to be established in Germany. Prior authorisation was also required

from the German authorities. The Commission brought an action against Germany in the ECJ under art.258.

## Held

❖ (ECJ) The requirement for the providers of insurance services to be established in Germany infringed art.49. However, the requirement for prior authorisation was justified in so far as it protected policy holders and insured persons. [1986] E.C.R. 3755.

## Commentary

[1] The single market in financial services has since *Commission v Germany* and other cases been completed with the adoption of a number of directives including measures to harmonise safeguards and standards in insurance.

[2] In *Gebhard v Consiglio Dell'Ordine Degli Avvocati Procurator di Milano* (Case C-55/94) a German member of the Stuttgart Bar was subjected to disciplinary proceedings by the Milan Bar for practising in Italy using the title "avvocato". The ECJ in an art.267 reference held that where national measures restrict one of the fundamental freedoms, they must be:
  (a) non-discriminatory;
  (b) justified by imperative requirements in the general interest;
  (c) suitable for attaining the objective;
  (d) not disproportionate.

[3] In *MacQuen v Grandvision Belgium SA* (Case C-108/96) the ECJ held that art.49 does not in principle preclude a prohibition under national law which prohibits opticians from carrying out certain optical examinations where it is justified by the protection of public health.

[4] In *Wouters v Algemeine Raad van der Nederlandse Ordre van Avocaten* (Case C-309/99) the ECJ held that a national regulation prohibiting multi-disciplinary partnerships between members of the Bar and accountants was not contrary to arts 49 and 56, since such regulations could reasonably be considered necessary for the proper practice of the legal profession as it was organised in the country concerned.

# THE PROVISION OF SERVICES

## Qualifications and residential requirements

**Key Principle** ...........................................................................................
Restrictions on the freedom to provide services shall be prohibited in respect of nationals of Member States who are established in one Member State and providing services in another Member State: art.56 TFEU.

> COMMISSION V GREECE (CASE C-198/89) 1991
> Greek law required tourist guides accompanying tour groups from other Member States to hold a licence granted only to diploma holders who had undertaken specific training. (A separate requirement for specialised professional guides covered visits to museums and other monuments.) The Commission brought an action in the ECJ under art.258 against Greece on the basis that the requirement for a licence infringed art.56.

**Held** ...........................................................................................
❖ (ECJ) While the general interest in the proper appreciation of the artistic and archaeological heritage of a country may justify a restriction on the provision of services, the requirement for a licence had a disproportionate effect. (It reduced the number of available tour guides, particularly those speaking the language of the tour group.) The measure infringed art.56. [1991] E.C.R. I-727.

**Commentary** ...........................................................................................
[1] A similar requirement in relation to tourist guides in France was also found to be disproportionate in *Commission v France* (Case C-154/89).

[2] Many cases on art.56 concern national requirements for professional qualifications which, without harmonisation or recognition, would severely limit both establishment and the provision of services. Directive 2005/36 applies to all nationals of a Member State wishing to pursue a regulated profession in a Member State other than that in which they obtained their qualification. It is a consolidating measure based on the principle of the mutual recognition of qualifications, and applies to both employment and self-employment. Recognition enables the individual to practise his or her profession on the same terms as a national of the host state under art.4(1) of the directive. A "regulated profession" is defined in art.1(a) as covering any professional activity where the possession of a diploma is required in the Member State. There are three routes to qualification: the general system for

the recognition of qualifications. Under art.13(1), where a regulated profession requires specific qualifications, the host state will allow access to the profession on the same terms as its own nationals where the applicant has attestation of competence or from a Member State or evidence of formal qualifications. Otherwise, the host state may require the applicant to undertake an aptitude test or period of adaptation. The second route applies to activities requiring only general or commercial knowledge, in which case the host state will recognise previous pursuit of the activity in another Member State (art.5). The third route applies to professionals previously covered by sectoral directives such as doctors, who are required to satisfy minimum training requirements as well as holding a formal qualification.

Where there is a substantial difference, an aptitude test or period of adaptation may be required by the host state.

## Key Principle

Restrictions such as a residential requirement may infringe arts 49 and 56 unless they are necessary to observe professional rules of conduct.

### VAN BINSBERGEN V BESTUUR VAN DE BEDRIFSVEERNIGING VOOR DE METAALNIJVERHEIED (CASE 33/74) 1974

Kortman, the legal adviser of Van B, was told that he could no longer represent his client before the Dutch courts when he moved from the Netherlands to Belgium. An art.267 reference was made.

## Held

❖ (ECJ) Article 56 was directly effective from the end of the transitional period (1961). A residence requirement contravenes art.56 unless it is objectively justified by the need to observe professional rules of conduct. [1974] E.C.R. 1299.

## Commentary

[1] The line of case law dealing with the possible objective justification of residential and other nationally based requirements, as in *Commission v Germany* (see above), is analogous to the "rule of reason" in *Cassis de Dijon*. (See p.97.)

[2] Lawyers seeking to provide services in other Member States continue to be covered by Directive 77/249 and Directive 98/5 (which seeks to make it easier for lawyers to practise on a self-employed or salaried basis in a state other than the one in which they qualified). In *Luxembourg v EP and Council*

(Case C-168/98) the ECJ dismissed the action by Luxembourg to annul **Directive 98/5** on the facilitation of practice of profession of lawyer in a state other than the state of qualification. The Court found that the directive did not infringe art.56, since the principle of a migrant lawyer practising in his home country title and that of a lawyer practising under professional title of the host state are not comparable.

[3] Article 56 is subject to **Directive 2004/38**. In *Omega Air* (Case C-36/02) the ECJ had to consider a referral from a German court arising from an appeal against a ban on human targets imposed by Germany on a German company operating a laser targeting installation. The ECJ found that the services were covered by art.49 (the equipment and technology were supplied by a British company). However, the ban had been imposed by the German authorities on grounds that the game posed a threat to public order as it infringed human dignity through the use of simulated killings. The derogation was therefore necessary to protect fundamental rights, even though the equipment was not illegal in the UK.

**Key Principle**
Where qualifications are not covered by a specific directive and are outside **Directive 2005/36**, the basic rules on recognition and equivalence continue to apply.

COLEGIO OFICIAL DE AGENTES DE LA PROPRIEDAD IMMOBILIARA V AGUIRRE, NEWMAN AND OTHERS (CASE C-104/91) 1992
Newman, a United Kingdom national and member of the Royal Institution of Chartered Surveyors, applied for membership of the Colegio, the body that regulated estate agency in Spain. Having received no response, he began practising as an estate agent in Spain. He was prosecuted by the Spanish authorities in 1991 before the implementation date of Directive 89/48 on the mutual recognition of qualifications. An art.267 reference was made.

**Held**
❖ (ECJ) In the absence of harmonisation measures, Member States may specify the knowledge and qualifications needed to pursue a profession and require the production of a diploma certifying the status of the holder's qualifications. [1992] E.C.R. I-3003.

## Commentary

In the circumstances, Spain would have been in a position to carry out a comparative examination of knowledge and qualifications. Full reasons for a refusal to recognise qualifications must be given.

## Key Principle

Where measures have been adopted to harmonise professional qualifications, national authorities must examine the experience of an applicant to a regulated profession to evaluate post-qualification experience.

> HAIM V KASSENZAHNÄRZTLICHE VEREINIGUNG NORDRHEIN (CASE C-319/92) 1994
>
> H was an Italian national who had qualified as a dentist in Turkey. He had practised in both Turkey and Belgium before seeking to practise in Germany. Professional qualifications for dentistry had been harmonised in an EC directive. The German authorities refused his application on the basis that he lacked the necessary qualifications. H challenged the refusal in the German courts, claiming that it infringed art.49. A reference to the ECJ was made under art.267.

## Held

❖ (ECJ) Failure to examine post-qualification experience may infringe art.49 where the effect is to hinder EU nationals from exercising the right of establishment. [1994] E.C.R. I-425.

## Commentary

[1] After harmonisation, Member States should consider relevant post-qualification experience as well as formal qualifications.

[2] The ECJ ruled on establishment in the absence of a directive in relation to the medical profession in *Hocsman v Ministre de l'Emploi et de la Solidarité* (Case C-238/98). It held that where an EU national applies to practise in another Member State, the host state must take into account all diplomas, other evidence of formal qualifications and relevant experience, by comparing the specialised knowledge and abilities certified by those qualifications and experience with the knowledge and experience required by national rules.

## Key Principle
Article 56 applies to services offered for remuneration across national borders. The right to provide services may only be restricted where there are overriding reasons and the restriction is not disproportionate.

### HM CUSTOMS AND EXCISE V SCHINDLER (CASE C-275/92) 1992
S, acting on behalf of four local state lotteries in Germany, sent letters from the Netherlands to the United Kingdom inviting the recipients to take part in the lotteries. They enabled purchasers to participate in the lottery on payment of the price of the ticket and were offered outside the state in which the operators were established. The Customs and Excise authorities seized the letters on the grounds that they infringed United Kingdom legislation on lotteries and gambling. Schindler challenged the seizure in the United Kingdom courts. An art.267 reference was made.

## Held
❖ (ECJ) The letters were not goods but were services under art.56. While legislation such as that applicable in the United Kingdom restricted the provision of services, it was justified in the public interest and was not disproportionate. [1994] E.C.R. I-1039.

### ALPINE INVESTMENT B.V. V MINISTER VAN FINANCIEN (CASE C-384/93) 1995
Dutch law prohibited "cold calling" (i.e. telephone contact by firms to potential customers without their prior written consent). The restriction applied to all firms established in the Netherlands, regardless of the location of their clients. Alpine Investments, a provider of financial services, was thus unable to canvass potential customers in the United Kingdom.

## Held
❖ (ECJ) While such a measure in principle infringed art.56 it was justified to protect consumers and the Dutch securities market. It was not disproportionate. [1995] E.C.R. I-1141.

## Commentary
[1] The ECJ distinguished *Alpine Investments* from *Keck and Mithouard*. (See Ch.9.) A restriction on cold calling, unlike legislation on selling arrangements, directly affects access to the market in other Member States and can hinder intra-EU trade.

[2] See also *Säger v Dennenmeyer* (Case C-76/90) in which a United Kingdom company was prevented from exercising patent renewal services in Germany by national legislation. Held (ECJ): Although the rules did not discriminate on grounds of nationality, they hindered D's access to the German market and were disproportionate.

[3] In *Laara v Finland* (Case C-124/97) a Finnish national challenged a grant of exclusive rights to operate slot machines, claiming that it infringed art.56. The ECJ held that, in the light of public interest objectives including the control of gambling, it did not infringe art.49.

[4] In *Déliege v Ligue Francophone de Judo* (Joined Cases C-51/96 and C-191/97) the ECJ had to consider art.56 in the context of participation of individuals known as judokas (professional or semi-professional judo players) in high-level sporting events which do not involve national teams competing with each other. The selection rules of the relevant sporting federations do not contain clauses restricting the number of players by nationality. Once selected, athletes compete on their own account, regardless of nationality. Such rules were found not to infringe art.56.

[5] In *Placanica* (Case C-338/04) the ECJ considered arts 49 and 56 EC in the context of Italian legislation providing that participation in games of chance (including the collection of bets) is subject to possession of a licence and a police authorisation. Infringement may result in imprisonment. Stanley, a UK company, provided betting services in Italy through independent operators, Placanica. However, Italy refused to grant licences to regulated companies such as Stanley. Placanica and others were charged with infringing Italian law by operating without a licence. The Court ruled under art.267 that national law prohibiting activities relating to betting without a licence or police authorisation restricted the right of establishment and the freedom to provide services. It held that arts 49 and 56 preclude national legislation imposing criminal liability on persons collecting bets without a licence or police approval, when such persons were unable to obtain licences in breach of EU law.

[6] The ECJ has given many rulings on games of chance and the provision of services. In *Ladbrokes Betting & Gaming and Ladbrokes International* (Case C-258/08), for example, it held that art.56 does not preclude Member States from granting a monopoly in organising and promoting games of chance, even where this prevents an operator from another Member State from providing services through the internet. This is an area which has not yet been harmonised and where Member States enjoy a wide discretion.

## FREEDOM TO RECEIVE SERVICES

**Key Principle**

Article 56 covers the freedom to receive as well as to provide services.

> **LUISI AND CARBONE V MINISTERO DEL TESORO (CASE 286/82) 1984**
> Luisi and Carbone had, independently of each other, taken money out of Italy in excess of the amount permitted under exchange control regulations to pay for medical and tourist services. An art.267 reference was made during their prosecution under Italian law.

**Held**

❖ (ECJ) Tourists, persons receiving medical treatment and persons travelling for the purpose of education and business are covered by art.56. [1984] E.C.R. 377.

**Commentary**

[1] The principle of non-discrimination: art.18 TFEU applies to the receipt as well as the provision of services. In *Cowan v Tresor Public* (Case 186/87) a United Kingdom national "mugged" on the Paris Metro claimed but was refused compensation for his injuries out of public funds. The ECJ held that as a tourist he was entitled to compensation on the basis of equal treatment.

[2] In *Commission v Spain* (Case C-45/93) the ECJ found that charging a discriminatory entrance fee for non-nationals to enter museums infringed art.18.

[3] The Court of Appeal ruled on the right to receive services in the EU in *R. v Human Fertilisation and Embryology Authority Ex p. Diane Blood* following a refusal to allow DB to obtain fertility treatment in another EU state using her dead husband's sperm as he had not given his consent. The CA granted an order in her favour without making a reference to the ECJ, stating that it considered that to have refused would have amounted to an unreasonable restriction on DB's right to travel to receive medical services under art.56.

[4] The ECJ had to consider the relationship between art.57 TFEU (ex 50) and the receipt of medical services in several recent decisions, *Geraets-Smits v Stichtun Ziekenfonds, Peerbooms v Stichtung CZ Grope Zorgverzekeringen* (Case C-157/99) and *Vanbraekel v Alliance Nationale des Mutualités Chrétiennes (ANMC)* (Case C-368/98). In *Geraets-Smits*, two applicants were insured for medical costs under an insurance scheme in the Netherlands. Both of the applicants received medical treatment outside the home state

without prior authorisation. Funding would only have been approved if the treatment was found to be both "normal" and "necessary". The ECJ (under art.267) found that these conditions amounted to a restriction on the freedom to provide and receive services. They were, however, capable of objective justification on several grounds, including the interests of maintaining a balanced medical service open to all. The conditions should be interpreted fairly, in a non-discriminatory manner. Treatment should only be refused on grounds of necessity where the same or equivalent treatment is available without undue delay from an establishment covered by the insurance fund's contractual arrangements.

[5] In *Vanbraekel* (Case C-368/98) the applicant, a Belgian national, had surgery in France despite being refused authorisation from the insurers, ANMC. V sought reimbursement through a tribunal in Belgium, appealing to a higher court when refused. The court ruled that the requirement imposed by the tribunal (certification by a Belgian professor of the need for treatment in France) was excessive. An expert report ordered by the court found that V required hospital treatment which could be better provided abroad. V died while undergoing surgery in Paris. The action was continued by her heirs. The ECJ (under art.267) ruled that national legislation which failed to guarantee a person within its social insurance scheme a level of payment equivalent to the rate to which he was entitled in the home state was contrary to art.56, where that person had prior authorisation to received hospital treatment in another Member State under Regulation 1408/71.

[6] The conditions for authorisation must not deprive an insured person from reimbursement where he is unable to apply for prior authorisation because of his health or who needs urgent treatment: *Commission v France* (Case C-512/08).

**Key Principle** ...............................................................................................
Medical services, including public services free at the point of delivery, are covered by art.56.

WATTS V BEDFORD PRIMARY HEALTHCARE TRUST (CASE C-372/04)
Mrs Watts had applied unsuccessfully to her local healthcare trust to travel to another EU Member State for hip replacement surgery, on the basis that it was a "routine" application (with a possible wait of up to one year). If the trust had found there would be "undue delay", it would have been obliged to grant the application in order to meet the

government target. As Mrs Watts' condition then worsened, the trust agreed to reduce the waiting period to three months, but refused to authorise the operation abroad. She failed to obtain judicial review and appealed to the CA, during which period she had the operation carried out in France.

## Held

❖ (ECJ) Medical services, including public services, are covered by art.56.

## Commentary

[1] The ECJ treated the services as paid, even if the payment was provided through state-funded healthcare such as the NHS.

[2] The rights of patients to cross-border healthcare are now covered by Directive 2011/24.

# THE ECONOMIC ELEMENT

## Key Principle

"Services" are normally provided for remuneration, in so far as they are not covered by other provisions on free movement of goods, persons and capital: art.57 TFEU (ex 50).

> SOCIETY FOR THE PROTECTION OF THE UNBORN CHILD (IRELAND) LTD V GROGAN (CASE C-159/90) 1991
> Officers of a student association in Ireland (where abortion is illegal) had distributed information without charge about the availability of abortion services in other Member States.

## Held

❖ (ECJ) In the absence of an economic element, the provision of information about abortion services in other Member States is outside the scope of art.56 TFEU (ex 49). [1991] E.C.R. 4685.

## Commentary

[1] Freedom to move around the EU, prior to the introduction of Union citizenship, remained largely dependent on economic status, whether exercising the rights of the worker, of establishment or the provision and receipt of services. Directives were adopted to provide residence rights for certain categories of individuals who are not economically active. These directives were all repealed and replaced by Directive 2004/38 (see Ch.10).

[2] *Carpenter v Secretary of State for the Home Department* (Case C-60/00) provides an insight into the relationship between art.56 and art.8 of the **ECHR** (respect for family life). The applicant, Mrs C, a national of the Philippines, overstayed her visitor's visa to the UK without permission, marrying a UK national the following year. Mr C ran a business selling space in medical and scientific journals, providing services across the EU. Mrs C appealed to the Immigration Appeals Tribunal (IAT) against a decision to deport her to the Philippines, arguing that she had a right in EU law to remain in the UK. This claim was largely based on art.56, in relation to indirect support she provided with childcare for Mr C's children. The ECJ (under art.267) held that art.56, read in the light of art.8 of the **ECHR** (respect for family life), precluded a refusal of the right of residence by the host state to the spouse from a third country of someone providing services in another Member State.

---

**THINK POINT**

When may national restrictions affecting the right of establishment or the freedom to provide services be acceptable, according to the decisions of the EU?

How far does the case law of the ECJ support the right of an individual who wishes to travel to another Member State to receive medical treatment, when no approval has been given in the home state?

# Competition Law 1

## Agreements and restrictive practices under art.101

........................................................................

### INTRODUCTION

Articles 101 TFEU (ex 81) and 102 TFEU (ex 82) establish a framework to regulate competition law throughout the EU. Detailed rules are provided by Regulation 1/2003 introduced as part of the programme to modernise competition law. Article 101 covers agreements and prohibits agreements and restrictive practices, whereas art.102 prohibits abuse of a dominant position (see Ch.13). The two articles should be seen as complementary, and are directly effective in the national courts.

Any agreement or concerted practice which infringes the prohibition in art.101(1) will be void under art.101(2), unless it has been declared inapplicable under art.81(3). Before **Regulation 1/2003** came into force in May 2004, the Commission alone was empowered under Regulation 17/62 to grant exemptions or decide on negative clearance following notification of individual agreements. After that date, art.101(3) became directly applicable. As a result, the enforcement of competition law was largely devolved to the national competition authorities (NCAs), in co-operation with the Commission (see p.xx).

........................................................................

### AGREEMENTS AND RESTRICTIVE PRACTICES UNDER ART.101

The prohibition

**Key Principle** ..................................................................
The following are prohibited as incompatible with the common market: all agreements between undertakings, decisions by associations of undertakings and concerted practices which may affect trade between Member States, and which have as their object or effect the prevention, restriction or distortion of competition within the common market: art.101(1).

# AGREEMENTS BETWEEN UNDERTAKINGS

## Key Principle

Agreements between undertakings are prohibited.

> ### ACF CHEMIEFARMA V COMMISSION (CASE 41/69) 1970
> Quinine producers entered into an export agreement relating to trade with third countries and a "gentlemen's agreement" in 1962 governing the conduct of its members in the common market. In the export agreement the parties agreed to be bound by the gentlemen's agreement. The Commission found that both agreements were an indivisible entity and contravened art.101. The applicants challenged the decision in the ECJ under art.263 TFEU.

## Held

❖ (ECJ) Having regard to the conduct of the parties in relation to sharing domestic markets, the fixing of common prices, determination of sales quotas and prohibition of making synthetic quinine, it was clear that the parties intended to be bound by the gentlemen's agreement which amounted to a restriction on competition contrary to art.101. [1970] E.C.R. 661.

## Commentary

[1] An agreement may be caught by art.101 even where it is not a legally binding contract. The ACF Chemiefarma (quinine producers) gentlemen's agreement was covered because it could be enforced through arbitration. The agreement is an example of a horizontal agreement, which seeks to partition the EU on national lines.

[2] An individual undertaking involved in a cartel may be held responsible for the overall cartel where the Commission can demonstrate that, during a given period, each undertaking consented to the adoption of an overall plan comprising the constituent elements of a cartel or that it participated directly in all these elements during the period: *Buchmann, etc.* (Cases T-295/94, etc.) ("Cartonboard").

[3] Any legal or natural person engaged in economic activity may be regarded as an undertaking, e.g. an opera singer in *Re Unitel* (Commission Decision, 1978).

[4] In *Wouters* (Case C-309/99) the Court found that the Bar of the Netherlands was not an undertaking for the purpose of art.102, as it did not carry out any economic activity.

[5] The competition rules in arts 101 and 102 are extended to public undertakings engaging in commercial activity by art.102: *Italy v Sacchi* (Case 155/73).

[6] Agreements between parent companies and subsidiaries are not regarded as agreements between undertakings where they form a single economic unit: *Viho Europe BV v Commission* (Case T-102/92). The CFI explained in *Akzo Nobel and others v Commission* (Case T-112/05, on appeal Case C-97/08P) that unlawful conduct may be imputed to a parent company or group of companies because they constituted a single undertaking, not because the parent company instigated the infringement or was otherwise involved.

[7] Decisions by associations usually involve trade associations, often acting informally. Such decisions may breach art.101.

[8] Where one undertaking succeeds another which has infringed art.10(1) EC and both are subject to the same public authority, the second entity may be penalised for the whole infringement: *Autorità guarantee della Concorrenza del Mercato* (Case C-280/06).

## CONCERTED PRACTICES

**Key Principle**
A concerted practice arises where positive steps short of an agreement have been taken to align the activities of undertakings.

IMPERIAL CHEMICAL INDUSTRIES LTD V COMMISSION ("DYESTUFFS") (CASE 48/69) 1972
ICI was one of 10 undertakings which together produced about 80 per cent of the market in dyestuffs in the EC. It was the first undertaking to announce a price rise in 1964, shortly followed by identical increases by the other dyestuff producers. Further increases took place in 1965 and 1967, again mirrored by the other producers. The Commission decided that there had been a concerted practice contrary to art.81 and imposed fines on the undertakings. The undertakings challenged the decision under art.263 in the ECJ, claiming that the price rises had not resulted from a concerted practice but from parallel behaviour in an oligopolistic market (i.e. in a market dominated by a few producers, with each producer following the "price leader").

## Held

❖ (ECJ) (1) From the number of producers concerned, it could not be said that the European dyestuffs market operated on the basis of oligopoly (dominance by a few producers). Price competition should have continued to operate, making it inconceivable that parallel pricing would occur.
(2) The general and uniform increase on the various markets could only have arisen as a result of a common intention by the undertakings to adjust prices and to avoid the risks of competition. [1972] E.C.R. 619.

## Commentary

[1] It is necessary to examine price rises, even where they are identical or very similar, to decide whether they reflect an independent response to the market or evidence of a concerted practice. The ECJ in *"Dyestuffs"* considered that the producers had eliminated uncertainty between themselves over future behaviour and, therefore, most of the risk inherent in independent change of conduct.

[2] The ECJ limited its stance on behaviour amounting to a concerted practice in *Ahlström OY v Commission ("Woodpulp")* (Joined Cases C-89, etc./85), a decision arising out of the practice of woodpulp producers of announcing maximum price rises on a quarterly basis to their customers. The ECJ found no breach of art.101, holding (on the facts) that the price announcements to users constituted market behaviour which did not lessen each undertaking's uncertainty as to the future attitude of its competitors.

## Key Principle

A single meeting may be a concerted practice.

T-MOBILE BV V RAAD VAN BESTUUR VAN DER NEDERLANDSE MEDEDINGINGSAUTORITEIT (CASE C-8/08) 2009
Five operators of mobile phone networks in the Netherlands met in 2001 to discuss various matters including standard dealer remuneration for post-paid subscriptions. The national competition authority considered that the operators had entered into a concerted practice. The operators appealed to the Administrative Court for Trade and Industry which sought guidance from the ECJ as to the meaning and scope of "concerted practice".

❖ (ECJ) (1) It is enough for a concerted practice to be regarded as having an anti-competitive effect if it has the potential to have a negative effect on competition, even where it has no effect on the price paid by end users.

(2) A concerted practice implies a causal link between the concerted practice and subsequent conduct on the market. Undertakings taking part in a concerted practice are presumed to have taken account of the information exchanged when determining their conduct on the market, a presumption which the national court must apply.

(3) A concerted practice may arise from a single meeting, if the exchange of information gave the parties the opportunity to determine their conduct on the market and knowingly substitute practical co-operation for the risks of competition. Where the parties remain active in the market in question, there is a presumption that the concerted practice caused the conduct of the undertaking on that market, even where the concerted practice arose from a single meeting.

## EFFECT ON INTER-MEMBER TRADE

**Key Principle**
There must be an effect on inter-member trade.

> SOCIÉTÉ TECHNIQUE MINIERE V MASCHINENBAU ULM GMBH (CASE 56/65) 1966
> MBU agreed to give STM exclusive distribution rights in France of heavy earth-moving equipment on condition that STM would not sell competing machines. The agreement was challenged before a French court, which made an art.267 reference to the ECJ.

**Held**
❖ (ECJ) "It must be possible to foresee . . . that the agreement in question may have an influence, direct or indirect, actual or potential, on the pattern of trade between Member States." [1966] E.C.R. 235.

**Commentary**
[1] The ruling demonstrates the wide interpretation placed by the ECJ in *STM v Maschinenbau* on "effect on trade between Member States". It means that an agreement will be covered by the prohibition even where it relates to a single Member State, provided there is a potential for exports to another Member State. See e.g. *Pronuptia v Schillgalis* (Case 161/84) in which a franchising

agreement intended to relate to a territory within Germany was found to have a potential effect on trade.

[2] A very different (potentially positive) effect on trade may be seen in *Publishers Association v Commission* (Case C-360/92P) where the ECJ overturned part of the CFI's decision to refuse exemption to the Net Book Agreements (a series of agreements between book publishers and retailers providing for certain books to be sold at fixed prices). The basis for the ECJ decision was that the CFI had failed to take proper account of the benefits to the book trade from the single language area formed by the British and Irish book markets. Soon after the ECJ decision, the Net Book Agreements collapsed due to commercial pressures.

## PREVENTION, RESTRICTION OR DISTORTION OF COMPETITION

**Key Principle**

An agreement is prohibited if its object or effect is to prevent, restrict or distort competition.

CONSTEN AND GRUNDIG V COMMISSION (JOINED CASES 56 AND 58/64) 1966

The German electronics company G entered into an exclusive distribution agreement with C whereby G agreed to supply C as sole distributor in France. In return C agreed not to sell any competing products in France or to re-export Grundig products. In addition, C was granted sole use in France of G's international trade mark (GINT). UNEF, another French company, bought Grundig products in Germany where they were sold more cheaply and resold them in France. C sued UNEF in the French courts for infringement of the GINT trade mark. UNEF applied successfully to the Commission for a decision that the agreement between G and C infringed art.101. G and C challenged the decision in the ECJ under art.263.

**Held**

❖ (ECJ) (1) The object of the distribution agreement was to eliminate competition to the detriment of consumers.

(2) There is no need to take account of the effects of an agreement once it appears that it has as its object the prevention, restriction or distortion of competition. [1966] E.C.R. 299.

[1] The use of the GINT trade mark could not be enforced by Consten because it had the effect of partitioning the market along national lines.

[2] The ECJ decided that the list of illegal practices set out after the prohibition in art.101(1) is illustrative rather than exhaustive. The practices include agreements to fix prices, limit production or markets, apply different conditions to equivalent transactions and impose unconnected supplementary obligation.

[3] The decision in *Consten and Grundig* has been criticised because it prohibits vertical agreements (i.e. agreements between undertakings at different levels of distribution, in this case between producer and distributor). Vertical agreements are seen as less damaging to consumers than horizontal agreements (i.e. agreements between undertakings at the same level of distribution, such as a cartel between retailers). Some commentators have thus taken the view that it is not necessary to ban agreements which restrict the availability of a particular brand where there is effective inter-brand competition (i.e. competition between brands).

## Key Principle

It is not necessary to carry out a market analysis where the object of the agreement is to prevent, restrict or distort competition.

> SOCIÉTÉ TECHNIQUE MINIERE V MASCHINENBAU ULM GMBH (CASE 56/65) 1966.
> For facts, see p.163.

## Held

❖ (ECJ) (1) The terms "object or effect" are "disjunctive" (i.e. alternatives).
(2) Exclusive distribution agreements do not necessarily restrict competition.
[1966] E.C.R. 235.

## Commentary

[1] Where it is not apparent that the object of the agreement is to restrict competition, a market analysis should be carried out to determine whether the effects of the agreement infringe art.101(1).

[2] The following factors were identified in *STM* as relevant for consideration in a market analysis:

(a) the market shares of the parties;

(b) whether the agreement formed part of a network;

(c) the nature or quantity of the products to which the agreement relates;

(d) the severity of the restrictions; and

(e) whether parallel imports or re-exports were prohibited.

[3] In *Competition Authority v Beef Industry Development Society Ltd and Barry Brothers (Carrigormore) Meats Ltd* (Case C-209/07) the reference to the ECJ arose in relation to the standard form of contract between the 10 main producers of beef and veal in Ireland, all of whom were members of the Beef Industry Development Society. The contract required members to reduce their processing capacity by 25 per cent. The ECJ held that such an agreement has as its object the prevention, restriction or distortion of competition, contrary to art.101(1). It followed that it was not necessary to consider the effects on competition of such an agreement.

## Key Principle

A distribution agreement will infringe art.101(1) where it substantially excludes other dealers.

### DELIMITIS V HENNINGER VRAU (CASE C-234/89) 1991

A tenant challenged the requirement under a beer supply agreement to buy all the beer for his bar from his landlord, claiming that it infringed art.101(1). An art.267 reference was made.

## Held

❖ (ECJ) (1) A full analysis was needed to establish whether so many outlets were tied to brewers that there were insufficient independent outlets to provide a viable market for a new brewer to supply.

(2) A selective distribution system does not infringe art.101(1) where resellers are chosen on the basis of objective criteria of a qualitative nature and the conditions for the application of such criteria are laid down for all potential resellers. [1991] E.C.R. I-935.

## Commentary

[1] *Delimitis* repeats the formula previously adopted by the ECJ in *Metro-Grossmarkte GmbH v Commission* (Case 26/76) in relation to selective distribution systems. The approach of the ECJ reflects the concept, borrowed from the United States' anti-trust law, known as the "rule of reason". Applying the rule of reason, agreements that are not automatically illegal are

considered within the context of the market to decide whether they are anti-competitive. Article 101(3) recognises this pragmatic approach by providing for exemption from the consequences of illegality under art.101(2)—see p.169.

[2] Other examples of a "rule of reason" approach include:
  (a) *Remia and Nutricia v Commission* (Case 42/84): restrictive terms in the sale of a business did not infringe art.101(1) if necessary to give effect to the sale; and
  (b) *Pronuptia v Schillgalis* (Case 161/84): restrictive clauses in franchise agreements did not breach art.101(1) if necessary to ensure the identity of the franchiser's network or to prevent know-how being transferred to competitors.

[3] The Commission issued a number of block exemption regulations in relation to common commercial agreements which would otherwise infringe art.101(1) where the conditions in the regulation are satisfied. Where an agreement is covered by a block exemption there is no need to notify the NCA as the agreement has full validity under art.101(3). Block exemption regulations were issued in areas including exclusive distribution, exclusive purchasing, research and development, specialisation, franchising and technology transfer. Most specify maximum turnover limits. If the undertakings' turnover exceeds the limit, it is not covered by the block exemption and will require an individual exemption to ensure validity.

[4] Vertical agreements are covered by the block exemption on vertical agreements, Regulation 330/2010. Vertical agreements are defined as "agreements or concerted practices entered into between two or more undertakings, each of whom operates, for the purpose of the agreement, at a different level of production or distribution chain, and relating to the conditions under which the parties may purchase, sell or resell certain goods or services". The regulation specifies threshold limits (30 per cent of the relevant market), above which notification will be necessary. Vertical agreements covered by other block exemptions are affected by the regulations.

**Key Principle**
A party to a contract which is liable to restrict or distort competition under art.101 can rely on the breach of that provision to obtain relief from the other party to the contract.

**COURAGE V CREEHAN (CASE C-453/99)**
Courage, the brewers, sued the tenant of a public house for breach of contract. The tenant claimed that the beer tie which applied to him was illegal, and that, in consequence, he should not have to pay damages.

**Held**
❖ (ECJ) (art.267) The national court must provide a remedy where someone is harmed by a breach of art.101. A ban on recovery under national law must be set aside, unless the party claiming bears significant responsibility for the breach of art.101. [2001] ECR I-6297.

## WITHIN THE COMMON MARKET

**Key Principle**
Anti-competitive agreements are covered by art.101(1) if they are between undertakings situated within the EC or between undertakings situated outside the EU, where the effects of the agreement are felt within the EU.

**ICI V COMMISSION ("DYESTUFFS") (CASE 48/69) 1972**
For facts, see p.161. Several of the undertakings engaged in concerted practices over price increases were based outside the EU, in Switzerland and in the UK (prior to membership).

**Held**
❖ (ECJ) Because the effects of their practices were felt within the EC, the undertakings were liable for breaches of art.101(1). The United Kingdom parent company, ICI (UK) Ltd, was liable for the breaches of its Dutch subsidiary.

**Commentary**
[1] *"Dyestuffs"* does not represent an entirely clear statement about the "effects" doctrine, since the issues were addressed mainly in terms of liability for the acts of subsidiaries.

[2] In *Ahlström OY v Commission ("Woodpulp")* (Joined Cases 89, etc./85) (see p.xxx) forestry undertakings in Finland, Sweden and Canada (all, at that time, outside the EC) challenged the Commission decision that their advance notification of price rises infringed art.101. The ECJ held that there was a breach of art.101 because the practices were implemented within the EU. It was immaterial whether they had used subsidiaries, agents or branches within the Member States.

# MINOR AGREEMENTS

## Key Principle
Agreements producing a negligible effect on trade do not infringe art.81(1).

> **VÖLK V VERVAECKE (CASE 5/69)**
> Völk, a producer of washing machines with about 0.2 to 0.5 per cent of
> the market in Germany and an even smaller market share in Belgium
> and Luxembourg, entered on agreement with Vervaecke. Under the
> agreement Vervaecke, a Dutch distributor of electrical products, was
> given exclusive rights to distribute Völk's products in Belgium and
> Luxembourg, with a further ban on parallel imports.

## Held
❖ (ECJ) There was no appreciable effect on competition and therefore no
breach of art.81(1). [1969] E.C.R. 295.

## Commentary
The Commission has adopted a series of Notices on Minor Agreements. As
Notices are non-binding, they may only be taken as indicative of the Commission's position. The most recent Notice was issued in 2001. It provides
that agreements between undertakings concerned with production or distribution do not infringe art.101(1) where the market share of the undertakings does not exceed 10 per cent (for agreements between competitors)
and 15 per cent (for agreement between non-competitors). A 10 per cent
threshold applies to agreements which are difficult to classify according to
these categories.

# ILLEGALITY AND EXEMPTION

## Key Principle
Any agreements or decisions prohibited under art.101(1) are automatically
void: art.101(2).

> **CONSTEN AND GRUNDIG V COMMISSION (JOINED CASES 56 AND 58/64)**
> **1966**
> For facts, see p.164.

## Held
❖ (ECJ) Only the parts of the agreement which restricted competition were
void (i.e. those relating to restrictions on parallel importation of goods).

## Commentary

[1] The decision in *Consten and Grundig* illustrates that the application of art.101(2) need not lead to the invalidity of the entire agreement (contrary to the earlier decision by the Commission).

[2] Before the repeal of **Regulation 17/62** in 2004 the prohibition under art.101(1) could be declared inapplicable by the Commission where two positive and two negative conditions were satisfied. The agreement was required to contribute to improving production or distribution of goods, or to promoting technical or economic progress.

[3] A new approach to exemption was introduced on May 1, 2004 when **Regulation 1/2003** came into effect. Under the regulation, much of the power currently held by the Commission devolved to the national competition authorities (NCAs), leaving the Commission free to concentrate on significant cases raising new issues. Notification to the Commission was abolished. The regulation implemented the 1999 White Paper on Modernisation which proposed extensive changes to the system of competition enforcement. Devolution to the national authorities was needed in order to deal with the volume of applications which exceeded the capacity of the Commission to respond.

[4] The UK passed the Competition Act in 1998, introducing a new regime for the administration of national competition rules based on arts 101 and 102 EC. Under the Act the UK competition authorities must ensure consistency with the principles of the Treaties, the case law of the European courts and the decisions and statements of the Commission. The prohibitions are mostly enforced by the Office of Fair Trading and a specialist tribunal, the Competition Appeal Tribunal, established under the Enterprise Act 2002.

[5] Under art.1 of **Regulation 1/2003** agreements caught by art.101(1) which do not satisfy art.101(3) are prohibited, no prior decision to that effect being required. Article 2 makes similar provision in relation to infringements of art.102. Undertakings should make their own assessments as to whether the agreement complies with EU competition law, applying established principles and Commission guidance. The Commission is empowered under art.4(2) of the regulation to adopt regulations requiring registration in relation to certain types of agreement caught by art.101(1). Registration will not provide any legal rights.

## Key Principle

The agreement must not impose any restrictions that are not indispensable.

> **CONSTEN AND GRUNDIG V COMMISSION (JOINED CASES 56 AND 58/64) 1966**
> For facts, see p.164.

## Held

❖ (ECJ) The use of the GINT trade mark in France was not required by the agreement. That part of the agreement was void.

## Commentary

It is possible to sever an illegal part of an agreement where the rest is valid.

## Key Principle

There must be no elimination of competition.

> **METROPOLE TELEVISION SA (M6) V COMMISSION (JOINED CASES T-185/00, T-216/00 AND T-300/00)**
> The CFI considered a complaint arising out of a Commission decision granting exemption to a set of rules adopted by the European Broadcasting Union for the granting of sub-licences to third parties for broadcasting rights to sporting events. The applicants were various television companies denied licences under the EBU rules. The Court confirmed the existence of an "upstream" market for the acquisition of rights and a "downstream" market for the televised transmission of sporting events. Television rights are normally granted on a territorial, exclusive basis. CFI found that the sub-licensing system did not guarantee the applicants, competitors of the members of the EBU, sufficient access to transmission rights for sporting events.

## Held

❖ (CFI) The Commission was wrong to decide that the sub-licensing scheme guaranteed access for third parties, avoiding the elimination of competition, even if a product market limited to certain major sporting events exists.

## THINK POINT

Are there any circumstances in which an agreement between a parent and a subsidiary company would be covered by art.101(1)?

Why and in what respects did the behaviour of the undertakings in *ICI v Commission* (Case 48/69) amount to a concerted practice? Is a concerted practice as serious a breach as a cartel?

# Competition Law 2

## 13

## INTRODUCTION

Article 102 TFEU (ex 82) prohibits abuse of a dominant position within the common market. The article should be read alongside art.101, as the two provisions are complementary. Terminology in relation to art.102 should be given the same meaning as art.101. It is important to appreciate that dominance is not illegal in itself. Article 102 is only infringed when an undertaking acts in a way which abuses that position of dominance.

The Commission published draft Guidance on Enforcement Priorities in applying art.102 in December 2008. The paper provides for an economic and "effects-based" approach, in line with the decisions in *Wanadoo (France Télécom), Microsoft* and *Téléphonica* (see below). This means that the Commission will undertake a careful examination based on convincing evidence and sound economic analysis, of the effects on consumers of the dominant undertaking's conduct.

The application of art.102 to mergers was confirmed in the *Continental Can* decision (see below). However, no separate procedure for notification of mergers was in place until 1989, from which date mergers (known as "concentrations" under the regulation) have been regulated. Mergers are currently governed by Regulation 139/2004, adopted as part of the programme to modernise competition law.

## ABUSE OF A DOMINANT POSITION UNDER ART.102

**Key Principle**
Any abuse by one or more undertakings of a dominant position within the common market or in a substantial part of it shall be prohibited under art.102 as incompatible with the common market in so far as it may affect trade between Member States.

# DOMINANCE

### Key Principle

Dominance results from a position of economic strength, which enables an undertaking to act independently of its competitors and consumers.

> HOFFMAN-LA ROCHE V COMMISSION ("VITAMINS") (CASE 85/76) 1979
> H-LR held the following market shares in relation to vitamins: A–47 per cent; B2–86 per cent; B3–64 per cent; B6–95 per cent; C–68 per cent; E–70 per cent and H–95 per cent, with 65 per cent of the worldwide market for vitamins in 1974.

### Held

❖ (ECJ) (1) H-LR could be presumed to be dominant in all vitamin markets except Vitamin A. Dominance could be shown in relation to A, as H-LR held substantially more of the market than the nearest competitor.

(2) "The existence of a dominant position may derive from several factors which, taken separately, are not necessarily determinative but among those factors a highly important one is the existence of a very large market share". [1979] E.C.R. 461.

### Commentary

[1] Size and turnover alone do not establish dominance. Other relevant factors identified by the ECJ include the absence of a significant competitor and the extent to which the sales network is developed.

[2] As the case law of the ECJ developed it became clear that dominance is a legal rather than an exclusively economic policy. It is established by carrying out an analysis of the relevant product, geographical and (where appropriate) temporal or seasonal markets.

[3] Note that to prove a breach of art.102, it is not enough merely to establish dominance. There must also be abuse of a dominant position.

# THE PRODUCT MARKET

### Key Principle

It is essential to identify the product market correctly before a breach of art.102 may be established.

Continental Can Co Inc (CC) were major producers of metal packages. In 1969 they took over a German company, Schmalbach (S). In 1970 CC agreed through its subsidiary, Europemballage, to acquire a majority holding in a Dutch company, Thomassen (T). At the time of the takeover of T, S and T were not in competition, although they were operating in adjacent geographical areas and were both making metal packaging. The Commission investigated the takeover of T, responsibility for which was imputed to CC by the enterprise entity concept (see p.xx: *Viho Europe*). The Commission decided that CC, through its holding in S, was dominant on the market for metal packaging for fish and meat and for metal closures for glass containers. It also found that the purchase of T amounted to an abuse of that position. CC and E challenged the decision under art.263.

**Held**

❖ (ECJ) The Commission had failed to identify the relevant product market and had not given reasons for its decision. The decision was annulled. [1975] E.C.R. 495.

**Commentary**

[1] While agreeing in principle that a takeover such as CC's acquisition of T could be a breach of art.102, the ECJ in *Continental Can* made it clear that the Commission's failure to take sufficient account of the relevant product market was a ground for annulment. The Commission should have analysed the undertaking's market power by defining the relevant market and then assessing the extent of dominance within that market. While there had been some consideration of possible substitutes on the demand side (meat and fish suppliers using plastic containers) it had not considered substitutes on the supply side (packaging manufacturers making alternative containers).

[2] Two key factors may be identified when identifying the product market: cross-elasticity of demand and cross-elasticity of supply (availability of demand/supply substitutes). In recent judgments the ECJ has focused more closely on cross-elasticity of substitutes on both the supply and demand sides, as in its judgment in *United Brands*.

## Key Principle

The product market should be defined by reference to product substitution (i.e. whether it is possible to interchange another product regarded by customers as identical).

> **UNITED BRANDS V COMMISSION (CASE 27/76) 1978**
> The Commission issued a decision that United Brands had infringed art.102 in the marketing of bananas grown by themselves in the EC. It considered that there was a separate market for bananas, which were not interchangeable with other fruit. United Brands challenged the decision in the ECJ on the basis that it did not hold a dominant position in the market, claiming that the relevant product market was fresh fruit and not bananas.

## Held

❖ (ECJ) The banana has special characteristics (e.g. taste, softness, ease of handling) which make it very suitable for the very young, old and sick. There is little substitutability between bananas and other fruit. The banana market is a distinct market, separate from other fruits. [1978] E.C.R. 207.

## Commentary

[1] The product market defined in *United Brands* was fairly narrow and related to substitutability from the demand side. An even more limited product market was identified in *Hugin-Kassaregister A.B. v Commission* (Case 22/78): spare parts to repair cash registers made by Hugin. See also *Hoffman-La Roche* (Case 85/76) (see p.xxx), in which each vitamin was found to occupy an individual product market. In some cases, it is the possibility of substitution from the supply side which is relevant. In *Tetra-Pak Rausing S.A. v Commission* (Case T-51/89), upheld by the ECJ in Case C-333/94P, the CFI held that the makers of milk packaging machines could not readily transfer to making aseptic packaging for UHT milk, justifying the finding that aseptic packaging was a distinct product market. In *France Télécom* (Case T-340/03, on appeal Case C-202/07P) the CFI (on appeal from the Commission) confirmed the Commission's decision that there was no substitutability between high- and low-speed internet access. The relevant product market was high-speed internet access for residential customers.

[2] In 1997 the Commission issued the Notice on Market Definition. This defined the relevant product market as "all those products and/or services which are regarded as interchangeable by the consumer, by reason of the products' characteristics, their prices and their intended uses". The Notice puts the question as to whether the parties' customers would switch to

readily available substitutes or to suppliers located elsewhere in the event of a hypothetical but permanent price increase (5–10 per cent) in the product and areas considered.

## THE GEOGRAPHICAL MARKET

**Key Principle**
It is necessary to show that dominance occurs within the common market or a substantial part of it.

> MICHELIN (N.V. NEDERLANDSCHE BADEN-INDUSTRIE MICHELIN) V
> COMMISSION (CASE 322/81) 1983
> The Commission found that there was an abuse of a dominant position arising out of the practices of the Dutch subsidiary of Michelin in the Netherlands. The Michelin group operated a policy of price discounts which made it difficult for their customers to obtain tyres for heavy vehicles from manufacturers competing with Michelin. The product market was identified by the Commission as tyres for heavy vehicles and the geographical market as the Netherlands, where the activities of the subsidiary were concentrated.

**Held**
❖ (ECJ) The Commission decision on the product and geographical markets was upheld and the abuse confirmed. [1983] E.C.R. 3461.

**Commentary**
[1] The geographical market may be, but is not always, the same as the sales area of the undertaking concerned. Where the product is readily transportable (in this case, nail cartridges) it may be the whole of the EU: *Hilti v Commission* (Case T-30/89). Some products may have a global market: "*Woodpulp*". The territories of most of the Member States have been found to be a substantial part of the common market (e.g. Ireland in *RTE, BBC and ITP v Commission* (Case C-241/91P)). The ECJ was prepared to define the geographical market very narrowly in *Corsica Ferries v Corpo dei Piloti del Porto di Genoa* (Case C-18/93) as the Port of Genoa.

[2] It is rarely necessary to define the seasonal or temporal market. The ECJ considered seasonal factors in *United Brands* (Case 27/76) but decided that they did not influence consumer choice to a significant degree. Temporal factors were considered but rejected in *Michelin* (Case 322/81). Issues such

as the need to build a new factory or for customers to assess the suitability of a new type of tyre were held to be too long-term to affect competition.

[3] The 1997 Notice on Market Definition defines the relevant geographical market as "the area in which the undertakings concerned are involved in the supply and demand for products and services, in which the conditions of competition are sufficiently homogenous and which can be distinguished from neighbouring areas because the conditions of competition are appreciably different in those areas".

## ASSESSING DOMINANCE

**Key Principle**

A detailed market analysis is needed to assess dominance, taking account of the market share of the undertaking and of competitors, control of production and distribution, and financial and technical resources.

UNITED BRANDS (CASE 27/76) 1978
For facts and decision, see p.176.

**Commentary**

Market share should be examined carefully in relation to competitors. Although the market share of United Brands was fairly low (about 40 per cent), the market was fragmented, with no competitor holding more than 16 per cent. United Brands was also identified by the ECJ as possessing superior technology to its competitors. United Brands controlled virtually all stages of production and distribution, owning the banana plantations, and controlling transportation, distribution and ripening of its brand "Chiquita". Taking all these factors into account, it was clear that United Brands was in a dominant position in the banana market in the EU.

## ABUSE OF A DOMINANT POSITION

**Key Principle**

Dominance is not illegal. Article 102 is only infringed where a dominant position is abused.

**Key Principle**

Abuse may be demonstrated by practices such as charging unfair prices, discriminating between customers and refusing to supply customers.

United Brands had engaged in a range of practices that the Commission had decided were abusive, including forbidding the sale of green bananas, refusing to supply a Danish wholesaler because it had engaged in an advertising campaign for a competitor (thus driving it out of business), charging customers in different Member States different prices, and charging excessive prices. United Brands challenged the findings of abuse in the ECJ.

## Held

❖ (ECJ) United Brands had engaged in abuse in relation to the ban on the sale of green bananas, the refusal to supply the Danish wholesaler and differential pricing. Abuse was not proved in relation to alleged excessive pricing.

## Commentary

[1] The prohibition in art.102 is followed by a list of examples of abuse similar to those in art.101 (imposing unfair prices or other trading conditions; limiting production, markets or technical development to the detriment of consumers; applying dissimilar conditions to equivalent transactions; and imposing unnecessarily supplementary obligations). The *United Brands* decision provides examples of most types.

[2] The ECJ and various academic commentators have divided abuses into exploitative abuses (taking advantage of a dominant position by imposing harsh trading conditions such as charging differential prices) and anti-competitive abuses (activities which are not necessarily unfair but which may reduce competition such as mergers: see below). Many examples of abuse show characteristics of both types.

[3] Another example of tying can be seen in *Van Den Bergh Foods Ltd v Commission* (Case T–65/98). Here, Van Den Bergh Foods Ltd, formerly HB Ice Cream Ltd (HB) a manufacturer of ice cream, supplied retailers with freezer cabinets either free or at a nominal charge on condition that the freezers were used exclusively for HB products. The relevant product market was single wrapped impulse ice cream. At least 40 per cent of the retail outlets of this type of ice cream had freezers supplied by HB under its exclusivity agreements. The CFI found that the HB arrangements constituted tying and were an abuse. The practices of the company restricted commercial freedom of choice of retailers of ice cream in relation to the products which they stocked.

[4] An example of a practice which may be abusive (both exploitative and

anti-competitive) is the granting of discounts. In *Hoffman-La Roche* the ECJ distinguished between loyalty and quantity discounts. Loyalty discounts were granted to customers on the proportion of the customer's requirement for vitamins purchased. This had a "tying" effect, compelling customers to buy from H-LR, and was abusive. Quantity discounts were granted on the basis of volume of vitamins bought from the same firm and were legal. In *BA v Commission* (Case C-95/04P) the ECJ held that it is necessary to consider all the circumstances, especially the basis on which grants or discounts are granted, to determine whether it is an abuse for a dominant undertaking to offer discounts which are unrelated to quantity or fidelity. The analysis should show whether or not the discounts or bonuses have an exclusionary effect (i.e. whether they make it more difficult for competitors to enter the market of the dominant undertaking, or for co-contractors to choose between different potential commercial partners) as well as whether there is an objective economic justification. There will only be a breach where the dominant undertaking discriminates against the other part, distorting the competitive relationship between the parties.

[5] Export and import bans are usually considered to be abusive: *BMW Belgium v Commission* (Joined Cases 32, etc./78) (export ban considered abusive even though there was national price control leading to particularly low prices in the country of export).

[6] Under a recycling scheme, an undertaking provided to collect, sort and recover all packaging bearing its logo on behalf of participating customers in Germany. However, the company required its customers to pay a fee for all packaging marketed in Germany bearing its logo, regardless of whether they used the system to dispose of their packaging. The CFI upheld the Commission decision that the conduct of the undertaking was an abuse: *Der Grüne Punkt-Duales System Deutschland (DSD) v Commission* (Case T-151/01, upheld on appeal Case C-385/07P).

## FURTHER EXAMPLES OF ABUSE

**Key Principle**
It is an abuse of a dominant position to refuse to supply a customer.

RTE, BBC AND ITP V COMMISSION (CASE C-241/91P) 1995
RTE, the BBC and the ITP refused to supply Magill, a publisher in Ireland, with information about weekly television listings for the purpose of producing an independent guide. The Commission and CFI found

that the refusal was an abuse of a dominant position. A further challenge was brought by the television companies in the ECJ.

## Held

❖ (ECJ) The ECJ accepted that weekly television listings amounted to a distinct market in which the television companies were dominant. The companies could not rely on intellectual property rights to justify refusal to supply the information, such refusal amounting to an abuse. [1995] E.C.R. I-743.

## Commentary

[1] See also *Commercial Solvents* (Joined Cases 6 and 7/73) in which a dominant undertaking refused to supply a former competitor with an essential chemical, driving it out of business. This was held by the ECJ to be abusive.

[2] Refusal to supply was also at the heart of the Court's decision in *IMS Health* (Case C-418/01). The case arose in the context of a dispute between two companies specialising in market analysis of pharmaceutical products and health care. One of the companies, NDC, claimed that it was entitled to use a "brick structure" (a system for storing data on pharmaceutical products) developed by the other company, IMS Health, which refused to grant a licence to use the structure. On a referral under art.267 from the German court, the ECJ found that, in order to decide whether the refusal of a licence was abusive, it should consider the degree of participation by users in developing the system, particularly in terms of cost. A refusal to grant a licence could be abusive where the applicant for the licence intends to offer new products or services on the supply of data in question for which there is a potential consumer demand, the refusal is not justified by objective considerations and the effect of the refusal will be to eliminate all competition in the relevant market.

## Key Principle

A position of overwhelming dominance carries special responsibilities.

### MICROSOFT CORPORATION v COMMISSION (CASE T-201/04) 2007

Microsoft enjoyed a share of more than 90 per cent of the market for desktop operating systems for personal computers and more than 60 per cent for group servers, a position of "overwhelming dominance" which the Commission considered carried special responsibilities. The company supplied its desktop operating system with Windows Media

Player already installed, a form of "tying" which the Commission considered was an abuse. Microsoft had extended its dominance over Windows to adjacent areas such as worktop servers, but refused to supply "interoperability" information to customers, although it had done so previously. This change virtually excluded competition on workplace servers.

**Held**

❖ (CFI) Tying Windows Operating System to Windows Media Player was an abuse, as was refusal to supply interoperability information to customers.

**Commentary**

[1] The CFI upheld the Commission decision in relation to tying and the refusal to supply. It also upheld the fine of just under €5 million, finding that the Commission had not erred in relation to the gravity and duration of the infringement. The CFI, however, dismissed the Commission's decision in so far as it required Microsoft to appoint a monitoring trustee with independent access to documents.

[2] Following the *Microsoft* decision, the Commission instigated a discussion paper in 2005 to review the operation of art.102. After extensive consultation, it produced draft guidance in December 2008 on the enforcement priorities in applying art.102 to exclusionary conduct by dominant undertakings. The guidance emphasises the need to focus on consumer welfare when examining abuses by dominant undertakings, in accordance with an "effects-based" approach to the identification of enforcement priorities.

[3] Refusal to supply may arise in the context of the so-called "essential facilities" doctrine (an expression not used by the ECJ). Oscar Bronner, a publisher of a low-circulation newspaper in Austria, sought access to the distribution network of Mediaprint which controlled about 36.8 per cent of the newspaper market in Austria. When Mediaprint refused, Oscar Bronner brought an action in the Austrian courts, claiming that the refusal was an abuse of a dominant position. The Austrian court sought guidance from the ECJ in order to avert possible conflict between Austrian and EC law. The ECJ held that it was not enough for a facility to be desirable, it must be essential. There were other ways to distribute newspapers in Austria outside Mediaprint's network. Thus, the refusal was not an abuse. An abuse might arise where refusal would be likely to eliminate all competition in the downstream market; the refusal was unjustified; access was indispensible to the other party; and there was no alternative, actual or potential: *Oscar Bronner v Mediaprint* (Case C-7/97).

## Key Principle

"Predatory" pricing is an abuse under art.102.

> ### AKZO CHEMIE V COMMISSION (CASE C-62/86) 1991
>
> ECS, a small undertaking in the United Kingdom producing benzyl peroxide, supplied its product to customers for use as bleach in flour refining. In 1979 it decided to widen its market and sell to users in the polymer industry. AKZO, a Dutch undertaking dominant in polymers, told ECS that it would lower its prices in the flour additive market to a level with which ECS could not compete. AKZO duly reduced its prices. The Commission found that AKZO's price reduction was "predatory" and imposed an exemplary fine. The Commission took account not only of the cost in comparison to the price, but also whether it was part of a strategy to eliminate competition, what the effects of the price reduction would be and the likely reaction of the competitor. AKZO appealed to the ECJ.

## Held

❖ (ECJ) (1) The Commission's finding under art.102 was upheld: AKZO's behaviour amounted to predatory pricing and was an abuse of a dominant position.

(2) Prices below average variable cost give rise to a presumption of predatory pricing.

(3) The amount of the fine was reduced. [1991] E.C.R. I-3359.

## Commentary

While price competition usually benefits the consumer, predatory pricing does not. Its aim is to drive the competitor out of business, thus reducing consumer choice. The reasoning of the ECJ in *AKZO* was followed by the ECJ in *Tetra Pak International v Commission* (Case C-333/94P) where Tetra Pak's pricing of non-aseptic cartons was found to be predatory.

## MERGERS AND CONCENTRATIONS

## Key Principle

Mergers and takeovers may be an abuse of a dominant position under art.102.

EUROPEMBALLAGE CORPORATION AND CONTINENTAL CAN CO INC V
COMMISSION (CASE 6/72) 1973
For facts and decision, see p.175.

**Commentary**
[1] Although the ECJ annulled the Commission's decision that the takeover of
Thomassen by Europemballage was an abuse of a dominant position under
art.102 (due to inadequate definition of the market and failure to give reasons), it established in principle that art.102 may be invoked to control
mergers and takeovers.

[2] Article 102 does not provide any mechanism for notification comparable to
notification under art.101(3), making it difficult for undertakings engaged in a
merger to protect themselves in the event of a merger being considered
abusive. In *BAT & Reynolds v Commission* (Joined Cases 142 and 156/84) the
ECJ raised the possibility of mergers being subject to art.101. This decision
opened up the possibility of adopting the **Merger Regulation** (see below)
which provided for advance notification of mergers.

## CONTROL OF CONCENTRATIONS

**Key Principle**
"Concentrations" (as joint ventures such as mergers and takeovers are
known under the regulation) must be notified to the Commission if they have
a Community dimension and satisfy specified turnover limits under **Regulation 139/2004**.

**Key Principle**
Factors to be considered by the Commission in deciding whether to clear a
concentration include the structure of the markets, the market position of the
parties, competition inside and outside the EU, barriers to entry, technical
and economic progress and the interests of consumers.

AEROSPATIALE/ALENIA/DE HAVILLAND 1991
Aerospatiale, a French undertaking, and Alenia, an Italian undertaking,
agreed to take over from Boeing the assets of the Canadian division of
De Havilland. The proposed concentration was notified to the
Commission.

**Held** .............................................................................................................

❖ (Commission) Clearance under Regulation 4064/89 was refused on the basis that the move would create a new undertaking with an overwhelmingly powerful position in the market for commuter aircraft (holding 50 per cent of the world market and 67 per cent of the EC market). The Commission's analysis found that the merger would be likely to have the following consequences:

(a) to increase the new undertaking's market share without leading to economies of scale;

(b) to cause the withdrawal of some competitors from the market; and

(c) to create barriers to entry for potential competitors. [1992] 4 C.M.L.R. M.2.

**Commentary** ............................................................................................

[1] *Aerospatiale* is an early example of a merger being refused clearance under Regulation 4064/89. This regulation has now been amended and recast by Regulation 139/2004.

[2] Concentrations are covered by Regulation 139/2004 where:

- the undertakings concerned have a combined aggregate worldwide turnover of at least €5 thousand million;
- the EU-wide turnover of at least two of the undertakings exceeds €100 million;
- the combined aggregate worldwide turnover of all the undertakings concerned is more than €25 million;
- in each of at least three Member States, the combined turnover of all undertakings concerned exceeds €100 million;
- in each of the three Member States (where relevant) the turnover of at least two exceeds €25 million;
- the aggregate EU-wide turnover of at least two of the undertakings concerned is more than €25 million, unless each of the undertakings concerned achieves more than two thirds of its aggregate EU-wide turnover in one and the same Member State.

Concentrations that are not cleared are illegal; undertakings responsible for them are to be fined.

[3] In *Gencor v Commission* (Case T-102/96) the CFI ruled that Regulation 4064/89 applies to collective dominant positions. It dismissed an application for annulment of a Commission decision prohibiting a concentration involving Gencor Ltd, a South African mining company and Lonrho Plc. The basis of the CFI's decision was that the concentration would have led to the

creation of a dominant oligopoly position between the entity resulting from the concentration and another company in the world platinum and rhodium markets, as a result of which effective competition would have been significantly impeded in the common market. The ECJ also ruled on collective dominance in *France v Commission/SCPE and EMC v Commission* (Joined Cases C-68/94 and C-30/95). However, in this case the ECJ held that the Commission had misapplied the concept by failing to establish that the concentration in question would in fact give rise to a collective dominant position in the relevant market. The Commission decision was annulled.

**Key Principle**

A full economic analysis is necessary before the Commission can reach a decision in relation to a proposed merger.

AIRTOURS PLC V COMMISSION (CASE T-342/99) 2002

Airtours (A), a UK company selling package holidays to short-haul destinations such as Spain and Italy, launched a bid to take over First Choice (FC). FC was one of A's main UK competitors, the others being Thomsons (T) and Thomas Cook (TC). The bid was notified to the Commission which found in September 1999 that it was incompatible with the common market as it would give the merged company, along with T and TC, collective dominance; leading to higher prices, restricted market capacity and increased profits. The Commission considered that the bid would increase the share of A, T and TC in the short-haul market from 68 per cent to 78 per cent. A challenged the decision of the Commission before the CFI.

**Held**

❖ (CFI) The Commission had failed to prove that the merger would have adverse effects on competition, owing to a series of errors as to whether a collective dominant position might be created.

**Commentary**

[1] The errors arose (to a substantial degree) as a result of the Commission's approach to economic analysis before it reached a decision. The Commission considered (wrongly) that customers did not switch between short- and long-haul holidays, thus reaching a wrong decision about the market.

[2] The CFI identified three conditions that must be met before a finding of collective dominance may be made:

(a) given the characteristics of the relevant market, each member of the oligopoly must know how the other members are behaving in order to be able to adopt the same policy;

(b) members of the oligopoly must be deterred over time from departing from the policy thus adopted;

(c) that policy must be able to withstand challenge by other competitors, potential competitors or customers.

Overturning the Commission decision, the CFI found that the Commission had not established that the three leading tour operators would have an incentive to stop competing with each other. Contrary to the view of the Commission, consumers may exercise significant buying power, switching to other operators or destinations in response to price rises.

[3] The CFI overturned two further Commission decisions on proposed mergers in *Schneider Electric SA v Commission* (Case T-310/01) and *Tetra Laval BV v Commission* (Cases T-5/02 and T-80/02), both in October 2002. The Commission was found to have failed to produce sufficient evidence in its economic analysis of the anti-competitive effects of both proposed mergers. The ECJ upheld the decision of the CFI on appeal in *Commission v Tetra Laval* (Cases C-12/03P and C-13/03P).

[4] The Commission was concerned at the implications of three major decisions being overturned in the CFI in this way. In December 2004 it adopted a comprehensive package in relation to EU merger control. The central element of the package was a new merger regulation—**Regulation 139/2004,** which amended and recast **Regulation 4064/89**. Key features of the new regulation seek to:

(a) clarify that the merger regulation may apply to situations of oligopoly which may give rise to competition problems;

(b) rationalise the timing of applications to the Commission for proposed mergers;

(c) simplify the system for transfer of cases between the Commission and national competition authorities;

(d) introduce greater flexibility especially into the investigation of complex cases;

(e) strengthen the investigative powers of the Commission.

[5] Other elements of the merger reform package included the appointment of a Chief Competition Economist within the Commission to provide advice on mergers and other competition investigations, the adoption of a notice on mergers between competing firms and speedy review by the courts of merger decisions.

[6] A proposed merger between Sony and Bertelsmann was initially considered by the Commission in May 2004 to be incompatible with the common market, on the basis that it would have strengthened the parties' collective dominance in the recorded music market. However, the Commission changed its position later in 2004, after hearing evidence from the parties, and allowed the merger. A third party, Impala (an organisation of independent music publishers), applied for the merger to be annulled. The CFI overturned the Commission decision. It found that collective dominance could have been inferred indirectly from various indicators, particularly price over a long period. It also found that the Commission's economic analysis was flawed: *Impala v Commission* (Case T-464/04). However, on appeal, the ECJ found that the CFI had examined only two of the five pleas put forward by Impala. It therefore annulled the decision and referred the case back to the CFI (Case C-413/06P).

## ENFORCEMENT OF THE COMPETITION RULES

**Key Principle**
Investigations into breaches of competition law may be either compulsory or voluntary.

> NATIONAL PANASONIC (UK) LTD V COMMISSION (CASE 136/79) 1980
> Suspecting an infringement (a concerted practice) of art.101, the Commission carried out a compulsory investigation of National Panasonic (UK) without warning.

**Held**
❖ (ECJ) The Commission was entitled under art.14 of **Regulation 17** to investigate without prior notice where a breach was suspected. A concerted practice was found. [1980] E.C.R. 2033.

**Commentary**
[1] This investigation was carried out under **Regulation 17/62**, now repealed and replaced by **Regulation 1/2003**.

[2] Under art.20 of **Regulation 1/2003** the Commission continues to be empowered to inspect premises. The main change under the new regulation is the requirement for the Commission to consult NCAs before making a decision to investigate. The CFI held in *France Télécom* that the Commission is not required to hold back from making an inspection where the NCA is dealing in parallel with a case (see above).

[3] Powers of entry and search relate only to the undertaking and not to the individual. Thus, they enable the Commission to enter the business premises of an undertaking under suspicion, but not to enter the home of, say, one of the directors, even if they believe that the individual has removed papers to his home. See *Hoechst v Commission* (Joined Cases 46 and 227/87) in which the search of the home premises of a senior member of staff was found to be illegal, being in breach of the principle of the inviolability of the home, contrary to the **European Convention on Human Rights**. See also *Orkem v Commission* (Case 374/87) and *Dow Benelux N.V. v Commission* (Case 85/87), the latter upholding the decision in *Hoechst*.

[4] In order to improve the quality of evidence on cartels, the Commission introduced a "leniency" programme in 1996, currently regulated by a Notice of 2006. Under the programme, an undertaking may "blow the whistle" on a cartel to which it belongs provided its own involvement in the cartel has ended and it has not coerced other undertakings to participate in the infringement. Immunity from fines is available to the first undertaking to blow the whistle.

## Key Principle
The ECJ must have regard to the legitimate business interests of undertakings in protection of their business secrets and must not disclose information acquired to the national authorities.

### ADAMS V COMMISSION (CASE 145/83) 1985
The Commission disclosed information about Adams, an informant, to the Swiss authorities, as a result of which A was charged and convicted by the Swiss courts. (For full facts, see p.79.)

## Held
❖ (ECJ) The Commission was liable for breach of the principle of confidentiality (although damages were reduced by A's contributory negligence).

## Commentary
See also *Australian Mining & Smelting Co Ltd (AM&S) v Commission* (Case 155/79): limited professional privilege applies to communications between lawyer and client. In *Akzo Nobel and Akros Chemicals v Commission*, the CFI held that an undertaking is entitled to refuse to allow the Commission to take "even a cursory look" at documents for which confidentiality is claimed, providing the undertaking gives appropriate reasons and considers that such

a look would be impossible without revealing the content of the documents. The CFI maintained the position in *AM&S* that communications between undertakings and lawyers employed by those undertakings are not covered by professional privilege.

## Key Principle

As arts 101 and 102 are directly effective, they may be enforced in the national courts.

> ### CUTSFORTH V MANSFIELD INNS 1986
>
> C sought to rely on art.101 in relation to a term in agreement between the tenants of tied houses and the brewer which had taken over the chain of public houses. Under the agreement the tenants would only be permitted to obtain their equipment from authorised suppliers. C, who had previously supplied gaming equipment to the public houses, was not authorised.

## Held

❖ (HC) There was a serious prima facie case between the parties. An interlocutory order restraining the application of the offending term was granted. [1986] 1 C.M.L.R. 1.

## Commentary

[1] Although it was suggested in *Garden Cottage Foods v Milk Marketing Board* (HL 1983) that damages should be available for breach of art.102, the position was not made clear in that case. Subsequently, the *Francovich* decision (Joined Cases C-6/90 and 9/90) has established that Member States are liable in damages for breaches of EU law (see p.15).

[2] The implementation of **Regulation 1/2003** has completely changed the power of the national courts to apply EU competition law. Under art.6 of the regulation, national courts are empowered to apply art.101 in its entirety, including art.101 (3). They must, however, under art.10, seek to avoid making a decision which conflicts with a Commission decision: art.16. In the event of uncertainty, national courts may (as they could under existing law) make a preliminary reference under art.267. They may also ask the Commission to provide information in its possession (art.15(1)) or for an opinion on the application of EU competition rules. The Commission may submit observations before the national courts on arts 101 and 102 on matters of EU interest.

In what circumstances is it a breach of art.102 to refuse to supply a customer?

Why did the decisions in *Airtours*, *Schneider* and *Tetra Laval* demonstrate that the regime for merger regulation within the EU needed to be reformed? Do you think that **Regulation 139/2004** provides a satisfactory solution to the problems in these cases?

# Equal Pay and Treatment

## 14

## INTRODUCTION

The **TFEU** provides for the principle of equal pay for equal work for men and women in art.157 (ex141), placing an obligation on Member States which is both economic and social. As the principle of equal pay in art.157 is a directly effective Treaty provision, claims for equal pay may be brought in the national courts against both public and private bodies. By contrast, equal treatment is recognised through a series of directives, and may thus only be enforced nationally against the state or a public body. **Directive 2006/54** repealed and recast **Directive 76/207** in 2009, providing for equal treatment of men and women as regards access to employment and vocational training, as well as to working conditions. **Directive 86/378** (equal treatment in occupational pension schemes) and **Directive 75/117** (implementing the equal pay principle) were repealed and recast by **Directive 2006/54**. **Directive 79/7** implements the equal treatment in relation to social security. It has not been repealed by **Directive 2006/54**.

The **Treaty of Amsterdam** introduced a new legal base for action to combat discrimination on grounds under art.19 TFEU (ex 13). **Directive 2004/43** prohibits discrimination on grounds of racial or ethnic origin. **Directive 2000/78** provides a general framework to combat discrimination on grounds of religion or belief, disability, age or sexual orientation.

## EQUAL PAY

**Key Principle**

Member States must ensure and maintain the application of the principle that men and women receive equal pay for equal work: art.157.

> DEFRENNE V SABENA (CASE 43/75) 1976
> For facts, see p.7.

**Held**

❖ (ECJ) Article 157 is directly effective from the date of the judgment (April 8, 1976). [1976] E.C.R. 455.

## Commentary

[1] Equal pay claims within art.157 may be enforced against both public and private bodies, as Treaty provisions are effective both vertically and horizontally. By contrast, equal treatment claims under the relevant directive may only be enforced against public bodies as directives are vertically but not horizontally effective (see p.7 on *Marshall*).

[2] The original economic emphasis of the **Treaty of Rome** has shifted towards a greater recognition of the social dimension. In *Deutsche Post Ag v Sievers and Schrage* (Joined Cases C-270 and 271/97) the ECJ held that the economic aim pursued by art.157 is secondary to the social aim under the article, which constitutes the expression of a fundamental human right.

[3] Recast **Directive 2006/54** covers equal pay in a single chapter, with a single article. It provides for the elimination of discrimination, either direct or indirect, on grounds of sex in relation to all aspects and conditions of remuneration: art.4(1).

## Key Principle

"Pay" means the ordinary basic or minimum wage or salary and any other consideration, in cash or kind, which the worker receives, directly or indirectly, in respect of his employment: art.141.

### WORRINGHAM V LLOYDS BANK LTD (CASE 69/80)

Lloyds Bank operated two retirement schemes, one for men and one for women. Male employees under 25, but not female employees, received a notional additional sum for the purpose of calculating the level of employer contributions towards pension entitlement.

## Held

❖ (ECJ) Even though the payment was notional and was immediately removed to the pension scheme, it was "pay" under art.157. [1981] E.C.R. 767.

## Commentary

[1] The payment in *Worringham* was "pay" because it was repaid to employees leaving the scheme early and was included in gross pay to calculate other entitlements such as redundancy pay.

[2] The grant of special travel facilities to former employees was held to be "pay" in *Garland v BREL* (Case 12/81).

[3] Contributions paid into a statutory social security scheme are not pay: *Defrenne v Belgian State* (Case 80/70), upheld in *Barber v GRE* (Case 262/88), unlike contributions paid into an occupational pension scheme, which are covered by art.157 (see p.196).

[4] A judicial award of compensation for breach for the right not to be unfairly dismissed is pay under art.157: *R. v Secretary of State for Employment Ex p. Seymour-Smith and Perez* (Case C-167/97) (see p.200).

## MATERNITY SCHEMES

### Key Principle
To assess the maternity scheme of a public body it is necessary to consider the scheme in relation to art.157, as well as the equal treatment directives.

> BOYLE V EQUAL OPPORTUNITIES COMMISSION (CASE C-411/96)
> B and six others were employed by the EOC and were of childbearing age. They had all worked at the EOC for more than one year and were not employed on casual or short-notice or fixed-term (of less than two years) contracts. At least three had recently taken maternity leave. They sought a declaration before an industrial tribunal that the maternity scheme operated by their employers contravened art.157 (and the three directives **75/117** on equal pay and equal treatment, **76/207** on equal treatment and 92/85 which is intended to improve the safety and health at work of pregnant workers and workers who have recently given birth or are breastfeeding). The tribunal referred questions to the ECJ under art.267.

### Held
❖ (ECJ) (1) A clause in a contract of employment making the application of a maternity scheme which was more favourable than the statutory scheme conditional on the pregnant woman's return to work after the birth of the child or the woman would be required to repay the difference between statutory and occupational scheme was not discriminatory.
(2) Although the right to the minimum period of 14 weeks' maternity leave provided for by **Directive 92/85** may be waived by the worker (apart from the two weeks' compulsory maternity leave), if a woman becomes ill during statutory maternity leave and moves to more favourable sick leave which terminates before the maternity leave, the period of maternity leave remains unaffected by the sick leave. [1998] ECR I-6401.

## Commentary

[1] **Directive 75/117** implemented and defined the scope of the equal pay principle in art.157. It introduced the principle of equal pay for equal value in art.1. It was repealed by **Directive 2006/54** in 2009, but case law under **Directive 75/117** remains relevant for interpretation.

[2] A lump sum payment made exclusively to female workers who take maternity leave where the payment is designed to offset the occupational disadvantages arising for workers due to their absence from work is pay under art.157. However, as male and female workers are in different situations, there is no breach of art.157: *Abdoulaye v Regie Nationale des Usines Renault SA* (Case C-218/98). Note that maternity pay should not be so low as to undermine the protective purpose of leave: *Gillespie v Northern Ireland Health and Social Services Board* (Case C-342/93). Any pay rise awarded to a woman on maternity leave between the beginning of and the end of the maternity leave in the period covered by the reference pay should be treated as pay under art.157 and must be included in the elements of pay taken into account in calculating the amount of maternity pay: *Alabaster v Woolwich Plc Ex p. Secretary of State for Social Security* (Case C-147/02).

## PART-TIME WORKERS

### Key Principle

Exclusion of part-time workers from entitlements such as sick pay may contravene art.157 where there are more female than male part-timers.

> RINNER-KUHN v FWW (CASE 171/88) 1989
> Part-time employees whose contracts limited their work to 10 hours a week or 45 hours a month were excluded from entitlement to sick pay.

### Held

❖ (ECJ) As more women than men worked part-time, such a restriction infringed art.157 unless it was objectively justified. [1989] E.C.R. 2743.

### Commentary

The ECJ rejected as inadequate the "justification" of the German government that part-time workers were less integrated into their employment and upheld its decision in *Bilka Kaufhaus* (Case 170/84) (see p.xxx).

**Key Principle**

The principle of equal pay applies to part-time workers in the United Kingdom, enabling them to claim for redundancy pay on the same terms as full-timers under United Kingdom law.

### R. v SECRETARY OF STATE FOR EMPLOYMENT EX P. EOC 1994

The Equal Opportunities Commission (EOC) brought an action in the United Kingdom courts claiming that provisions for redundancy under United Kingdom law infringed art.157 and **Directive 75/117** and that the conditions governing conditions for unfair dismissal for part-time workers infringed **Directive 76/207** on equal treatment.

**Held**

❖ (HL) The exclusion of part-time workers from redundancy benefits and protection against unfair dismissal infringed art.157 of **Directive 75/117** and **Directive 76/207** respectively. [1995] A.C. 1.

## OCCUPATIONAL PENSIONS

**Key Principle**

Payments under occupational pensions schemes are "pay" under art.157.

### BARBER v GUARDIAN ROYAL EXCHANGE (CASE C-262/88) 1990

Mr Barber belonged to a pension fund established by his employers, Guardian Royal Exchange. The scheme was non-contributory and "contracted-out" (i.e. a private, non-statutory scheme approved by UK law). Under the scheme women were entitled to receive their pension at the age of 57 years, whereas men had to wait until they were 62. In the event of redundancy women received an immediate payment at 50 and men at 55. Mr Barber was made redundant at the age of 52. He received severance pay, statutory redundancy pay and an ex gratia payment, but was told that he would not receive his pension until he reached pensionable age (i.e. 62 years). Mr Barber brought proceedings in an industrial tribunal based on the **Sex Discrimination Act**, claiming unlawful discrimination. (A woman in his position would have received an immediate pension.) His action initially failed but reached the Court of Appeal in appeal proceedings brought by his widow after Mr Barber's death. The Court of Appeal referred questions to the ECJ.

**Held** ...........................................................................................

❖ (ECJ) (1) A pension paid under a contracted-out, private occupational scheme is "pay" under art.157.

(2) It is a breach of art.157 in a contracted-out scheme to impose an age condition which differs between men and women, even where permissible under national law. To enable national courts to identify and eliminate any discrimination between the sexes, all elements of a remuneration package must be transparent.

(3) Equality in pension claims may only be claimed from the date of the judgment (May 17, 1990) except for claims initiated before the judgment. [1990] E.C.R. I-1889.

**Commentary** ...........................................................................

[1] *Barber* has been an immensely important decision as it required occupational pension schemes to harmonise the retirement ages for men and women. Before equality measures are taken, equalisation must be achieved without reducing existing entitlements. After measures are taken, equality may be fixed at any level: *Van den Akker v Stichting Shell Pensioenfonds* (Case C-28/93).

[2] The ECJ limited the temporal effect of the judgment, as it did in *Defrenne*. This restriction was confirmed in a protocol to the **Maastricht Treaty**.

[3] The *Barber* decision caused **Directive 86/378** (equal treatment in occupational pensions schemes) to become largely irrelevant, as most issues relating to differences between men and women in retirement ages or pension entitlement are now covered by art.157. The directive was repealed by **Directive 2006/54** in 2009.

[4] Pensions paid to the spouses of deceased employees are within art.157: *Ten Oever v Stichting Bedrijfspensioenfonds Voor Het Glazenwassers* (Case C-109/91).

[5] The arrangements for funding occupational pensions are outside art.141, thus permitting schemes to require different levels of contribution from men and women based on actuarial factors such as life expectancy: *Neath v Hugh Steeper* (Case C-152/91). Statutory social security schemes are also outside art.157: *Barber*; as are "single sex" schemes: *Coloroll Pension Trustees Ltd v Russell* (Case C-200/91).

[6] The ECJ in *Deutsche Telekom v Schröder* (Case C-50/96) and other joined cases found that exclusion of part-time workers from an occupational

pension scheme amounted to discrimination contrary to art.157, if the measure affects a considerably higher percentage of female than male workers, unless objectively justified. (This is known as indirect discrimination—see *Seymour Smith*;, below.)

[7] Another instance of indirect discrimination in relation to pensions arose in *Preston v Fletcher* (Case C-78/98). This time the workers in question were prevented from pursuing their claim for retrospective membership of the pension scheme by a national (UK) law requiring them to bring their claim within six months of completing their employment and restricting the period of retrospective membership of the pension scheme to the two years before their claim was instituted. The Court found that the six-month requirement for a claim did not infringe EU law, since it supported the principle of effectiveness and legal certainty. The restriction of membership, however, did contravene the principle of effectiveness since it excluded from the record of service the period before the two-year point.

[8] In *Griesmar* (Case C-366/99) the ECJ found that exclusion of civil servants who are fathers from entitlement to the service credits paid to retired civil servants who are mothers infringes the principle of equal pay if the fathers can prove that they brought up the children. In *Voß v Land Berlin* (Case C-300/06) the ECJ considered art.157 in relation to national legislation defining "overtime" as hours worked over and above normal working hours for both part-time and full-time civil servants where the overtime rate was less than the normal hourly rate of pay and there were more female than male part-time staff. It found that such legislation indirectly discriminated against women and was not objectively justified.

[9] In *Menaur* (Case C-379/99) the ECJ interpreted art.157 as meaning that bodies such as German pension funds entrusted with providing an occupational pension scheme must ensure equal treatment for men and women, even if the employees discriminated against have a protected right against their employers in the event of insolvency that excludes all discrimination.

## DIRECT AND INDIRECT DISCRIMINATION

### Key Principle
Direct discrimination is illegal under art.157. Indirect discrimination may be legal if it is objectively justified.

## Bilka-Kaufhaus GmbH v Weber von Hartz (Case 170/84) 1986

Part-time workers were excluded from an occupational pension scheme unless they had been employed for 15 years. Full-time employees were not similarly restricted. As nearly all the part-timers were female, the effects were felt disproportionally by women. A female part-timer challenged the exclusion in the German courts, which made a reference to the ECJ.

**Held**

❖ (ECJ) (1) Exclusion of part-time workers from a pension scheme infringes art.157 where:

(a) a considerably smaller proportion of the workforce is employed part-time;

(b) the difference in treatment is based on sex; and

(c) the exclusion is not objectively justified.

(2) A measure will be objectively justified if it corresponds to a real need on the part of the undertaking, it is appropriate to achieve the objective pursued and it is necessary. [1986] E.C.R. 1607.

**Commentary**

[1] Direct discrimination occurs where one sex is treated disadvantageously compared with the other sex. (See *Dekker v Stichting Vormingscentrum Voor Jonge Volwassenen* (Case C-177/88), discrimination on grounds of pregnancy was held to be direct discrimination.)

[2] Indirect discrimination involves practices which are not apparently discriminatory but which have an adverse effect which is felt disproportionately by one sex, as in the exclusion of the part-time (female) employees from the pension scheme in *Bilka-Kaufhaus*, upholding the earlier decision in *Jenkins v Kingsgate (Clothing Productions) Ltd* (Case 96/80) (paying part-time employees, most of whom were female, less than men did not infringe art.141 if objectively justified and not based on discrimination on grounds of sex).

[3] In the UK the House of Lords ruled in *R. v Secretary of State for Employment Ex p. EOC* (HL, 1994) that the requirement for part-time workers to be employed for five years (compared with two years for full-time workers) before gaining certain employment protection rights was indirect discrimination which was not objectively justified.

[4] The use of factors which vary between the sexes to determine the number of additional years that may be credited to an official under the Community

pension scheme is discrimination on grounds of sex which is not objectively justified by the need to ensure sound financial management of the pension scheme: *Lindorfer v Council* (Case C-227/04P).

## Key Principle

In assessing whether a measure adopted by a Member State has a disparate effect on men and women so as to amount to indirect discrimination, the state should consider the respective proportions of men in the workforce able to satisfy the requirement and those unable to do so, and compare these proportions as regards women in the workforce.

### R. V SECRETARY OF STATE FOR EMPLOYMENT EX P. SEYMOUR SMITH AND PEREZ (CASE C-167/97) 1999

The applicants were two women, each of whom had been dismissed from their employment before completing the two-year period required for protection against unfair dismissal under a UK Order of 1985. They claimed before the Divisional Court that the Order was indirectly discriminatory against women, contrary to the **Equal Treatment Directive 76/207**, and before the Court of Appeal, that the Order infringed art.157. After a misleading declaration by the CA, the House of Lords requested a ruling from the ECJ under art.267.

## Held

❖ (ECJ) It is for the national courts to assess the factors and reach a conclusion. The onus was on the Member State to show that:
(1) the alleged discriminatory rule reflected a legitimate aim of social policy;
(2) the aim was unrelated to any discrimination based on sex;
(3) the Member State could reasonably consider that the means chosen were suitable for attaining that aim.

## Commentary

[1] The House of Lords applied the ruling in February 2000. After analysing the statistics it held that the impact of the UK legislation was debatable but that, at the time of the action, it was objectively justified. The HL decision was, by then, overtaken by events, as the two-year qualification period had been abolished.

[2] A national rule limiting entitlement under art.157 to two years before the commencement of proceedings had the effect of preventing proper

enjoyment of EU law rights: *Magorrian v Eastern Health and Social Services Board* (Case C-246/96).

[3] While it is for the national courts to lay down detailed rules on the protection of employment rights under EU law, such rules may not be less favourable than those covering comparable domestic claims and may not make it virtually impossible to exercise those rights: *Levez v T.H. Jennings (Harlow Pools) Ltd* (Case C-326/96). The ECJ held that, where an employer misinformed a female employee as to the salary of her male predecessor, a restriction on arrears of pay to two years prior to the commencement of proceedings could not be applied.

## Key Principle
Men and women have equal rights to join an occupational pension scheme under art.157.

> DIETZ V STICHTUNG THUISZORG ROTTERDAM (CASE C-435/93) 1996
> Dietz was employed by the defendants part-time until November 6, 1990 when she agreed to retire early at the age of 61. At that time part-timers were excluded from occupational pension schemes. She claimed she would have retired later if she had known about imminent changes to the pension scheme of benefit to her. The Dutch court made a reference to the ECJ.

## Held
❖ (ECJ) The right to join an occupational pension scheme is covered by art.157 and can be enforced against the scheme's administrators. [1997] 1 C.M.L.R. 199.

## Commentary
[1] The ECJ in *Dietz* followed *Vroege v NCIV Institut Voor Volkshuisvesting* (Case C-57/93) in placing no restrictions on the temporal effect of art.157 in this context (cf. *Barber*). However, it ruled that national time limits may be invoked in relation to art.157 provided the limits are no less favourable than those relating to comparable domestic actions.

[2] On equality of access to pension schemes, see also *Fisscher v Voorhuis Hengelo* (Case C-128/93) where the exclusion of married women from an occupational scheme was found to infringe art.157.

# REDUNDANCY PAY

BARBER V GRE (CASE C-262/88)
For facts, see p.196.

**Held**

❖ (ECJ) Redundancy pay is "pay" under art.157, whether paid under a contract of employment, by virtue of legislative provisions or on a voluntary basis.

**Commentary**

After *Barber*, the earlier decision of the ECJ in *Burton v British Railways Board* (Case 19/81) would appear to have little relevance. In *Burton* the ECJ held that discrimination between the sexes in terms of age of entitlement to voluntary redundancy was calculated by reference to the statutory retirement age (60 for women and 65 for men). As **Directive 79/7** (see p.192) permitted Member States to exclude the statutory retirement age from equal treatment, the claim under **Directive 76/207** failed. Such a claim could now be brought under art.157. United Kingdom law permitting different statutory retirement ages for men and women was amended by the Sex Discrimination Act 1986 which made discrimination between the sexes in retirement ages illegal and by the Employment Act 1989 which provides for a single retirement age of 65 years for both sexes for redundancy benefit.

# EQUAL WORK

**Key Principle**

Equal pay for equal work means the elimination of all discrimination on grounds of sex for the same work or for work to which an equal value is attributed, with regard to all aspects and conditions of remuneration: art.1, **Directive 75/117**.

BILKA-KAUFHAUS GMBH V WEBER VON HARTZ (CASE C-170/84) 1986
For facts and decision, see p.199.

**Commentary**

[1] **Directive 75/117** was adopted to clarify art.157 and to provide a mechanism for comparing work of equal value. It did not alter the scope of art.141: *Jenkins v Kingsgate* (Case 96/80) (see above). Thus, all considerations applying to art.141 also apply to **Directive 75/117**, including the decisions of the ECJ on direct and indirect discrimination and on objective justification.

[2] Where men and women are engaged in the same work, as in *Bilka-Kaufhaus* and *Jenkins v Kingsgate*, discrimination infringes art.157 where it is based exclusively on the difference of sex of the worker.

[3] Where statistics show a significant difference in pay for jobs of equal value where one (in this case pharmacy) is carried out almost exclusively by men and the other (speech therapy) by women, the employer must establish that the difference is objectively justified by factors other than sex: *Enderby v Frenchay Area Health Authority and Secretary of State for Health* (Case C-127/92).

[4] Where people perform seemingly identical tasks but draw on knowledge and different skills and do not have the same qualifications to perform other tasks that may be assigned to them, they do not do the "same work" for the purpose of art.141: *Angestelltenbetriebsrat der Wiener Gebietskrankencasse* (Case C-309/97). In this case social insurance institutions in Austria employed three different classes of psychotherapists, paid at different rates: doctors, graduate psychologists and others with a specialised training in psychology.

[5] See also *Brunnhofer v Bank der Österreichen* (Case C-381/99) in which it was held that it is not permissible to put together the personal qualities of the employee with the way in which she worked in order to support the view that she was not engaged in similar work or work of equal value to the work of other employees.

**Key Principle**
Equal work need not be identical work but must display a high degree of similarity.

MACARTHYS LTD V SMITH (CASE 129/79) 1981
Mrs Smith was appointed by Macarthys as a warehouse manager. She complained that she was paid less than her male predecessor, who had left four months before she took up the job. The Court of Appeal made a reference to the ECJ to clarify the meaning of art.157 in such circumstances.

**Held**

❖ (ECJ) The principle of equal pay for equal work is not confined to situations where men and women are contemporaneously doing equal work for the same employer.

**Commentary**

While the ECJ did not rule in *Macarthys* on the meaning of "the same work", Advocate General Caportorti submitted that it included jobs which were highly similar but not identical. There must always be a real (not hypothetical) comparator, even if that comparator is not employed at the same time.

## WORK OF EQUAL VALUE

**Key Principle**

Where a job classification scheme is used to determine pay, it must be based on the same criteria for men and women, and must exclude discrimination based on sex: art.1(2), **Directive 75/117.**

> RUMMLER V DATO DRUCK (CASE 237/85) 1986
>
> The applicant challenged the criteria under a job classification scheme, claiming that she should have been placed in a higher paid category covering heavy physical work, because packing parcels was a heavy task for her. The employer considered that the job placed only light physical demands on her. A reference was made to the ECJ.

**Held**

❖ (ECJ) (1) A job classification scheme based on strength or physical hardship does not infringe **Directive 75/117** provided the system precludes discrimination on grounds of sex and the criteria employed are objectively justified.

(2) "Objectively justified" means appropriate to the tasks to be carried out and corresponding to a genuine need of the undertaking.

**Commentary**

[1] The ECJ in *Rummler* approached the issue as one of indirect discrimination, which may be capable of objective justification. It would be discriminatory to calculate the physical effort required for a job by reference to the average characteristics of one sex. However, the applicant's subjective experience of effort was not relevant.

[2] Article 4(2) of **Directive 2006/54** provides (in identical terms to art.1(2) of

Directive 75/115) that job classification schemes, where these are used, shall be based on the same criteria for men and women, and drawn up so as to avoid discrimination on grounds of sex.

[3] The criteria in a job evaluation scheme must be "transparent" (i.e. clearly displayed): *Handels-Og Kontorfunktionaernesforbund v Dansk Arbejdsgivforening for Danfoss* (Case 109/88). (If the criterion of "flexibility" meant quality of work, it was neutral unless it systematically discriminated against women. If it meant adaptability to work schedules it could discriminate against women due to their family responsibilities.) Each element in a remuneration package will need separate consideration in an equal value claim. See also *Barber*: p.196.

[4] In *Lawrence v Regent Office Care Ltd* (Case C-320/00) the applicants were Mr Lawrence and 446 other workers employed as cleaners, nearly all women. Female workers had brought an action against Regent Office which led to a ruling in the HL, stating that their work was of equal value to the male workers. As a result, pay for women increased. The appellants were workers employed by the respondent undertakings, and were regarded as performing work of equal value. The Court held that, as a result, the work and payment of these workers could not be compared. Where the differences identified in the pay conditions of workers of different sex performing equal work or work of equal value cannot be attributed to a single source, the situation is not covered by art.157.

**Key Principle**

Member States must provide a means of assessing equal value claims if they do not provide a job classification scheme.

COMMISSION V UK (RE EQUAL PAY FOR EQUAL WORK) (CASE 61/81) 1982
United Kingdom law provided for equal pay for people doing "like work" or work rated as equivalent in a job evaluation scheme. Such schemes were only instituted with the agreement of the employer. The Commission brought proceedings against the United Kingdom in the ECJ under art.258.

**Held**

❖ (ECJ) (1) Job classification is only one of several ways to determine equal value.
(2) The United Kingdom's interpretation of **Directive 75/117** denies the

existence of the right to equal pay for work of equal value where no classification has been made, contrary to the general scheme and provisions of the
directive. [1982] E.C.R. 2601.

## Commentary

Under art.6 of the directive, Member States must take the necessary measures to ensure that the principle of equal pay is applied. Effective means
must be available (not necessarily by a job classification scheme).

## EQUAL TREATMENT

### Key Principle

Men and women are entitled to be treated equally as regards access to
employment, including promotion, and to vocational training and as regards
working conditions and social security: art.1, **Directive 2006/54**.

### Key Principle

There shall be no direct or indirect discrimination on grounds of sex in the
conditions, including selection criteria, for access to all jobs or posts,
whatever the sector or branch of activity, and to all levels of the occupational
hierarchy: art.14(1)(a) of **Directive 2006/54**.

---

DEKKER V STICHTUNG VORMINGSCENTRUM VOOR JONGE VOLWASSEN
PLUS (CASE 177/88) 1990
Ms D applied for a job at a youth training centre in the Netherlands.
Although the selection committee considered Ms D to be the most
suitable applicant for the post she was not offered employment
because she was pregnant. (The centre's insurers had refused to
reimburse sickness benefits in the event of taking on an employee
known to be pregnant.) The Dutch courts referred questions to the ECJ
under art.267.

---

### Held

❖ (ECJ) Discrimination based on pregnancy was direct discrimination contrary to art.3 of **Directive 76/207**. [1990] E.C.R. I-3941.

### Commentary

[1] **Directive 76/207** was repealed and recast by **Directive 2006/54**, on
August 15, 2009. Article 14(1) of the recast directive prohibits direct and
indirect discrimination in relation to conditions for access to employment,
self-employment or occupation, including promotion, as well as to access to

vocational training and retraining, employment and working conditions including dismissals and membership of an organisation of workers or employees. Article 14(2) allows only one exception, enabling Member States to treat men and women differently where, by nature of particular occupational activities or the context in which they are carried out, a characteristic constitutes a "genuine and determining occupational requirement", provided the objective is legitimate and the requirement is proportionate.

[2] There was no need in *Dekker* to compare the position of men and women, since women alone may be refused employment because they are pregnant. Such a refusal is therefore direct discrimination and incapable of objective justification.

[3] By contrast, where a woman becomes ill as a complication of pregnancy and is dismissed, the ECJ has held that the dismissal is indirect discrimination and is thus capable of objective justification: *Handels-Og Kontorfunktionaerer-Nes Forbund I Denmark (Acting for Hertz) v Dansk Arbejdsgivforening* (Case 179/88).

[4] In *Mahlburg* (Case C-207/98) the ECJ ruled that **Directive 76/207** precludes a refusal to appoint a pregnant woman to a post for an indefinite period on the ground that a statutory prohibition on employment attaching to pregnancy prevents her from being employed in that post from the outset and for the duration of pregnancy.

## PREGNANCY AND MATERNITY

**Key Principle**
There shall be no discrimination on grounds of sex either directly or indirectly in the public or private sectors, including public bodies: art.14(1) of **Directive 2006/54**.

> WEBB V EMO AIR CARGO (UK) LTD (CASE C-32/93) 1994
> This decision concerned a woman who was dismissed when she became pregnant while employed on an indefinite term during the maternity leave of another employee: see p.12. The fundamental issue

was whether she was unlawfully dismissed. Ms Webb claimed that the dismissal amounted to discrimination contrary to s.1 of the **Sex Discrimination Act 1975** and that the Act should be interpreted subject to the **Equal Treatment Directive 76/207**. The House of Lords decided to refer questions for interpretation of the directive to the ECJ under art.267.

**Held** ....................................................................................................

❖ (ECJ) Article 2(1) read with art.5(1) of **Directive 76/207** precludes dismissal of an employee who is recruited for an unlimited term with a view, initially, to replacing another employee during the latter's maternity leave and who cannot do so because, shortly after recruitment, she herself is found to be pregnant. [1994] E.C.R. I-3567.

**Commentary** ....................................................................................

[1] The ECJ ruled that no comparison should be made between the situation of a woman incapable of working due to pregnancy and a man similarly incapable for medical or other reasons. Pregnancy is not a pathological condition comparable to non-availability for work on non-medical grounds (which would otherwise justify dismissal without discrimination on grounds of sex).

[2] The ruling makes it clear that dismissal of a pregnant woman recruited for an indefinite period cannot be justified on grounds related to her inability to fulfil a fundamental condition of her employment contract. The wording appeared to provide a loophole allowing dismissal in circumstances where a woman becomes pregnant having been engaged for a definite period of time (e.g. as a maternity leave replacement).

[3] This anomaly was resolved by **Directive 92/85** on pregnant workers and working mothers, which provides protection for all pregnant employees against dismissal, regardless of the nature of contractual service. The directive does not cover refusal to employ a pregnant woman. However, in *Mahlburg v Land Meckleburg-Vorpommern* (Case C-207/98) refusal to appoint a pregnant woman for an indefinite period in line with a national prohibition was found to be in breach of **Directive 92/85**. See now art.14(1)(c) of **Directive 2006/54**.

[4] See also *Melgar v Ayuntamiento de Los Barrios* (Case C-438/99) and *Tele Danmark A/S* (Case C-109/00). M had been recruited by the municipality of Los Barrios in Spain for three months, her contract being renewed twice. After signing a fourth contract for a fixed term on a part-time basis in May 1999,

she was issued with a letter stating that her contract would terminate in June 1999. She was pregnant at the time and gave birth in September 1999. M brought proceedings in the national courts against the municipality, leading to referral under art.234. *Tele Danmark A/S* (Case C-109/00) also involved an employee on a fixed-term contract (six months, in this case) who was dismissed on account of pregnancy. Tele Danmark claimed that the applicant should have informed them that she was due to give birth before the end of the six-month period. Clarification was sought by the Danish court under art.234. The ECJ held (in *Melgar*) that the prohibition on the dismissal of pregnant women applies to both fixed-term and part-time appointments. In *Tele Danmark* the ECJ confirmed that a refusal of employment on account of pregnancy cannot be justified by financial loss which the employer may suffer, if he recruits a woman during her maternity leave or because the woman he has recruited cannot occupy the post during her pregnancy.

[5] Applying the principle of non-discrimination, pregnant workers require protection against unfair dismissal throughout the period of pregnancy: *Brown v Rentokil* (Case 394/96). In *Paquay* (Case C-460/06) the ECJ held that **Directive 92/85** prohibits the notification of a decision to dismiss on grounds of a pregnancy and/or birth of a child during the period of protection in art.10(1) of the directive.

[6] **Directive 2006/54** provides in art.15 that a woman on maternity leave is entitled to return to her job or an equivalent post on terms and conditions no less favourable and to benefit from any improvement in working conditions to which she would have been entitled during her absence. Member States which recognise rights in relation to paternity and adoption are required under art.16 to protect the beneficiaries of such rights on a similar basis to art.15.

**Key Principle**
Men and women must be treated equally in terms of working conditions, including conditions governing dismissal: art.14(1)(c), **Directive 2006/54**.

MARSHALL V SOUTHAMPTON AND SOUTH WEST HAMPSHIRE AREA HEALTH AUTHORITY (NO.1) (CASE 152/84) 1986
For facts, see p.7.

## Held

❖ (ECJ) Article 5 of **Directive 76/207** (replaced by art.14(1)(c), **Directive 2006/ 54**) does not entitle Member States to limit the application of the equal treatment principle and may be relied upon by an individual against the state before the national courts. [1986] E.C.R. 723.

## Commentary

[1] Ms Marshall could rely on art.5 of the directive against a public body, the Area Health Authority, when compelled to retire at an earlier age than her male counterparts (a practice permitted at that time in the United Kingdom under the **Sex Discrimination Act 1975**). The *Marshall* decision is important most notably because the ECJ confirmed that directives may have vertical but not horizontal effect. Article 5 was deleted by **Directive 2002/73**.

[2] Article 9(1) of recast **Directive 2006/54** provides that fixing different retirement ages for men and women infringes the principle of equal treatment.

[3] The retirement age for receiving an occupational pension is not necessarily the same as the age of entitlement to state retirement benefits. The exception in the **Social Security Directive 79/7** (permitting different ages for the receipt of state pensions for men and women) must be interpreted strictly so as to be inapplicable to the fixing of retirement ages under occupational pension schemes. This approach was confirmed in *Roberts v Tate and Lyle Ltd* (Case 151/84) in relation to the fixing of different retirement ages for both sexes under an early retirement scheme, held to be illegal under art.5 of **Directive 76/207**.

[4] Recast **Directive 2006/54** provides in art.17 that Member State are required to ensure that judicial procedures are available to all persons who consider themselves wronged by failure to apply the equal treatment principle, after recourse to other competence authorities including conciliation, where appropriate. Article 23 requires national abolition of measures which conflict with the principle of equal treatment, while art.24 requires Member States to introduce measures to protect employees against dismissal and other action following a complaint. Further general horizontal provisions are set out in arts 25–29 to cover the prevention of discrimination, minimum requirements for equal treatment, gender mainstreaming (i.e. taking into account the objective of equality when formulating or implementing laws or policies) and the dissemination of information.

# REMEDIES

Member States must introduce into their legal systems the necessary procedures and remedies to enforce the equal treatment principle: art.17, **Directive 2006/54** (previously art.6, **Directive 76/207).**

> VON COLSON AND KAMANN V LAND NORDRHEIN-WESTFALEN (CASE 14/83)
> 1984
> For facts, see p.10.

**Held**
❖ (ECJ) While art.6 of **Directive 76/207** does not satisfy the requirements for direct effect, Member States are obliged by the principle of effectiveness to interpret national law to comply with the relevant directive. [1984] E.C.R. 1891.

**Commentary**
[1] In the context of art.6 of the directive, the obligation under *Von Colson* is for national authorities to interpret implementing legislation so as to ensure that it provides for appropriate procedures and remedies.

[2] See *Marshall v Southampton and South West Hampshire Area Health Authority (No.2)* (Case C-271/91) in which the ECJ held that art.6 was directly effective and was infringed where a Member State imposed an upper limit on compensation in relation to EU law. The effect of this ruling was to remove the ceiling previously applied by industrial tribunals in equal treatment claims.

# EXCEPTIONS TO THE EQUAL TREATMENT PRINCIPLE

**Key Principle**
Member States may exclude from the operation of the equal treatment principle, occupational activities and training where the sex of the worker is a determining factor, provided the objective is legitimate and the means proportionate: art.14(2), **Directive 2006/54.**

> COMMISSION V UK (RE EQUAL TREATMENT OF MEN AND WOMEN) (CASE 165/82) 1983
> The Commission brought enforcement proceedings against the United Kingdom under art.258 in relation to the implementation of **Directive 76/207.** The claim contained three main complaints:

(1) UK legislation failed to provide that collective and other agreements which contravened the principle of equal treatment were void;

(2) the exclusion under s.6(3) of the **Sex Discrimination Act 1975** from the equal treatment of employment in private households or where five or fewer individuals were employed infringed **Directive 76/207**;

(3) s.20 of the 1975 Act wrongly excluded midwives from the equal treatment principle.

**Held**

❖ (ECJ) The United Kingdom was found to be in breach of EU law in relation to the first two complaints, but not the third, due to the sensitivity of the midwife/patient relationship. [1983] E.C.R. 3431.

**Commentary**

[1] Article 2(7), **Directive 76/207** allowed an exception for the protection of women, particularly during pregnancy and maternity. This right has been extended to cover women who adopt children, but not men: *Commission v Italy* (Case 163/82). A similar distinction between the sexes was taken in *Hofmann v Barmer Ersatzkasse* (Case 184/83) in which extra maternity leave granted to mothers was not extended to fathers, the leave recognising both the biological condition of giving birth and the relationship between mother and child.

[2] Article 3 of recast **Directive 2006/54** permits Member States to maintain or adopt measures within the meaning of art.57 (4) TFEU with a view to ensuring full equality in practice between men and women in working life. The only exception under **Directive 2006/54** is set out in art.14(2) in relation to a "genuine and determining occupational requirement" (see p.211).

## EQUAL TREATMENT AND THE ARMED FORCES

**Key Principle**

National decisions on the management of the armed forces must normally observe the principle of equal treatment between men and women.

JOHNSTON AND THE CHIEF CONSTABLE OF THE RUC (CASE 222/84)

J, a female member of the RUC, challenged the RUC's refusal to renew her contract, as it had made a policy decision not to train women in the use of firearms.

**Held** .......................................................................................................................

❖ (ECJ) Any claim to depart from **Directive 76/207** must be decided by the national court only in the light of the directive and not in the light of art.45(3) TFEU (ex 39(3)). [1986] E.C.R. 1651.

**Commentary** .....................................................................................

[1] In *Sirdar v the Army Board and Secretary of State for Defence* (Case C-273/97) the applicant was a woman excluded from joining the Royal Marines. Unlike other units of the British armed forces, each individual, regardless of specialisation, must be able to serve at any time in a commando unit. The ECJ held that the Royal Marines were combat units pursuing activities for which sex is a determining factor.

[2] In *Kreil v Bundesrepublik Deutschland* (Case C-285/98) the ECJ considered a national (German) exclusion of women from military posts, including the use of arms. Women were permitted access only to the medical and military-music services. It held that such exclusion infringed **Directive 76/207** and was disproportionate. The exclusion of women from a post was not justified by the directive on the ground that women should be given greater protection than men against risks to which both sexes are equally exposed.

[3] In *Dory v Germany* (Case C-186/01) the ECJ held that **Directive 76/207** does not preclude military service being reserved to men.

## EQUAL OPPORTUNITIES AND POSITIVE DISCRIMINATION

**Key Principle** ...............................................................................

Member States may maintain or adopt measures within the meaning of art.157(4) with a view to ensuring full equality in practice between men and women in working life: art.4, **Directive 2006/54**.

> KALANKE V FREI HANSEATADT BREMEN (CASE C-450/93) 1995
> German law operated a rule requiring the appointment of the female applicant for a job in the event of applicants being equally qualified in areas where women were under-represented. Mr Kalanke, a landscape gardener with the Bremen Parks Department, claimed that he had been refused promotion in favour of an equally qualified female applicant. The German court made an art.267 reference to the ECJ.

## Held

❖ (ECJ) Article 2(4) of **Directive 76/207** (now replaced by art.2(8)) permits measures giving a specific advantage to women with a view to improving their ability to compete on the labour market and to pursue a career on an equal footing with men. It does not permit "absolute and unconditional priority" to be given to women. [1996] 1 C.M.L.R. 175.

## Commentary

[1] The wording of the *Kalanke* ruling found its way into art.157 TFEU which now reads: "With a view to ensuring full equality between men and women in working life, the principle of equal treatment shall not prevent any member state from maintaining or adopting measures providing for specific advantages in order to make it easier for the under-represented sex to pursue a vocational activity or to prevent or compensate for disadvantage in professional careers". (Note the change from *Kalanke*: the substitution of "under-represented sex" for "women".)

[2] A national rule requiring preference to be given to the promotion of women where there are fewer women than men at the higher level of the relevant post in the public service does not infringe the directive, unless reasons specific to the male candidate tilt the balance in his favour. This exception may only be invoked where there has been an objective assessment of the candidatures which takes account of each candidate's specific circumstances: *Marschall v Land Nordrhein Westfalen* (Case C-409/95).

[3] A plan to fill more than half the posts in a sector where women are under-represented by women, either by appointment or promotion, did not infringe the directive, provided it satisfied an objective assessment by the national court in line with *Marschall*: *Georg Badek* (Case C-158/97).

[4] The ECJ in *Abrahamsson v Fogelqist* (Case C-407/98) interpreted art.141(4) which allows Member States to take measures for special advantage to ensure full equality between men and women in professional life. The Court held that **Directive 76/207** and art.157(4) preclude national legislation which automatically grants preference to candidates from the under-represented sex, if they are sufficiently qualified, subject only to the proviso that the difference between the merits of the candidates of each sex is not so great as to result in a breach of the requirement of objectivity in making appointments.

# GENDER REASSIGNMENT, SEXUAL ORIENTATION AND EQUAL TREATMENT

## Key Principle
Protection against discrimination on grounds of sex includes the protection of transsexuals.

> P v S (CASE C-13/94)
> This case involved a claim for unfair dismissal following gender reassignment. (For facts, see Ch.3.)

## Held
❖ (ECJ) Discrimination extends beyond the concept of whether an individual is male or female into the area of gender reassignment.

## Commentary
[1] *P v S* represents a bold step by the ECJ to extend the concept of discrimination beyond the differential treatment of men and women.

[2] The boldness did not, however, extend to equal treatment in homosexual relationships. In *Grant v South West Trains* (Case C-249/96) the ECJ held that same sex relationships were not covered by the **Equal Treatment Directive**. Sexual orientation is, however, within the scope of **Directive 2000/78**. *Grant* was followed by the CFI in *D v C* (Case T-264/97), upheld by the ECJ in Joined Cases C-122/99P and C-125/99P, a staff case, arising from a refusal to grant a household allowance to an EC official living with a same sex partner, on the basis that stable relationships between individuals of the same sex could not be equated to marriage.

[3] The two directives adopted under art.19 TFEU in 2000 amount to a radical departure in terms of scope from previous directives on equal treatment. **Directive 2000/43** provides for equal treatment between persons irrespective of racial or ethnic origin. **Directive 2000/78** provides a general framework for equal treatment in employment and occupation in order to combat discrimination on grounds of religion or belief, disability, age or sexual orientation. **Directive 2006/54** repealed and replaced **Directive 76/207**. Article 2(3) of **Directive 2000/43** prohibits "harassment" and "sexual harassment". Both directives were due for implementation by July 2003, although the UK was allowed up to December 2006 to implement **Directive 2000/78**.

[4] Directive 2004/114 was adopted in 2004 implementing the principle of equal treatment between men and women in the access of supply of goods and services. It followed a request by the European Council at Nice in December 2000 to the Commission to strengthen equality-related rights in areas other than employment and professional life.

## SEXUAL ORIENTATION AND EQUAL TREATMENT

**Key Principle**
Non-discrimination on grounds of sexual orientation is prohibited: arts 1 and 2, **Directive 2000/78.**

> TADAO MARUKO V VERSORGUNGSTALT DER DEUTSCHEN BÜNEN (CASE C-267/06) 2008
> After M's life partner (i.e. same sex partner under a registered partnership) died, he sought a survivor's pension from his partner's occupational pension fund. His application was refused on the basis that the scheme did not recognise life partners. M sued the pension fund which referred to the ECJ for guidance.

**Held**
❖ (ECJ) (1) A survivor's benefit under an occupational pension is pay under art. 141 EC.
(2) Legislation which treats a surviving life partner less favourably than a spouse in relation to survivorship benefit infringes arts 1 and 2 of **Directive 2000/78** (though it was left to the national court to determine whether a surviving life partner is in a position comparable to a spouse).

## DISABILITY AND EQUAL TREATMENT

**Key Principle**
Discrimination on grounds of disability is prohibited: arts 1 and 2, **Directive 2000/78.**

> COLEMAN V ATRIDGE LAW AND STEVE LAW (CASE C-303/06) 2008
> Ms Coleman returned to work from maternity leave after the birth of a disabled child. She accepted voluntary redundancy from her employers, after which she brought an action for unfair constructive dismissal. She claimed that she had been treated less favourably by her employer on the basis of her son's disability compared with the parents of

children who were not disabled by being denied the chance to return to the same job, as well as flexibility regarding working condition, that she was described as "lazy" when she took time off to care for her son and other allegations. The employment tribunal sought clarification from the ECJ under art.267.

**Held**

❖ (ECJ) (1) The prohibition of direct discrimination under arts 1 and 2 of **Directive 2000/78** is not limited to persons who are themselves disabled. It is direct discrimination for an employer to treat an employee who is not disabled but who is the parent of a disabled child less favourably on the basis of the child's disability than another employee in a comparable situation.

(2) The prohibition of harassment under arts 1 and 2(1) and (3) of the directive covers not only unwanted behaviour towards those who are disabled but also towards employees who are not disabled but who are a disabled child's primary carer.

## AGE DISCRIMINATION AND EQUAL TREATMENT

**Key Principle**

Discrimination on grounds of age is contrary to arts 1 and 2 of **Directive 2000/78**.

WERNER MANGOLD V RÜDIGER HELM (CASE C-144/04)
A German law adopted in 2000 authorised the conclusion of fixed-term contracts of employment once the worker has reached the age of 52, except in specific cases of continuous employment. Mr Mangold, a 56-year-old lawyer, entered into a contract in Germany by which he was employed by Mr Helm for a fixed period from July 2003 until February 2004. He brought proceedings arising from the contract before the German courts which referred several questions to the ECJ for clarification on the interpretation of **Directive 2000/78**.

**Held**

❖ (ECJ) The principle of non-discrimination on grounds of age is a general principle of Community law. The purpose of **Directive 2000/78** is to lay down a general framework for certain forms of discrimination, including in particular discrimination on grounds of age, as regards employment and occupation. A difference of treatment on grounds directly of age constitutes direct discrimination prohibited by EU law, unless it is objectively and reasonably justified by a legitimate aim, particularly by legitimate employment policy and labour market objectives. The means to achieve such objectives must be appropriate and necessary.

## Commentary

[1] The ECJ recognised in *Mangold* that the purpose of the German legislation was to promote the integration into working life of unemployed older workers, in so far as they met difficulties in finding work. While such an objective could be objectively and reasonably justified, the German provision exceeded what was appropriate and necessary to achieve this objective.

[2] While acknowledging in *Mangold* that Member States enjoy broad discretion in adopting measures to achieve objectives in social and employment policy, the universal application of the national legislation to all workers of 52 and over was seen to have resulted in the exclusion of a significant body of workers from the benefits of stable employment, itself a major element in the protection of workers. In the Court's view, the fixing of an age threshold had not been shown to be objectively justified.

[3] The case law of the ECJ on age discrimination is developing rapidly. The existence of non-discrimination on grounds of age as a general principle was confirmed in *Kücükdevici* (Case C-555/07). In this case the ECJ held that national legislation which does not take account of employment below the age of 25 years in calculating notice for dismissal infringes the principle. However, it is for the national court to ensure the full effectiveness of the principle and disapply conflicting national law, if necessary. *Kücükdevici* places a different complexion on age discrimination, as the decisions immediately after *Mangold* did not cite the case. In *Lindorfer* (Case C-227/04P) the Court ruled on sex discrimination but not age discrimination. In *Palacios de la Villa v Cortefiel Services SA* (Case C-411/05) the Court held that a compulsory retirement age of 65 years agreed through collective bargaining was lawful where it was objectively justified by a legitimate aim relating to employment policy and was proportionate.

[4] In *Bartsch* (Case C-427/06) the alleged age discrimination arose in relation to an occupational pension scheme which excluded spouses more than 15 years younger than the deceased employee. The Court distinguished *Mangold* on the basis that national rules in that case had been adopted to transpose a directive (**Directive 1999/77** on fixed-term work), whereas in *Bartsch* the directive had not been transposed. The prohibition on age discrimination was found not to be mandatory where there was no link with

EU law. No such link could be found before the deadline for transposition of **Directive 2000/78** has passed.

[5] Further clarification of **Directive 2000/78** followed when the Court ruled on *The Incorporated Trustees of the National Council (Age Concern England) v Secretary of State for Business, Enterprise and Regulatory Reform* (Case C-388/07). The ECJ held that that a rule such as that in the UK Equality (Age) Regulations 2006 permitting employers to dismiss employees aged 65 years or over if the reason for the dismissal is retirement can be justified under art.6(1) of the directive if the aim is objectively justified in the context of national law by a legitimate aim relating to public policy and the labour market and it is proportionate. It found that it was for the national courts to decide whether national legislation reflects such a legitimate aim and whether the means of implementation were appropriate.

[6] The ECJ held in *Wolf* (Case C-229/08) that national legislation setting a maximum age for recruitment to the first service at 30 years amounted to a difference in treatment under **Directive 2000/78**, but was proportionate and justified by operational considerations under art.4. Fixing a maximum age of 68 years to practise as a panel dentist is not justified to protect the health of patients, but may be justified to share out employment opportunities if it is proportionate: *Petersen* (Case C-341/08). An automatic retirement age does not infringe art.6(1) of the Directive where it is objectively justified to achieve a legitimate aim of the labour market provided it is proportionate: *Rosenbladt* (Case C-45/09).

## EQUAL TREATMENT IN SOCIAL SECURITY

**Key Principle**

Men and women should be treated equally in matters of social security: art.1 of **Directive 79/7** on equal treatment in matters of social security.

**Key Principle**

The equal treatment principle applies to the working population, defined as "self-employed persons, workers and self-employed persons whose activity is interrupted by illness, accident or involuntary unemployment and persons seeking employment (and to retired or invalided workers and self-employed persons": art.2, **Directive 79/7**.

**DRAKE V CHIEF ADJUDICATION OFFICER (CASE 150/85) 1986**
The applicant gave up her job to care for a disabled mother. An art.234 reference was made to clarify the scope of art.2 of the directive.

**Held** ...............................................................................................................................

❖ (ECJ) Article 2 covers all benefits designed to maintain income where any of the risks specified in the directive have been incurred. [1986] E.C.R. 1995.

**Commentary** .........................................................................................................
[1] Article 3 of the directive (providing that the equal treatment principle applies to statutory schemes to protect against sickness, old age, etc., and social assistance schemes set up to supplement or replace statutory schemes) has been held to apply to schemes exempting persons of pensionable age from prescription charges: *R. v Secretary of State for Health Ex p. Richardson* (Case C-137/94). Housing benefit was not, however, covered: *R. v Secretary of State for Social Security Ex p. Smithson* (Case C-243/90) because the benefit was not directly and effectively linked to one of the risks in art.3(1). Similar reasoning was employed by the ECJ in *Atkins v Wrekin District Council* (Case C-228/94) in which a 63-year-old male was refused public transport concessions, which were available to women at 60. The concession was held to be outside art.3(1), as was a winter fuel scheme for pensioners: *R. v Secretary of State for Social Security Ex p. Taylor* (Case C-382/98).

[2] The ECJ held in *Jonkman* (Joined Cases C-231–233/06) that rules intended to allow one sex, originally discriminated against, to become eligible for the pension scheme of the other sex on payment of sums representing the difference in contributions between the sexes did not infringe **Directive 79/7**. It also observed that where the Court provides a reference from which it is clear that national law conflicts with Community law, the national authorities must take the necessary measures to ensure compliance with Community law, so as to give full effects to the rights of individuals.

[3] The equal treatment principle has also been extended to cover occupational pension schemes (**Directive 86/378**) and self-employment (Directive 86/613). **Directive 86/378** has largely been superseded by the *Barber* decision that pensions paid under occupational pension schemes are "pay" under art.141: see p.196. **Directive 86/378** was repealed in August 2009 by **Directive 2006/54**.

Why was the decision in *Barber* so important in relation to equal pay?

Why did the ECJ in *Webb v EMO* find that a pregnant woman should not be compared to a sick man in terms of non-availability for work?

# Index

This index has been prepared using Sweet and Maxwell's Legal Taxonomy. Main index entries conform to keywords provided by the Legal Taxonomy except where references to specific documents or non-standard terms (denoted by quotation marks) have been included. These keywords provide a means of identifying similar concepts in other Sweet & Maxwell publications and online services to which keywords from the Legal Taxonomy have been applied. Readers may find some minor differences between terms used in the text and those which appear in the index.
Suggestions to **taxonomy@sweetandmaxwell.co.uk.**